African Chieftaincy in a New
Socio-Political Landscape

A publication of the
African Studies Centre
(Leiden, The Netherlands)

LIT

African Chieftaincy in a New Socio-Political Landscape

edited by

E. Adriaan B. van Rouveroy van Nieuwaal
and
Rijk van Dijk

LIT

Die Deutsche Bibliothek – CIP-Einheitsaufnahme

African Chieftaincy in a New Socio-Political Landscape /
E. Adriaan B. van Rouveroy van Nieuwaal; Rijk van Dijk (eds.).
– Hamburg : LIT, 1999
  (African Studies Centre, Leiden, The Netherlands)
  ISBN 3-8258-3549-9

NE: GT

© LIT VERLAG Münster – Hamburg – London
  Grindelberg 15a 20144 Hamburg Tel. 040–44 64 46 Fax 040–44 14 22

Distributed in North America by:

Transaction Publishers New Brunswick (U.S.A.) and London (U.K.)	Transaction Publishers Rutgers University 35 Berrue Circle Piscataway, NJ 08854	Tel.: (732) 445–2280 Fax: (732) 445–3138 for orders (U.S. only): toll free 888-999-6778

CONTENTS

Introduction: The Domestication of Chieftaincy in Africa: from the imposed to the imagined   1
Rijk van Dijk & E. Adriaan B. van Rouveroy van Nieuwaal

Chieftaincy in Africa: Three Facets of a Hybrid Role   21
E. Adriaan B. van Rouveroy van Nieuwaal

The Elusive Chief: Authority and Leadership in Surma Society (Ethiopia)   49
Jan Abbink

Modern Local Administration and Traditional Authority in Zaïre Duality or Unity? An Inquiry in the Kivu   75
Dirk Beke

Nkoya Royal Chiefs and the Kazanga Cultural Association in Western Central Zambia today – resilience, decline or folklorization?   97
Wim van Binsbergen

Traditional Chiefs and Modern Land Tenure Law in Niger   135
Christian Lund & Gerti Hesseling

"One Chief, One Vote": The Revival of Traditional Authorities in Post-Apartheid South Africa   155
Ineke van Kessel & Barbara Oomen

The "Anglophone Problem" and Chieftaincy in Anglophone Cameroon 181
Piet Konings

Obscured by Colonial Stories. An Alternative Historical Outline of Akan-Related Chieftaincy in Jamaican Maroon Societies 207
Werner Zips

About the authors 241

Index of cited authors 245

Acknowledgement

In appreciation of his stimulating interest for the study of traditional authorities in Africa, the Editors express their gratitude towards the Netherlands' Minister for Development and Cooperation, his Excellence Drs. J. Pronk, for his generous support of this publication.
This support follows an earlier subvention to the organisation of a study-day on chieftaincy in Africa, organized by the Africa Studies Center and held in Leiden in March 1996, which has formed the intellectual basis of this volume.

INTRODUCTION: THE DOMESTICATION OF CHIEFTAINCY: THE IMPOSED AND THE IMAGINED

Rijk van Dijk
and
E. Adriaan B. van Rouveroy van Nieuwaal

The study of chieftaincy in Africa is currently facing something of a loss of paradigm – a crisis in the modernist assumptions of 'traditionality'. Many critics have been unmasking and unravelling the artificiality of 'tradition' in African societies. Many 'traditions' and 'customs' there have been found to be products of codification, petrification and coercion under modernist projects of colonial rule, missionary activity and postcolonial state formation. A body of literature has emerged since the early 1980s which regards all 'tradition' as a specific construction at a specific time for specific purposes. Ever since the pioneering work of Hobsbawm and Ranger (1983), the mainstream of these 'invention of tradition' studies has been exploring the ways in which such modernist projects imposed certain 'traditions' on African societies. And indeed, quite a number of the studies have brought to light deliberate attempts by colonial rulers to *create* 'African chiefs' and impose them on subjected populations. 'Tradition' and 'custom' in Africa, in other words, have become a culturally specific, historical phenomenon and event. The codification of certain practices as 'authentic traditions' by colonial rulers, missionaries or anthropologists and their writings led to many instances in which local leaders themselves began trying to legitimise their positions along such lines. This appropriation of inventions of tradition often helped them to curb 'internal' rivalry and fluidity in their societies with regard to their disputed claims to power.

Three theoretical positions have emerged out of the invention-of-tradition approach, as scholars have attempted to understand the 'traditionality' or 'primordialness' of chieftaincy in Africa. The first argues that chieftaincy existed in some cases prior to the arrival of European rulers and missionaries (a well-known example is the Asantehene of Kumasi; see McCaskie 1995). In such cases the arrival of colonial rule had all sorts of ramifications in terms of internal divisions, alliances, bureaucratic arrangements, and above all encapsulation of chiefs into a system of indirect rule. In general terms, colonialism favoured the codification of one line of power in local society, which was then fortified against rival or more fluid forms of power brokering, ultimately creating an artificial 'tradition' of hereditary power. European rulers could pride themselves on creating something that seemed to resonate deeply with locally held cultural perceptions, while strategically placed individuals in society could venture into the new opportunities for salaried positions and upward social mobility that such codification created.

The second approach emphasises that in acephalous societies, colonial rulers did not hesitate to impose an 'African' form of 'traditional' rule. In cases described by Geschiere (1993, 1996) for Cameroon and by Hawkins (1996) for Northern Ghana, colonial administrators randomly selected individuals for the role of communication channel, and gradually started calling them chiefs. In so doing, colonial administrators tended to overlook, or remain unaware of, the significance of other types of non-political officeholders such as earth-shrine priests or warlords. 'Tradition' here, as Ranger maintained in later writings (1993), was truly a colonial and modernist invention.

A third position deriving from the invention-of-tradition approach focuses on those situations in which modernist projects of power were absent and therefore did not impose such invented traditions. Some remote areas remained unaffected by colonial and missionary endeavours, and no externally inspired 'traditions' and 'customs' were created in Western writings and representation. However, as Abbink's contribution (this volume) on Ethiopia shows, it was not just in Western modernising projects that traditions were invented, but this invention took place in other, non-Western hegemonic projects as well (such as the expansion of Islam).

One and a half decades have passed since the invention-of-tradition approach was introduced to the study of African chieftaincy, and counterviews have meanwhile emerged. Obviously the main problem with the invention-of-tradition approach is the question of acceptability and legitimacy. How can something that is imposed ever be acceptable to a local population? Inventing and creating a structure is one thing, but it is entirely something else to give meaning and significance to it and imbue it with respect and awe. Discussing Ndebele chieftainship in Zimbabwe in his 1993 article, Ranger revised his position on the invention of traditions on this issue of acceptability. Referring to Anderson's work *Imagined Communities* (1983), Ranger now preferred to speak of 'imagined traditions' to indicate that there was a desire in local society to share in the construction of new models of authority, and to imagine new vistas that could be opened by appropriating one's own tradition in a new world. As Feierman (1990) has demonstrated in great detail, local intellectuals in Tanzanian peasant societies had been

Introduction: The Domestication of Chieftaincy: The Imposed and the Imagined

debating 'tradition' and 'chiefs' all along, producing different imaginations of how interaction with (colonial) state rule had developed in the past and how it might develop in the near future. Ranger writes:

> Some traditions in colonial Africa really were invented, by a single colonial officer for a single occasion. But customary law and ethnicity and religion and language were imagined, by many different people and over a long time. These multiple imaginations were in tension with each other and in constant contestation to define the meaning of what had been imagined – to imagine it further. Traditions imagined by whites were re-imagined by blacks: traditions imagined by particular black interest groups were re-imagined by others. The history of modern tradition has been much more complex than we have supposed (Ranger 1993: 81-82).

Hence, Pels has recently shown for the Waluguru in Tanzania how discourses developed, both on the side of the colonial administration and on that of local political leaders, in which the images of authority, rule and governance to be produced by each 'community' were debated and negotiated (Pels 1996). Interestingly, Pels describes the emergence of a specific 'language' between the superstrate political discourse of the colonial regime and the subaltern political discourse of the Waluguru, a language that both domains could share (a process which Pels denotes as the 'pidginisation of Luguru politics').

The crux of the matter, though, is that the act of invention becomes lost to memory. Still the invention itself is then reintegrated into the new vistas of power. From the contemporary, postcolonial perspective to which this book is devoted, African chiefs' imaginations about the colonial experience have become valuable assets in their claims to authority. Usually they construct a narrative which claims that colonial bureaucracies, missionary conversion projects, and their accompanying schooling and education programmes were all directed at creating a past/inferior versus present/superior dichotomy, within which the cultural and political power of the chiefs was assigned to a category of social evil. Missionaries were out to 'save' the younger generation from the clutches of traditional, heathen rituals controlled by chiefs, by providing educational facilities over which chiefs held no sway. Colonial and postcolonial bureaucracies are claimed to have encapsulated chiefly power in systems of customary law, curtailing their decision-making authority and preparing chiefs a place in society that would not go beyond the 'honorary' and the 'ceremonial'.

Although a substantial number of studies are providing evidence to corroborate this narrative of the encapsulation of chiefly tradition by external powers, in today's postcolonial predicament the same narratives fulfil a special transformative function. With the advent of postcolonial state formation, the narrative of the colonial encapsulation of chiefs was transformed into one about the brokerage role that most chiefs in Sub-Saharan societies still find themselves locked into. In particular, recent contributions to the *Journal of Legal Pluralism,* edited by van Rouveroy van Nieuwaal and Ray (1996), have explored the continuing narrative of encapsulation in terms of how chiefs visualise themselves between the emerging state and the local population. The postcolonial state has seen itself compelled to enlist chiefly support in order to acquire some measure of legitimacy for implementing its policies and laws; chiefs similarly need the state to defend their position in local government and the legitimacy of their power to act. Postcolonial states are in the business of inventing traditions all the time, as by launching new national festivals that put rigidly selected elements of particular cultural traditions on show while purposely ignoring others. Since local chiefs, for their part, may also flaunt government officials and their regalia, ultimately the question becomes: Who has captured whose imagination of power? Referring to De Boeck's views on the 'uncaptured' kings of Zaire, Werbner writes:

> The point is that the cross-dressing is mutual: for the kings, spectacles like the president's and for the president, the regal leopard bonnet.... On the one side the kings are flown to the presidential palace, invited to party congresses and rallies, and given cars and residences at the capital. People's representatives, party functionaries and high officials of state attend upon the king's shrines, their enthronements and other meetings at court, on the other side (Werbner 1996: 17).

We thus witness a mutually perpetuating invention of traditions whereby post colonial states seek no enlist chiefly support by creating national councils, conferences and consultations. On their turn, chiefs create similar avenues for the enlisting of state support for their position in society.

Nonetheless, in the debate about what position chiefs held under colonial rule, the invention-of-tradition approach to the brokerage of chiefly power in its contemporary context would fall short of understanding its imagined status. The purpose of this book is to determine the overlay of different chiefly power bases (the imposed and the imagined) in present-day society, and how this has been affected by the recurrent experiments at nation-building and by ideologies of democracy, liberalisation, development and the like. Obviously there can be no one answer to such questions. We are well aware of the local specificity of power fields. Not only are the regional differences in Africa substantial, but so is the diversity in colonial and postcolonial governmental histories (or 'governmentality' to invoke Foucault in passing) within which institutions of chieftaincy have evolved. In other words, to understand how chiefs mediate the link between past, present and future, it is important to understand first how their authority relates to differently conceptualised worlds (the state, the local, the west, the secretive, etc), and to what people imaginge about these worlds. Clearly, chiefs mobilize resources from their power in these differently conceptualised worlds (van Rouveroy van Nieuwaal 1996).
It would therefore be a mistake to try to explore the plurality of power formations in postcolonial Africa solely from the point of view of its *imposed* nature, thereby

Introduction: The Domestication of Chieftaincy: The Imposed and the Imagined

disregarding what is imagined, desired, sought after and longed for. Chiefs in Sub-Saharan Africa seem to occupy a position as brokers between what is imposed and what is imagined. Useful concepts for exploring the present-day transformative role of chiefs in the interaction between state and society and between the imposed and the imagined respectively are that of 'mediation', used by Bayart (1993), and that of 'mutational work' used by Bourdieu (1977). Although these two terms may seem to refer to similar processes of exchange and transformation between two fields, there is one difference between them which is crucial to the understanding of chieftaincy. Bayart's work and that of others writing about state-society relations in Africa is predicated on a sharp vertical dichotomy between state and society. Hence, Bayart's emphasis on 'politics of the belly' refers to a bottom-up perspective on state power. Civil society and chiefs are seen to occupy a middle level. Von Trotha (1996: 103) perceives a development from what he calls 'administrative chieftaincy' (chiefs incorporated in the state apparatus) towards 'civil chieftaincy', whereby limited independence from the state is accepted, as though chiefly office were turned into a parastatal. As De Boeck (1996: 96) and Werbner (1996) have been arguing, however, this dichotomy between state and society, with traditional authorities residing somewhere in the middle, is highly problematic. For one thing, the state is seldom the *only* source of power and legitimate authority (consider the case of the 'uncaptured kings'), and furthermore the public realm where state control is supposed to operate is often weak, limited and highly vulnerable to exploitation for individual gain. Chiefly and state authority could also stand side by side, and politics from below could be directed in a non-hierarchical sense against both domains.

The term 'mutational work', in contrast to 'mediation', is more horizontal in its connotations, referring to the often highly respected activities of certain agents in society, actors who are capable of transferring one form of power from one domain to a different form of power in another domain. For instance, kinship relations may be 'mutated' to enhance someone's chances of finding employment in the job market – being someone's nephew may be turned into an asset in a non-kinship domain, that of paid employment. In the same way, other symbolic capital, such as the custodianship of certain initiation rituals, can be turned into an advantage in regional or even national politics (for an example of such mutational work, see de Jong 1997). Invoking Bourdieu, we can interpret chiefs as 'converters' in African societies today, because they convert the power of the 'past' to that of the present, the power of the secretive into public power, the law of 'tradition' into codified 'customary' law, and the power of ritual into manifest political activity. The question is how the chiefs' mutational work between the imposed and the imagined in the African postcolonial situation actually functions: what is its language, what are its claims and (symbolic) representations. This is the analytical profile of the present collection of contributions to the study of chieftaincy in Africa – an analysis focusing on the various dimensions of such mutational work, which changes the representation of chieftaincy from a static into a dynamic, ever-changing phenomenon. Hence we might coin the verb 'chiefing' to reflect the creative nature of the mutational work chiefs perform in their present-day role of 'converters'.

The most important context of chiefly mutational work today is the interaction of the global with the local in political culture, in law and legal pluralism, and in society as a whole (De Boeck 1996). The democratisation of African political culture was superimposed from the global level by the international community. Here again, the imposed has met the imagined, as massive support for the move to multiparty democracy and parliamentary representation has subsequently emerged from within African societies. The spread of a specific form of nation-state, at once liberal and democratic (at least in its manifest political ideology), has led in many places to extremely complex interactions between that state and local officeholders such as chiefs. Hence, when it comes to democracy and representation, one topic of consideration for chiefs and scholars alike has become the issue of just what the democratic content of chiefly authority is or should be (van Kessel & Oomen in this volume). In other words, to what extent does the imagination of a democratic political culture (if such can ever be fully realised) *produce* the authority of imposed chiefs? Moreover, the presence of international initiative, of international intervention and aid, is now felt more strongly than ever in Sub-Sahara Africa. Postcolonial society in Africa has experienced swift 'encroachment' by a variety of global social and political formations, of which the waxing and waning of the nation-state is only one out of many. It is now engulfed in global processes such as the application of uniform international legislation. Another area for viewing the mutational activities of chieftaincy is the presence of international organisations, such as NGOs, from the national all the way down to the village level. They appear to have turned chiefly office into an arena of brokerage, thus opening new perspectives and avenues for entrepreneurial activity.

A literature has emerged that critically reflects on this state of affairs, focusing on the interplay between chiefs and the postcolonial African nation-state, and especially on the domains of power where chiefs show themselves able to control their mutational work to their own advantage (see, for example, van Rouveroy van Nieuwaal 1996; Fisiy 1995; Geschiere 1993; 1996; Bekker 1993). In such domains, their nostalgic claims to authentic ritual power are effectuated in terms of real political power in African societies today. In brief, there appear to be two such domains. The first concerns the management of natural resources, and in particular the allocation of land. In most cases chiefs succeed in invoking ritual rights from the 'past', which they then translate into instruments for 'hard' political brokerage. Chiefs negotiate their positions in the context of global discourses on sustainability, environmental awareness and national and international interest in ecological preservation (see Daneel 1996 and Lund & Hesseling in this volume).

The invention or rerouting of historical truths about the political say of the chiefs in land issues, law, and the ritual representation of the political claims of certain ethnic or social groups still offers one of the primary angles from which chieftaincy and its mutational agency can and should be studied.

Introduction: The Domestication of Chieftaincy: The Imposed and the Imagined

The second key chiefly domain is that of ritual and symbolism in society as they relate to identity politics. Here chiefs can help foster a sense of primordialness and authenticity. The first domain is addressed by studies on topics such as land tenureship, dispute settlement and their resonance in national politics; the second domain is covered largely by studies on the construction of communal identities, conflict resolution and mediumship.

As dispute settlers and local administrators, chiefs exercise a firm ritual and moral authority over their people, which is enshrined in mystic and sacred attributes and faculties belonging to the cosmological notions of chieftaincy. In terms of imaginary worlds, some chiefs are involved in witchcraft, are considered witches themselves or act as witch-hunters (van Rouveroy van Nieuwaal 1988). As Geschiere (1996) and others have shown for Cameroon, the increasing rationalisation of bureaucracy, government, the economy and social life in general has by no means resulted in 'disenchantment', reflected in a decline of witchcraft and the occult in Africa. Rather, the encroachment of modernity on African societies appears to produce a greater social and political awareness of the presence and the problem of witchcraft and the occult in their modern manifestations. The advance of modernity has prompted an intensified search for ritual protection, which seems to be offered in some cases by new forms of fundamentalism (see van Dijk & Pels 1996; van Dijk 1998; Meyer 1995); in other cases this has strengthened the position of chiefs. Chieftaincy increasingly usurps the position of the custodians of social order and public discipline by enacting and re-enacting certain rituals and other symbolic practices. There is symbolic capital in social order and public discipline (see van Binsbergen, this volume), a capital which in Africa's current 'weak states' (see Ellis 1996) certainly pays off in hard political currency. Some chiefs even succeed in forging links between the cosmological orders of their own local community and the worlds of modern economy and politics, successfully using the changing social, political and economic structures to become part of a new entrepreneurial elite (von Trotha 1996). Especially when it comes to modern health care, chiefs may offer mediumship between local, cosmological conceptions of illness, affliction and misfortune and the things Western medical organisations may have to offer.

Outside these 'traditional' political domains of chiefly authority, many others can be distinguished which outline a new social and economic landscape for the mutational work of 'chiefing'. The point is that not only should we stop emphasising the demise of African chieftaincy and its dependence on a politics of nostalgia, but we should no longer hold it to be 'traditional', either, a residual of something authentic. Agreeing with Chabal (1996) we state that the current preoccupation of outside observers with a 're-traditionalisation' of African politics reveals more about Western stereotypes than about actual processes taking place in Africa. Chieftaincy is rapidly turning itself into a perplexing new phenomenon which appears capable of negotiating and modifying modern institutional arrangements to its own ends. Chiefs' claims to authenticity, to being legitimate 'representatives of their people', are balanced and negotiated against achievements such as institutional qualities and skills (sometimes even academic ones), links with global networks, and shrewd dealings with the political powers, parties and bureaucracies in their countries.

The social sciences, and legal anthropology in particular, tend to concentrate on the type of chieftaincy that is located, in political terms, at the tops of highly stratified societies. But there are many other forms of 'chiefship' we need to deal with, such as the religious leaders and earth priests who have manifest political power (for example, Abbink in this volume). Furthermore, the rapid rates of urbanisation, the growth of schooling and education, and the rise of modern sectors of non-rural employment have long been deeply affecting the outlook and the application of postcolonial chiefly authority. Though the majority of Africans still live in rural areas, cities in Africa have been growing fast as a result of global processes. This has led to the formation of specific forms of urban chieftaincy, which should be included in our analysis of present-day traditional authority.

Particularly in cities, chiefs are confronted with immigrant populations which did not belong to the chief's social, political and cultural traditions in the past, and never will in the future. Some recognise no chiefs at all and others have chosen rural-urban migration to escape the chiefly order of their village and try to start new lives as more autonomous citizens. In other words, there are limits to the imagined quality of chiefly power as well as to the domains of their mutational work.

It would be a serious mistake, though, to think of urban areas as 'modern', and thus unsuited to 'traditional' chiefly authority, while regarding the village as 'traditional' and as such the playground for that authority. As Mbembe has argued, there is a fractured play of identity politics in the postcolony, in which the urban and the rural are caught up together:

> The postcolony is made up not of one coherent public space, nor is it determined by any single organising principle. It is rather a plurality of 'spheres' and arenas, each having its own separate logic yet nonetheless liable to be entangled with other logics when operating in certain specific contexts: hence the postcolonial 'subject' has had to learn to continuously bargain and improvise. Faced with this, ... the postcolonial 'subject' mobilizes not just a single 'identity', but several fluid identities which, by their very nature, must be constantly 'revised' in order to achieve maximum instrumentality and efficacy as and when required (Mbembe 1992: 5).

Although the individual subject in the postcolonial predicament may appear to be a mere *homo economicus* – a transactionalist maximising on choices based on a continual cost-benefit analysis, the essence here is that chieftaincy cannot escape from this entanglement. For certain aspects of social life in both rural and urban areas, subjects imagine themselves as living under chiefly authority. It is, however, a lost paradigm of hegemony (if such a hegemony ever existed in the first place). The present postcolonial subject seeks 'chiefing' for specific social purposes, specific moments of identification, specific needs. For other facets of life, the current fractured state of African societies and identities provides the subject with a wide array of opportunities to 'opt out' and turn to other models of power brokerage. Looking at present-day chieftaincy from this bottom-up vantage point may, as this collection aims to show, help move research out of the conundrum of viewing state and chiefly power as interlocked forces. In portraying their relations as a zero-sum game, with chiefly power increasing when state power diminishes and vice versa (see van Rouveroy van Nieuwaal & Ray 1996: 29), a top-down perspective leaves little room for the play of imagination and individual agency. The different spheres and arenas that Mbembe refers to in the quoted passage reflect a far more open, fluid situation. As the work and criticism of De Boeck (1996) has revealed, the postcolonial African state, aware of the limitations of its power, is mainly active in certain domains, and the same is true of chiefly authority.

What, then, is the future for 'chiefing' in Africa? Clearly the imagination angle has taught us that chieftaincy cannot do without power from below. Chieftaincy has to be desired by the population. Sweeping reforms have been carried out in many 'democratised' African states in recent years. What will be an appropriate role for chiefing when all such constitutional, legal and land reforms have been successfully implemented? In some quarters of African societies today, people feel that a rejuvenation of chieftaincy would be in their interest (see in this volume Konings on the struggle of anglophone Cameroonians for decentralisation; and van Kessel and Oomen on the calls for an election procedure for local chiefs in the new democratic South Africa). Predictably, many African states will be decentralising their power and authority structures and bureaucratic hierarchies in the very near future. They seem to have no other alternative now that Structural Adjustment Programmes have demanded the scaling down of their administrative systems and have imposed an uncompromising ideology of efficiency and accountability. Shorter lines of decision-making, greater effectiveness of local participation, and power-sharing are increasingly desired. This is a context in which chiefing may prove to be of increasing value in the near future. There is one aspect of chiefing for which no shortcuts exist for enhancing efficiency, and no adjustment programmes for enhancing governmentality: the task of conflict resolution. Conflict resolution is an area where demands from 'below' and governance from 'above' seem to concur in their appreciation of chiefing (for a recent example of mediation by the Asantehene in a violent ethnic conflict in Northern Ghana seems to confirm this trend; see Skalník 1996).

Intervention by chiefs can and does occur in more situations than only cases of armed violence (séminaire-atelier Niger, 25-26 June 1996). It can also be of strong symbolic and ritual significance in conflicts over cultural heritage, nature conservation, and rights to food, shelter and integrity of human life.
The desire from below to involve chieftaincy in such a crucial task can be interpreted as a

conscious, public move towards the *domestication of chieftaincy*. This means that there should be a popular say in what is expected of chiefs, in how their tasks should be 'trimmed' to fit the needs of certain sectors of a population. It also reflects signs that the public has a stricter moral gaze on the achievements and failures of chiefing in today's African societies. The domestication of the state in Africa, which has included the appropriation of its exploitative potential by the political elite, is now being followed by a popular domestication of chieftaincy, with chiefs confronted by a heightened sense of public morality. The basis of such a moral judgment can sometimes be found in history (see Zips's contribution on diasporic chieftaincy among the New World Maroons) or in ritual (van Binsbergen, this volume). Chiefs in Africa have entered a postmodern society and are increasingly becoming nuclei in the development of local popular 'arena's', where the processes of domestication are giving rise to complex figurations of leadership. The contributions to this collection explore the two central elements in our understanding of chieftaincy in Africa – mutation and domestication – in a wide range of social, political and economic contexts. We will now highlight each of these contributions.

Overview

In his article 'Chieftaincy in Africa: Three Facets of a Hybrid Role', *E. Adriaan B. van Rouveroy van Nieuwaal* argues that the bureaucratic position of chieftaincy in Africa today reflects the hybrid nature of the phenomenon 'chief'. It has never been easy to classify chiefs into different categories, for their political and administrative tasks in bureaucracies cannot readily be distinguished from the political, judicial and socioreligious roles they play in African societies. Not only have colonial regimes and the postcolonial state tended to conflate the bureaucratic tasks of the chiefs with their social positions in society, but chiefs have actively sought this hybridity and have imagined a sociopolitical space created by it. The variety and hybridity of chiefly positions and roles today has made the phenomenon of chieftaincy into a much greater enigma than it ever was in precolonial times. The present-day chief in Africa is a new sociopolitical phenomenon. He, and occasionally she, has become a syncretic leader, forging a synthesis between antagonistic forces issuing from different state models, bureaucracies and world views.

Since the colonial era, the African chief has been subjected to a process of political and administrative enclosure at the hands of the state. Using Togo as an example, van Rouveroy van Nieuwaal shows how chiefs have been given top-down support and legitimisation through the principle of devolution, first introduced by the French colonial government. This operated through a firmly hierarchical organisation of traditional chiefs, which implemented governmental policies and administrative decisions using its own language, directives and rituals. In Togo this also resulted in the implementation of the Territorial Administrative Redivision Act.

Such processes in Togo and elsewhere in Africa led to the development of an 'administrative chieftaincy' (Beck 1989; von Trotha 1996). Although this did include the role of mediation which chiefs would later propagate so strongly during the so-called 'democratisation process', the chiefs were also increasingly coerced into carrying out closely circumscribed administrative duties. In Togo, nevertheless, one of the most important characteristics of chieftaincy, which is now still recognised by the population, has been an active involvement in dispute settlement, even in the face of efforts by both the colonial and postcolonial governments to curtail and marginalise such 'traditional' responsibilities.

On the other hand, popular esteem for the office of chief were seriously and deliberately undermined after independence by a despotic politicisation of the chief's role. Paying respect to the chief became part of the oppressive system of political control in Togo in the years that followed independence. Moreover, the administrative duties the chief was to perform in the name of the state ultimately relegated him to the status of a low-ranking officeholder. Chiefs have become conscious of this process, which has seriously affected their role as a representative of a local order. Some fear a real loss of power – estrangement from the local population and ineffectuality vis-à-vis the state. And chiefs are also wondering whether they are not becoming mere folklore, just one of the attractions travel agencies put on their programmes for Western tourists in Togo. Van Rouveroy van Nieuwaal shows that the chiefs are keenly aware of this process, which is undermining the intermediary power position the chiefs acquired in the French colonial era. It is the subject of vehement debate amongst them.

African chieftaincy assumes widely varied forms, both in the nature of chiefly authority and executive power, and in its autonomy of action vis-à-vis the postcolonial state. *Jan Abbink*, in his contribution entitled, The Elusive Chief: Authority and Leadership in Surma Society (Ethiopia)', describes recent developments in a society *without* conventional 'chiefs': the Surma agro-pastoralists of southern Ethiopia. He first links his discussion of a 'chiefless' society to the renewed anthropological attention to local chieftaincy in Africa – its potential role in postcolonial state formation in areas such as local-level democratisation, power-sharing and decision-making. The nature of the authority and legitimacy of Surma leaders is restricted largely to the ritual domain. A consideration of the three major political periods of 20th-century Ethiopia illustrates how the Ethiopian state's grip on local leadership has been steadily strengthening: authority and decision-making have moved decisively away from their local base, and the autonomy of local leaders has diminished. In addition, state-sponsored young leaders with 'non-traditional' qualifications (such as elementary state education, military experience in the national army, or knowledge of the national *lingua franca*) are replacing the 'traditional' ritual leaders and elders, giving the state and its agents more control over local developments.

Although postcolonial states elsewhere in Africa are regarded as increasingly weak, thus creating room for chieftaincy to stimulate greater decentralisation, Ethiopia does not seem to fit the pattern. Obviously Ethiopia has never had a colonial experience, and the inventions of chiefly traditions that occurred elsewhere in Africa were not a factor here. Nevertheless, as Abbink shows in his contribution, forms of leadership did exist that are comparable to the earth priests or territorial mediums of Southern Africa (Daneel 1996). Such leaders have not been the object of indirect colonial rule. Likewise the Ethiopian state never delegated any bureaucratic and administrative tasks to them. Abbink concludes by showing that the modern Ethiopian state is currently in the process of inventing traditions by selecting officials with non-traditional characteristics. It remains to be seen whether this modern invention of tradition will gain legitimacy among local populations.

Dirk Beke's contribution examines the differences between rural and urban areas when it comes to accepting invented traditions. In his contribution 'Modern Local Administration and Traditional Authority in Zaire. Duality or Unity? An Inquiry in the Kivu', he approaches this issue from the angle of legal anthropology, highlighting the different administrative strategies that have arisen to cope with the rural-urban differential. Probably the most fundamental characteristic of Belgian colonial administration in the Congo was the formal distinction it made between the 'traditional' or 'indigenous' administration and modern 'Western' administration. The basic premise was that 'traditional' African forms of administration and chieftaincy – sometimes forcefully altered – were suited to the small-scale rural units at the lowest levels of local administration, but that larger units, and especially urban areas, required a modern type of administration.

For postcolonial, independent Congo/Zaire, the author argues that regional and local government was subject to a series of reforms aimed at modernisation, centralisation and domination by Mobutu's party bosses. Notably, however, a popular restoration – or public recognition – of the 'traditional' form of African chieftaincy took place in the early 1980s. It reconfirmed the colonial concept of duality of administration, under which traditional chieftaincy was to be retained only for the small rural entities.

The study examines various reforms of regional and local government in Congo/Zaire in the light of both the formal and the actual place of traditional chieftaincy in the rural areas of Kivu. It shows that the weakening and ultimate demise of central authority in the country, underway since the 1980s, has generated spontaneous, broadly supported forms of local autonomy. In the popular imagination, a revival of 'traditional' forms of administration under the prevailing bleak socioeconomic conditions has been seen as an important element of self-reliance. Another element is the proliferation of NGOs in the area. But Beke's contribution also shows how the revival of 'traditional' powers in the precarious Kivu context has fostered an ethnicisation of public consciousness. Rwandan-speaking residents and refugees struggle for political power, and they compete with 'original' ethnic groups for the control of land. While the role of 'traditional' chieftaincy in these ethnic conflicts is important, Beke also shows that significant forms of 'non-traditional' solidarity, such as the *mutuelles tribalo-regionales,* have also been established in urban areas. In other words, popular support and imagination with regard to local self-organisation are fed not only from rural areas; urbanites contribute to them as well.

Since the distinction between rural and urban in the acceptance of chieftaincy seems to be fading in the present-day context, it is odd that most governmental reforms still adhere to the old divisions: chieftaincy in the villages, 'modern' government in the towns. The penetration of many forms of modernity into rural areas, together with the imagination or awakening of 'traditional' elements in the towns, warrant serious reconsideration of this approach.

The contribution of *Wim van Binsbergen,* 'Nkoya Royal Chiefs and the Kazanga Cultural Association in Western Central Zambia Today - *resilience, decline or folklorisation?*' goes further in examining the oppositions between chiefs and the postcolonial state and the growing appreciation of chiefly roles in rural and urban areas. The main aim of this paper is to examine the thesis of the 'resilient chief' by considering an illuminating case from western Central Zambia. Van Binsbergen first describes the unique position of contemporary African chiefs, who seem to function on a plane different from that of legislation, the political process and the bureaucratic structure of the postcolonial state. He then traces the succession of approaches to African chieftaincy in the course of the 20th century, contrasting the dualistic and the transactionalist models.

This provides a further descriptive framework for chieftaincy in western Central Zambia. The author examines in detail the power base of local chiefs and their room for manoeuvre. That power base is weakening, and the chiefs are desperately experimenting with new strategies of survival; conspicuous among these is a retreat into nostalgic cultural forms. Chiefs are driven into the arms of a variety of new actors on the local scene (including national-level politicians, churches, foreign commercial farmers) against whom they are rather defenceless. One such new actor is an ethnic voluntary association, the Kazanga Cultural Association, founded and controlled by the chiefs' most successful urban subjects (often the chiefs' own kinspeople). This non-governmental organisation was surprisingly successful at first in linking indigenous politics to the state in a process of ethnicisation; gradually, however, the revival of chieftaincy brought about by this NGO has resulted not in resilience but in an impotent folklorisation – if not the very destruction – of chieftaincy. As a consequence, tensions are mounting between chiefs and the ethnic organisation.

In concluding, van Binsbergen examines the implications this episode has for the general Africanist argument about the resilience of chiefs today. In the specific context of rural Zambia, Kazanga has provided a viable alternative to chieftaincy in the task of linking local communities to the national state and the world at large. While chiefs in other parts of Africa are active in forging such links in their dealings with actors such as international NGOs, in Zambia the chiefs' activities appear confined to the ceremonial and ritualistic. Hence, one key to the resilience of chiefs seems to be their success at sparking the imagination of urbanites. Chiefs who are unable to link their symbolic capital – their ceremonial functions – to the experiential worlds of the urbanites, seem limited in their 'mutational' capacities. They find themselves locked into a position of declining significance.

In South Africa, by contrast, democratic procedures may be laying the grounds for mutational work. As *Ineke van Kessel* and *Barbara Oomen* show in "One Chief, One Vote": The Revival of Traditional Authorities in Post-Apartheid South Africa, the post-apartheid situation has created new space for chiefly imaginations.

In the apartheid era, chiefs were denounced as puppets of Bantustan rule. In ANC-related circles it was widely assumed that chieftaincy would not survive in the post-apartheid era. But the institution of traditional leadership has proved highly flexible. Far from being shunted off as relics of premodern times, chiefs are now reasserting themselves in the new South Africa. Contrary to van Binsbergen's observations on the dwindling resilience of chiefs in Zambia, the South African chiefs appear to have survived the post-apartheid changes through a strategy of shifting alliances.

By the end of the 1980s, they were substantially reorienting themselves towards the ANC, correctly perceived by them as the ruling party-in-waiting. Combining their symbolic resources of 'tradition' with a discourse of liberation politics and development, they secured constitutional and other legal guarantees for the position of traditional leaders and for their representation in local, provincial and national government after the ANC's accession to power. In a sense, chiefs invented and imagined their own tradition. For its part, the ANC had an interest in wooing chiefs to its side, in order to forestall a potential conservative alliance in which Bantustan elites would join forces with traditional leaders. The article by van Kessel and Oomen analyses these developments, focusing on the principal topics of debate between the government, the ANC and the chiefs both before and after the democratic changes. Their brief case study of chieftaincy issues in northern Transvaal makes clear once again that urban, educated elites played a central role in the invention of the post-apartheid tradition of chieftaincy.

Access to land, along with democratic power-sharing in the decision-making relating to it, remains a bone of contention. It is the most crucial space where chiefs now vie for political power.

Introduction: The Domestication of Chieftaincy: The Imposed and the Imagined

This issue of debate and contestation, often perceived as the 'traditional' area of chiefly power, is also the main focus of *Christian Lund* and *Gerti Hesseling's* contribution on the present-day significance of chieftaincy in French-speaking Africa. In 'Traditional Chiefs and Modern Land Tenure Law in Niger', they review the French-language literature on chieftaincy. The insights of the invention-of-tradition approach have failed to gain the prominence there that they have in English-language research. A strong sense of the realness, the 'non-inventedness' of tradition seems to predominate, both in the actual discourse and practices of chiefs and in academic representations. Clearly the act of invention has become lost to memory in Niger. On the subject of land reform, both planner-administrators and academics engage in a discourse that seems to take Tradition as an undisputed given. The remarkable thing is, this appears to work: land reforms that present tradition as an undisputed, non-invented fact have borne fruit. In a new *Code Rural*, legislators and rural development planners in Niger have succeeded in modernising tenure laws by appealing to tradition.

Local tenure arrangements in Niger have long guaranteed that diverse groups of users could exercise claims, either simultaneously or in sequence, on the available but limited natural resources in a given territory. Many such arrangements were largely implicit, not recorded in any codified form. The local population and the transhumant groups that frequent the area regard these implicit arrangements as tradition, and they firmly believe such a tradition guarantees the survival all groups involved. In the process of codification now underway, chiefs are regarded as the key interpreters of tradition, mutating the implicit into the explicit. But they have discovered that their position is laden with ambiguity, and that land tenure reform under such conditions is therefore not without its contradictions. Lund and Hesseling examine some of these contradictions and explore how they translate into legislative challenges. One important issue is how chiefs are to maintain a level of flexibility and dynamism within the codified, rigidified form that the local tenure arrangements will have once they are made explicit.

The flexibility and dynamism of the implicit local arrangements have clearly served as an effective safety valve in a situation where natural resources vary in quality and quantity each year. Another issue is therefore how a chief is to determine which implicit local customary practice is to have primacy in a codified form, since their parameters are always changing from season to season and year to year. The complexities inherent in the very nature of local resource management seem to defy any modernist state project of inclusion, codification and legalist rigour. At any given point in time, local groups clearly desire and imagine that someone will 'chief' for their interests, but the chiefs find themselves in awkward positions, since they never can be sure whose rights are to be defended or constrained. Although the authors believe the idea of modernising tenure rules on the basis of what is implicitly known to the population is worth pursuing, they feel it is naïve to place undue confidence in the ability of 'custom' and chiefs to steer towards good governance, rule of law and social justice. We again witness a postcolonial invention of tradition in which chiefs play a central role – not so much because they are a

- 15 -

'tradition' now in the process of being invented, but more because they are party to the founding of new (legal) traditions of tenure law.

The extraordinary predicament of chiefs in postcolonial society – acting in the interest of particular groups but thereby becoming involved in inventing new traditions – also features in *Piet Konings'* contribution, 'The 'Anglophone Problem' and Chieftaincy in Anglophone Cameroon'. He draws attention to the remarkable actions of some chiefs on behalf of a specific section of the Cameroonian population in the late 1980s. His study examines the role chieftaincy has played in the current Anglophone struggles for self-determination and autonomy. In the aftermath of political liberalisation in Cameroon in the early 1990s, parts of the Anglophone elite began openly setting up organisations and pressure groups to protest against the alleged subordinated position of the Anglophone minority in the Francophone-dominated state. They demanded either a return to the federal state or outright secession. Both options were to have permitted a return to a nostalgically perceived situation of chiefly autonomy.

Konings observes that most Anglophone chiefs have strongly resisted persistent efforts by the Francophone-dominated state to enlist them in defence of the unitary state. They have instead backed Anglophone calls for federalism or secession. Whereas the French and the British colonial systems differed in the roles they assigned to chiefly authority, the French-style system was extended to the former British sector after independence as a sort of internal colonialism. The current call for decentralisation, a most sensitive issue in present-day Cameroonian politics, has been incorporated into the Anglophone chiefs' imaginations about the position they can occupy to resist the state's hegemonic efforts towards unity. Thus, the language of the former British oppressors now serves as a uniting force in the struggle 'from below' against Francophone control. This leaves the reader wondering how chiefs who happen to live in Francophone territory perceive these struggles. Will they go on supporting the state or will they see opportunities to secure for themselves a new political space in Cameroonian politics in the near future? Konings concludes his contribution with some speculations about their role and position.

The final contribution to this volume, by *Werner Zips,* gives us rare insights into a historical process of domestication of chieftaincy in transatlantic milieux. In his 'Obscured by Colonial Stories. An Alternative Historical Outline of Akan-related Chieftaincy in Jamaican Maroon Societies' he describes how the diasporic Maroon communities once appropriated chieftaincy to turn it against British indirect rule, and then successfully developed it in relative harmony with the colonial rulers who had tried to impose it in the first place. The first black freedom fighters in the African diaspora drew on their historical experiences in their motherland to reorganise themselves socially and politically. Chieftaincy was already a firmly ingrained system of governance in West African societies when Maroon social entities emerged in Jamaica, Surinam and elsewhere in the New World. At the turn of the 17th century, powerful African kingdoms such as Asante were on the rise, and they waged armed struggle against competing West

Introduction: The Domestication of Chieftaincy: The Imposed and the Imagined

African nations on the Gold Coast such as the Denkyira and the Fante. When the Europeans began conducting a massive slave trade with these kingdoms, they exported into the diaspora these same skills of militancy, organisation, and social and political structuring that were to sustain the Maroons' military action.

In 1738, after 85 years of guerrilla warfare, the British colonial regime finally had to admit that Africans who had organised themselves in the mountainous inland regions of Jamaica had indeed created systems of self-government. It signed a peace treaty with the Maroons, guaranteeing them political and territorial autonomy, administration of justice, economic endeavour, various privileges and the right to govern themselves through their chiefs. The treaty further specified a line of succession to Captain Cudjoe, the most powerful Maroon commander in the rebellion. Historical records have revealed that the British were hoping to establish a system of 'traditional authority' based on West African models. But the indirect rule they envisaged failed to come about. The Maroons domesticated chieftaincy, severed all its ties with indirect rule, and managed to keep their political autonomy intact for the next 250 years. Still today the Maroons protect their chieftaincy system against state interference, and control the selection of their leaders, even receiving assistance from the Jamaican state electoral committee.

Zips argues that chieftaincy is a dynamic system which, after its reintroduction in Jamaican Maroon societies, was able to undergo many changes because it was free from British colonial control. The author examines the creation of this so-called 'traditional authority' in processual terms, linking the way the Maroon societies imagined West African chieftaincy to the British attempts to impose indirect rule. In an interesting comparative perspective, Zips takes the experiential West African sources of governance into consideration, and he also compares the Jamaican organisational forms with their Surinamese Maroon counterparts. What comes to light is that one important factor in the appropriation and subsequent imagination of chieftaincy is the primus-inter-pares ideological discourse of chiefly authority. In all three cases, the discourse and practice of traditional authority appear to have been characterised by a rhetoric of democratic rule, in the form of consensus-oriented political and legal decision-making. The primus-inter-pares ideal of chieftainship is still frequently cited by the Maroons in support of the egalitarian communicative standards of their political processes.

In conclusion it is important to note that while all contributions stress the significance of chieftaincy for understanding social and political processes in Africa today, there is more to chieftaincy than that. As the Zips contribution shows, chieftaincy is, and probably always has been, important in 'Africa outside Africa'. Chiefs can be found holding office in places throughout the new diaspora, in Germany, England and the USA, where many African communities have arisen in recent decades as a result of global labour migration and intercontinental travel. Further inquiry is needed into how African chieftaincy interacts with external forces, such as international organisations and diasporic African communities. Alongside the powerful process of domestication of chieftaincy highlighted here, there is also a forceful trend towards globalisation of its meaning, significance and modes of operation. The relationship between chieftaincy and one global phenomenon – democratisation – is explored here within the confines of the African continent; the globalisation of the chiefly office itself, however, is a subject for further investigation. We hope this volume will help establish a new agenda for research on this unique social and political development.

References

ANDERSON, Benedict
1983   *Imagined Communities: Reflections on the Origin and Spread of Nationalism.* London: Verso

BAYART, Jean-François
1993   *The State in Africa: the Politics of the Belly.* London: Transl. by M. Harper, C. Harrison & E. Harrison. London: Longman

BECK, Karl
1989   Stämme im Schatten des Staates: Zur Entstehung administrativer Häuptlingstümer im nördlichen Sudan. Pp. 19-35. In: *Sociologus, Zeitschrift für empirische Soziologie,* 39

BEKKER, Jan C.
1993   The Role of Chiefs in a Future South African Constitutional dispensation. Pp. 200-204. In: *Africa Insight,* 23 (4)

BOURDIEU, Pierre
1977   *Outline of a Theory of Practice.* Cambridge: Cambridge U. P.

CHABAL, Patrick
1996   The African Crisis: Context and Interpretation. Pp. 29-54. In: *Postcolonial Identities in Africa.* R. Werbner & T. Ranger (eds.). London: Zed Books

DANEEL, Martinus L.
1996   Environmental Reform. A New Venture of Zimbabwe's Traditional Custodians of the Land. Pp. 347-376. In: *Journal of Legal Pluralism,* nos 37-38

DE BOECK, Filip
1996   Postcolonialism, Power and Identity: Local and Global Perspectives from Zaire. Pp. 45-106. In: *Postcolonial Identities in Africa.* R. Werbner & T. Ranger (eds.) London: Zed Books

DIJK, Rijk van
1998   Pentecostalism, Cultural Memory and the State. Contested Representations of Time in Postcolonial Malawi. In: *Memory and the Postcolony.* R. Werbner (eds.) London: Zed Books, forthcoming

DIJK, Rijk van & Peter PELS
1996   'Contested Authorities and the Politics of Perception'. Pp. 245-270. In: *Postcolonial Identities in Africa.* R. Werbner & T. Ranger (eds.). London: Zed Books

ELLIS, Stephen (ed.)
1996   *Africa Now.* Leiden: African Studies Centre

FEIERMAN, Steven
1990   *Peasant Intellectuals. Anthropology and History in Tanzania.* Madison: Univ. of Wisconsin Press

FISIY, Cyprian F.
1995   Chieftaincy in the Modern State: An Institution at the Crossroads of Democratic Change. Pp. 49-62. In: *Paideuma*, 41

GESCHIERE, Peter
1993   Chiefs and Colonial Rule in Cameroon; Inventing Chieftaincy, French and British Style. Pp. 151-175. In: *Africa*, 63 (2)

1996   Chiefs and the Problem of Witchcraft. Varying Patterns in South and West Cameroon Pp. 307-327. In: *Journal of Legal Pluralism*, nos. 37238

HAWKINS, Sean
1996   Disguising Chiefs and God as History: Questions on the Acephalousness of Lodagaa Politics and Religion . Pp. 202-247. In: *Africa,* 66 (2)

HOBSBAWM, Eric & RANGER, Terence (eds.)
1983   *The Invention of Tradition.* Cambridge: Cambridge Univ. Press

JONG, Ferdinand de
1997   Playing With Politicians. The Politics of Ethnicity in a Jola Initiation Ritual.' *Paper* presented at the Conference 'Identity in Africa, 22-23 april, African Studies Centre: Leiden

McCASKIE, Thomas C.
1995   *State and Society in Pre-colonial Asante.* Cambridge: Cambridge Univ. Press

MBEMBE, Achille
1992   Provisional Notes on the Postcolony. Pp. 3-37. In: *Africa*, 62 (1)

MEYER, Birgit
1995   Delivered from the Powers of Darkness. Confessions about Satanic Riches in Christian Ghana. Pp. 255-263. In: *Africa,* 65 (2)

PELS, Peter
1996   The Pidginization of Luguru Politics: Administrative Ethnography and the Paradoxes of Indirect Rule. Pp. 1-24. In: *American Ethnologist,* 24 (4)

RANGER, Terence
1993 The Invention of Tradition Revisited: the Case of Colonial Africa In: *Legitimacy and the State in Twentieth Century Africa. Essays in honour of A.H.M. Kirk-Greene*. T. Ranger & O. Vaughan (eds.). London: MacMillan

ROUVEROY VAN NIEUWAAL, E. Adriaan B. van
1996 Chiefs and States. Are Chiefs Mere Puppets? Pp. 39-78. In: *Journal of Legal Pluralism*, nos. 37 & 38

ROUVEROY VAN NIEUWAAL, E. Adriaan B. van
1990 Sorcellerie et justice coutumière dans une société togolaise: une quantité négligeable? Pp. 433-453. In: *Recueil Penant*, année 99, no. 801

ROUVEROY VAN NIEUWAAL, E. Adriaan B. van & Donald I. RAY
1996 Introduction. The New Relevance of Traditional Authorities in Africa'. Pp. 1-38. In: *Journal of Legal Pluralism*, nos. 37 & 38

SÉMINAIRE-ATELIER
1996 Prévention et gestion des conflits nationaux et sous-régionaux en Afrique de l'Ouest, tenu à Niamey (Niger) du 25 au 26 juin 1996.

SKALNÍK, Peter
1996 Authority versus Power. Democracy in Africa Must Include Original African Institutions. Pp. 109-121. In: *Journal of Legal Pluralism*, nos. 37 & 38

TROTHA, Trutz von
1996 From Administrative to Civil Chieftaincy. Some Problems and Prospects of African Chieftaincy. Pp. 79-107. In: *Journal of Legal Pluralism*, nos. 37 & 38

WERBNER, Richard
1996 'Introduction. Multiple Identities, Plural Arenas'. Pp. 1-26. In: *Postcolonial Identities in Africa*. R. Werbner & T. Ranger (eds.). London: Zed Books

CHIEFTAINCY IN AFRICA: THREE FACETS OF A HYBRID ROLE[1]

E. Adriaan B. van Rouveroy van Nieuwaal

Introduction

In this article I want to draw attention to a number of general principles that govern in many African States the interplay between chiefs and governments. In addition to these principles African chiefship reflects the hybrid nature of the phenomenon "chief". It is never easy to assign chiefs to different categories or to clearly define their political and administrative tasks as distinct from the socio-religious and judicial roles they play in African society. Moreover, the intermediary role chiefs have by definition played since colonial oppression also resists classification. This variety of positions and roles has made the phenomenon of chieftaincy into a bigger enigma than it had ever been in pre-colonial times. The present-day chief in Africa has become a syncretic leader. By this I mean that he is a socio-political phenomenon which forces a synthesis between antagonistic forces stemming from different state models, bureaucracies and world views. We often characterize these, for the sake of convenience, as "modern" and "traditional", but the value of such concepts is very limited, as von Benda-Beckmann concluded years ago (1979). A key future of syncretism is constant change, which forces the chief to use two different languages belonging to two radically different worlds (see Pels 1996) in which he has been received since colonial oppression. This situation also creates a certain duality in the chief's behaviour.
The following example will illustrate this:

---

[1]   This article is partly based upon the author's States and Chiefs: are chiefs mere puppets? In: van Rouveroy van Nieuwaal and Ray 1996

In early December 1987, I gave the highest traditional leader of the Têm from Sokodé (North-Togo) a lift as we were both heading for the executive meeting of the bureau of the Union Nationale des Chefs Traditionnels du Togo[2]. Once we got there, the chief mysteriously retreated to take off his Western clothes, reappearing, several hours later traditionally dressed as Paramount Chief of the Têm. The puzzling nature of this event lay not so much in the way he withdrew from my observation, but in the fact that one of the people at the meeting whispered to me that the chief had ritually washed himself in seclusion, to protect himself from the evil influences of the alien environment he found himself in. Politely, but resolutely, I was refused any further information.

For state officials and the subjects of the chiefs syncretism has the disadvantage that the chief's conduct cannot be easily predicted. The advantage, however, is that this conduct reflects the entire social situation and cannot be identified with just one characteristic of it. Syncretic leadership stimulates some form of neo-traditionalism. It has its origin in the need of both the rural population and the government to dispose of a go-between (Fallers 1955: 290; Miller 1968: 184-187). The extent to which the chief is able to integrate in two political systems is important to the continued existence of this type of leadership (Skinner 1968: 200). Syncretism requires of the chief an ability to constantly adapt to change and it sometimes even forces him to subtly but profanely swap his traditional garment for a European outfit, or vice-versa as in the example above. But syncretism also enables the chief to mobilize a wide variety of resources and power instruments to attain goals that may be in his own interest or that of the people he represents. In some countries chiefs rank among the most powerful men, who often have direct access to the complex network of compliant authorities extending into public administration, the army command, the clergy and the business world (Vaughn 1988: 46; von Trotha 1994b: 4). By his syncretic conduct the chief gains access to economic resources and politico-legal means of power from separate worlds. This may include acquiring academic titles and engaging in many activities on an economic level. He is likewise also ensured of access to more traditional areas such as dispute settlement, allocation of land rights, elimination of witches or exactly the opposite: the *practice* of witchcraft. By analogy with other authors (Hesseling 1992; Spittler 1981; von Trotha 1994a), the chief can be described as exerting his power "in the shade of the state law and administration". Finally, he is assured of a ceremonial role in various local rituals. This role is well-defined and is embedded in local cosmological views, norms and values which are respected by everyone in the particular society[3]. This, of course, is one of the specific aspects of a chief, as he is not just a subordinate local administrator

---

[2] It has frequently changed its name since its foundation in 1968. As of 1992-1993 it is known as the Association des Chefs Traditionnels du Togo. See *Atopani Express*, weekly journal in Togo, no. 262, 24-30 March 1996, p. 2; and van Rouveroy van Nieuwaal n.d.

[3] These norms may even be laid down in a governmentally recognized customary constitution, as in the case of the Royaume Guin in Glidgi, led by the Bebe Foli in southern Togo (Gayibor 1991).

controlled by bureaucratic exercise of power - a role imposed on him since the colonial era by the government, acting in the interest of government. The chief is in many cases also a figure who aims to protect the welfare of his land and people through a widely divergent system of possibilities, such as "authoritatively supported law observance"[4], dispute settlement, or even imploring rain and fertility of the ancestors[5]. Fulfilling these duties according to prevailing standards, ensures the chief's authority and respect amongst the people. It is this diversity of positions and roles of chiefs on a political level which von Trotha recently summarized as "From administrative to legal and civil chieftainship..."[6]. In my opinion, the chief's socio-religious duties may also be added to this list.

The foregoing can be reformulated as follows. Because the modern chief in Africa has been accepted within the state bureaucracy (and sometimes, too) within the state's legal system through an extensive system of constitutional and governmental rules and because on the other hand he is part of a more or less "traditional" world, the chief disposes of two bases of power from which he is able to operate towards the state and towards his people. His position could be described as a linkage between both worlds. This is by no means always a pleasant position, since serving two masters demands certain juggling capacities which many chiefs do not possess (Holleman 1969: 117-118; van Rouveroy van Nieuwaal 1991: 123).

In both realms the chief often disposes (depending on his hierarchical level) of an extensive network of clients, relatives and in-laws. This network is clear insofar as the state is concerned. The state holds the view that chiefs are encapsulated in state bureaucracy by legislation, and have been reduced to mere civil servants who can be promoted, punished or even dismissed by means of payment, pension schemes or housing legislation. But this is only the surface. Underneath such regulations lies a more powerful model. This is a personalistic model, which has little to do with formal rules and laws, but rather dismisses such formalities. In a way, the legalistic paper-model serves only to legitimize the state to a wary outside world.

This bureaucratic logic, which had a strongly centralistic, hierarchical nature in the colonial era, bore democratic marks for some time after independence in a multi-party system. However, it then evolved into a strong presidential form of government, which

---

4   A well-known concept from Dutch-Indonesian customary (adat) law, meaning that by his presence at a legal transaction a chief in fact ratifies this transaction; cf. ter Haar 1939.

5   See in this context the story of Ollennu, who in the 1940's paid a visit to a former colleague, also a jurist appointed superior chief in Akwapin (in Ghana): "...he had expected to hear that the chief was finding life on the stool boring and a complete waste of precious time. To Justice Ollennu's surprise and enlightment, the Chief said: "I am kept busy from morning till evening; I thought chiefs were all rogues, idlers spending all their time drinking schnapps; I never realised that there was so great opportunity for service to my people waiting for me; what is more, my people are so appreciative" - quoted by Annor 1985: 156

6   In: van Rouveroy van Nieuwaal & Ray (eds.), 1996

soon gave rise to one-party states and military dictatorships. To the chief, all such forms of government are coincidental, externally imposed frills. In the domain of his own, simultaneously co-evolving customary administrative system, the chief is required to be the focus of traditional authority.

In this area the chief is assured of his role as the upholder of the traditional order and rules and as the guardian of traditional norms and values. He is the supreme dispute settler, allocator of rights to land, and through witchcraft he is able in some cases, to exercise real terrorist power upon his society. Against this background, the chief is a kind of spearhead, accosting the state and trying to divest it of its resources such as markets and development projects, but also using new or existing legislation, such as land law reform (Fisiy 1992; van Rouveroy van Nieuwaal 1995; 1998), or personal networks to achieve his goals.

The chief's dual basis of power however is, also characterized by an entirely different feature. That dual basis of power also entails a mutual dependence between state government and chiefs. It connects the protagonists in a strategic game of power, in which each of the leading figures tries to consolidate his own authority (van Rouveroy van Nieuwaal 1992). This is almost always accompanied by extensive negotiations.

The above can be summarized as follows. The chief finds himself in a sort of zero-sum relationship with the state and its institutions. Both actors struggle for power and respect among their followers, but due to factors which bind them to together and because they must operate within the same territory, they are obliged to negotiate. The chief must enter into these negotiations with the state and its institutions so as not to lose his position within the constitutional and administrative framework. But the chief seems also made for this role, as he has fulfilled an increasingly intermediary role between the state and its people from the colonial era onwards.
I will deal with these three aspects successively.

The African State and the Chief: a zero-sum game?

Concepts of power and authority are at the centre of any study about 'state' and 'chief. Upon closer examination it proves rather difficult to make an analytical distinction between the two concepts. Power is commonly conceived as the possibility of a person to impose his will on others by using physical or psychological violence or the threat of it[7]. Authority, by contrast, is seen to be based on the shared conviction of the subjects

---

[7] Claessen relates the concept of 'authority' to that of 'power', by intepreting the latter as the possibility to limit other people's behavioural strategies (Claessen, 1988: 4). In real terms it is hardly practicable to put a restraint on a person's behavioural strategies for a long, continuous period. For this reason, both the chief and the state authorities try to make their followers do what they approve of. If this aim is not achieved, this may result in a political crisis.

that the state authority imposes its will in a legitimate way. Blau (1963: 307ff) shows that no clear-cut distinction between these concepts can be made; it is a question of a sliding scale (van Laar 1991: 2/3). Violence is used, in the implementation of both power and authority not only to subjugate citizens but also to provide them collectively with goods and services. The very fact that the authoritative ruler provides them with goods and services makes subjects believe that his imposition of will over them and their reduction to obedience is founded on a legitimate base.

Within this context the relationship of "modern authority" with "traditional authority" is fundamental. If we consider this relation as a kind of "zero-sum game", expansion of the power of the one actor will always reduce the power of the other[8]. This is, not the case of course when it comes to power in different fields. This may be interpreted in a strictly territorial sense - state jurisdiction stops at the state's borders - and a functional sense - the church's authority is limited to religious matters, at least in those cases where state and church are separated.

However, I assume that between both actors the fields of authority can be demarcated and that there are areas where the two actors' authority overlap. In practice, this demarcation is not always easy as I illustrate concerning the administration of justice (van Rouveroy van Nieuwaal 1995).

Returning to the zero-sum game, we may assume that it does not apply in areas where the two actors' authorities do not overlap. For example, the government does not even aspire to the religious tasks performed by chiefs. For the zero-sum context it is the field of political (and judicial) authority over individuals that captures my interest. Chiefs can base themselves on legitimate structures to act as representatives of their people. Within an area mostly smaller than the state, they are considered to serve as guardians of the public interest and providers of collective goods, as well as administrators and judges.

Chief and state are profit-maximizing actors who constantly strive to expand or to at least stabilize their power. They will resist any attacks made on it. This is the key issue of the zero-sum game. As a consequence, they will compete in order to perpetuate or consolidate their position of power. But should neither actor be out to perpetuate or consolidate his position of power and both are seeking a status quo, there is no competition. Their relationship becomes well-balanced and stable. As soon as one of them tries to expand his power, however, it will be at the expense of the other. This means that if both "power-seekers" operate within the same domain, the expansion of one's power will always pose a threat to the other's position of power.

---

[8] Not all authors share this opinion. Bienen, for example, argues that both local and national government can be strengthened simultaneously and that "...power should not be conceived as existing in a zero-sum game" (1970: 120).

Nevertheless, competition is not the only factor that 'binds' the two actors together. They also need each other for various other things: they are mutually dependent. The government depends on the chief for the implementation of its policy, as well as for the flow of specific information about the local community over which the chief exerts authority. This specific information is used by the government in the implementation of its policy.

On the other hand, since colonial times the chief has been dependent on the government for the recognition of his legitimacy as representative of his people, as well as for obtaining economic or political favours to satisfy the people he represents. This situation of mutual dependency is at least as important as the competitive atmosphere between the two actors. It does, however, entail the danger that one of them may use his indispensability to consolidate his position and to achieve certain goals. Just one example:

> The Togolese head of state, Eyadéma, while backing his candidate for the highest traditional position in the Têm society in 1986, was obliged to confer upon this candidate the title "chef supérieur" (paramount chief), thus deviating from his policy at that time of granting chiefs at best the hierarchically lower-ranking title "chef de canton". A "chef supérieur" (paramount chief) not only has a larger group of followers than a mere "chef de canton" (district chief), but is also entitled to a considerably higher monthly state allowance.

In conclusion we may reiterate that the relationship between the chief and the modern government is based on two characteristics: competition and mutual dependence. Both actors aim at expanding their power, and this is always at the expense of the other actor. This is competition. But they also need each other to exercise their power. In this they are mutually dependent.

As we have seen, though chief and state are in this context mutually dependent, they would prefer to do without one another. This situation of having to put up with one another, but actually wishing it were otherwise, is an uneasy one. It also entails a constant fear that the 'opponent' will strengthen his position while the other, incapable of taking action, will see his position weakened. Furthermore, each actor will think that even if the other does not act, taking action himself may still prove advantageous. For in so doing, he will be one step ahead of his opposite number and will have built a stronger position. The parties cannot guarantee each other that they will leave their mutual relationship as it is. It is therefore best to go for the action-option. Since this is a less than suboptimal situation both would be better off leaving the relationship as it stands, in order to enjoy the benefits of stability. But because of fear and ignorance of the others behaviour, they will take action. In pre-emptive, both actors are each other's prisoner's. In the original prisoners dilemma, the "game" is only played once. Given the absence of a second round, the actors do not have to reckon with the consequences for a next meeting with their opponent. But such is not the case in the relationship between chiefs and government. In real terms the actors do come into contact and must constantly consider the other in their actions. The frequency of such contacts increases with decreasing territorial distance between the two actors. Thus I noticed that in Lomé, but also in other provincial capitals in Togo, chiefs and local administrators entertained contact, whereas contacts between administrators and chiefs in more remote places were considerably less frequent. In any event, all such successive contacts, dictated by their mutual dependence, put a restraint on the intensity of the power struggle. They will have to face each other in the following round, so improvement of the position of the one must not so disadvantage the other that the latter will sabotage the next round. Their interaction thus proves a very delicate matter. Legal studies in this field seem to give only a limited insight into this subtle game of implications, anticipations and playing the ball back and forth between chief and state administrator. The same hold for political science studies, dominated as they are by the notion that whatever is coming from the centre can effectively command, control and penetrate this entire civil society.

Returning to the theory of the zero-sum game and the prisoner's dilemma connected to this issue, attention must also be given to some other aspects. For instance, the reaction to a power decrease is related to the extent to which the actor whose position has been weakened is dependent on the other actor. The more the government depends on chiefs for the implementation of its policies, the greater the chiefs' opportunities to claim or regain territory[9]. To do this, the chief may adopt a certain "strategy of withdrawal": by insulating himself within in his own society and withdrawing from the governmental grasp, he can put himself in a position from where he can exact certain concessions.

This strategic option is not open to the government, since interference with and presence in society are defining characteristics of (national) government. A government which is unconcerned with its society, but is merely "floating" above it, essentially falls short of these defining characteristics. On the other hand, the government does have another strategy at its disposal: the monopoly on violence, resulting in a symbolic or material repression. This position of having the monopoly on violence can be put to use by the government to regain lost territory. Many a chief has fallen victim to this. Of course, repression does hold the risk of long-term adverse effects, and for this reason the government always needs to keep open the possibility of negotiations.

If, nevertheless, the government, by strengthening its position, also decreases its state of dependence upon the chief, the strategy of withdrawal will overshoot the chief's initial goal. The government is now less in need of him for the implementation of its policies and will go to no further trouble to coerce him into a constructive attitude for the next round of negotiation. If this situation is reached, the chief has few options left, unless he

---

[9] They also use this space for manoeuvring as inherent in their intermediary position. Cf. van Rouveroy van Nieuwaal n.d. Ch. VIII

takes the initiative to transform his position(s), in order to reduce, or even eliminate, the competition between him and the state. Elsewhere I have explaind what I mean by transformation (van Rouveroy van Nieuwaal 1996; n.d.): it means that the content of his position may change and that his field of authority may shift, but transformation does not necessarily imply a weakening or strengthening of the chief's position. Transformation in this context is limited to issues relating to the *content* of his position. The following example illustrates this:

> During the years of the democratization process in Togo (1989-1992), the district chief Togbui Kpelly III from Mission-Tové (South-Togo) distinguished himself from his colleagues by delivering a trenchant speech demanding attention for the constricted position of the Togolese chief during the Eyadéma regime. This was at one of the daily sessions of the *Conférence Nationale Souveraine* (held from 8 July to 28 August 1991). The speech resulted in his election, as the only chief, to the *Haut Conseil de la République*. From a local traditional administrator he suddenly became a member of a national legislative institution. He had to delegate other, more traditional duties to members of his council. This switch to state politics meant that in the field of dispute settlement, he stepped out of the competition with his direct rival, the Primary Court (=Tribunal de Première Instance).

The preceding simplified model of reality has been conceived to provide more insight into this intricate matter of struggle for power. Probably neither actor's course of action will exactly follow the lines sketched, but the model may help to discern the conduct characteristic of the prisoner's dilemma and it may serve to understand the consequences of a withdrawal or a repression strategy.

The question however remains to what extent we are dealing with a finite amount of power, either controlled or desired by a chief or a state, which the one party tries to take away or keep from the other. Chiefs and state prey on each other's power. It is not just one game, in fact, but several, in which both actors do not hesitate to attire themselves with the regalia belonging to the other's power in their pursuit of power. For instance, the head of state in Africa - the symbol of state power par excellence - adorns himself, with symbols and titles that belong to a chief. The chief himself on the other hand, does not hesitate, in his bid for power and respect, to make use of academic titles, or to put his economic interests in local, national or even international enterprises, his client relationships or even his skills in witchcraft to use if it will do him any good. Against this background their struggle for a prized possession as power is not so much a struggle for power itself but rather the pursuit of the approval of their citizens or followers, the pursuit of political support or - in the case of the state - the pursuit of the identification of the citizen with that state. The fact that this identification with the state is not great among the people can be explained if one considers that for many African people their constitutional horizon has for ages been limited to the confines of the ethnic group to which they feel most closely related. In the case where the citizen or follower observes a degree of dichotomy between state and chiefly power and suspects that the two actors are at odds with each other, loyalty to the one will automatically mean disloyalty to the other. But if the citizen has the feeling that both parties are sharing in each other's power - as in the case of the Nkoya chiefs in Zambia who meet at regular intervals, in the capital Lusaka as forming a sort of shadow cabinet[10] - a certain mingling of powers occurs and the dichotomy becomes to an extent invisible to the citizen . In this situation, the metaphor of the zero-sum game no longer holds, for it is applicable only if the matter over which the two actors are competing can be defined. An excellent example is the administration of justice:

> In many African states the legislator has taken over the administration of justice to the exclusion of chiefs whose traditional task of dispute settlement was marginalized as a result of legal measures. But in nearly all cases the chiefs did not let themself be pushed aside and kept on fulfilling these customary law tasks, thereby entering into full competition with the relevant state institutions. The paramount chief Na Tyaba Tyekura of Mango (North Togo), for instance, refused during his reign (1963-1977) his followers access to his court-room when he learned that they had previously brought their case before the then Tribunal Coutumier de Première Instance[11]. He hereby demonstrated an eagerness to enter into competition rather than a desire to avoid it. He wished to leave his followers no doubt as to who, in his opinion, was responsible for dispute settlement in the region. The consequences soon made themselves felt for the Tribunal: it had its role in judicial matters reduced primarily to administrative legal matters such as confirming birth certificates through the so-called "jugements supplétifs et rectificatifs" (van Rouveroy van Nieuwaal 1976: 235-237).

This example from my own field observations may readily be supplemented with examples from other African countries. In Tanzania, for instance, chiefs have been put out of action by legal measures and have disappeared in a formal legal sense from the administrative and judicial level (van Rouveroy van Nieuwaal 1987: 35). But Moore (1978: 55-73) shows that the Tanzanian traditional authority will not let itself be pushed into "a secluded corner where the chief could nurse", as Holleman once put it for Zimbabwe (1969: 117-118). Notwithstandig numerous Tanzanian legal measures, the Tanzanian traditional authority within the *sungusungu* movement appears to have made its comeback (Bukurura 1994). A similar situation obtains in the Republic of Benin, where a certain revaluation and revival of the position of chiefs is taking place, following a period of breakdown of chiefly authority which had already begun by the

---

10 van Binsbergen, personal communication in an interview on 18.09.1993

11 Since a reform of the administration of justice in 1978: Tribunal de Première Instance

end of the French colonial period. The socio-economical, but also the politico-judicial positions of chiefs are now continually being promoted by te state[12]. A similar process appears to be underway in Niger (Chaïbou 1994).

Negotiation

As I describe the relationship between state and chief as mutually dependent, what then is actually taken place? I have described that situation as uneasy, because both would prefer to do without the other, but they are obliged to put up with one another. It is what I referred to as the "prisoner's dilemma". Moreover, the two actors are in competition with each other, in a struggle for power and respect among the citizens or their followers. The following example shows just how uneasy this relationship can be:

> In September 1988, positive migration forced Lomé's city council to expand the city limits northwards. This expansion was to be at the expense of the territory of the neighbouring village of Agoe Nyivé. This provoked strong resistance from the villagers. The local district chief at the time was the chairman of the *"Union Nationale des Chef Traditionnels au Togo"* (see footnote 2) and as such also a member of one of the highest institutions of the United Party. During the negotiations with the city council he had pointed to the inhabitants' resistance to the city's expansion plans. He proved unable to undo the plans, nor did he succeed in calming his people. In the end, the government tried to enforce the city's expansion by bringing in the army. To no avail.
> The chief had suffered from both the nasty situation of having to deal with two differently directed loyalties and the failure of his negotiations with the government and his followers[13].

In this competition and rivalry between state (institutions) and chiefs, negotiations play an important part. Both actors must, whether they wish to or not, consult with the other, for instance in order to determine their socio-economic policies for the region in question. Both actors come into contact with each other in different ways and on different occasions to "talk business". One common guideline is the principle of "If you, chief, help me, state institution, I will not be disinclined to help you". Researchers who try to gain accurate insights into such negotiations are handicapped by the suspicions both players have towards them. In all fairness I must admit that I have almost never been allowed to be personally present during the actual negotiations. In almost all cases

---

[12] Personal communication from A. Tingbé-Azalou (University of Bénin - Cotonou) at the conference called Contribution of Traditional Authority to Development, Democracy, Human Rights and Environmental Protection: Strategies for Africa. Accra: 2-6 september 1994.

[13] It concerns Togbui Atsou Gléglédzi I who died on 22 February 1996. See also van Rouveroy van Nieuwaal n.d. ch. VIIII

where I became aware that negotiations between chiefs and state institutions were taking place, I had to content myself with reconstructions of these negotiations in subsequent interviews with the persons involved[14].

By analogy with the situation during dispute settlement, the relationship between the two partners in the present context can be of a simple or a multiplex nature. In the former case the focus is on one interest, whereas in the later case multiple interests are at stake. Thus, we speak of a simplex-relationship when negotiations are only to determine the extent of political authority itself. But since political authority involves not only a territory but also interpersonal relationships between chiefs and state institutions, the negotiations between them are almost exclusively multiplex. Ideally, a compromise agreeable to both parties will be sought, but because of the divergent interests, backgrounds and aims which state and chief by definition have, the negotiations will not always go smoothly and without tension. This also result from the difference in the two actors' socio-political positions and, of course, by the disposition of physical violence or politico-economic instruments of power. But also the use (or threat of) supernatural powers plays its own specific role, giving these negotiations and the relationships between the two actors their dynamic character.

> I recorded a striking example in October 1988 from the then prefect of Bafilo (North-Togo). When the prefect had moved into his official residence after his appointment, he was haunted by nightmares which he claimed were caused by the owls nesting in the ridge of his house. Their mournful hooting made his flesh crawl. When an employee told him of the supernatural powers of the local chief Essò Erateï, the prefect wasted no time in consulting him in order to silence the owls. My informant did not reveal the nature of the chief's magic, but the owls ceased their haunting nocturnal cries. Not only did this establish the chief's fame with regard to his mystical powers, but it also created a good relationship between prefect and chief from which the chief would later greatly benefit when he came into serious problems with the central authority.

The state itself does not have this kind of supernatural means at its disposal. It will therefore have to content itself with appealing to the constitution and other legal norms. Chiefs, on the other hand, will often refer to their traditional legitimacy and their - often externally imposed - role of guardian of traditions. After all, they have been referred to for ages as "the guardians of our traditions and customs". At this point we encounter a

---

[14] I must also admit that I have sometimes been led up the garden path, notwithstanding my many years of experience in the field. This happened, for instance, in a case concerning the problems of the district chief Essò Erateï in Bafilo (North-Togo). In September 1988 the then serving prefect of that time elaborately reconstructed matters for me. But exactly a year later, in a sequel to that interview, it emerged that he had kept certain information about the case from me because he "assumed that I was just another passing anthropologist merely collecting data to show off back home". My revisit inspired his confidence that my interest in the position of chiefs was sincere.

never-ending conflict about which negotiations are to take place. This is a structural aspect in the relationship between chiefs and state. If local administrators and chiefs maintain stable, regular and troubleless relations, these relations may be called symmetrical (cf. Kurczewski and Frieske 1977: 502). The consequence is mutual recognition of political authority and of each other's legitimacy. In this situation both actors exploit the other's position in order to validate or consolidate the legitimizing process and their own political authority. In this case, the local state representative tries to use the chief to secure his political legitimacy, whereas the chief attempts to put his collaboration with the prefect to use in securing his traditional legitimacy within his own territory. If relationships are unstable, irregular and conflictuous, however, that will not only make the negotiations toilsome, but it will call their legitimacy into question. Relationships are then asymmetrical and unbalanced. In many cases the central government will consider itself the superior party, exerting political power through legislation, administration of justice, pure physical (military) violence and threat of dismissal, with little consideration of their traditional opposite number, the chief. The following description of the situation in Sierra Leone by Tangri (1980: 183-184) may serve as an illustration of this point.

> The (British) government demanded little beyond the chiefs' being responsible for law and order, tax-collection and the settlement of civil and petty criminal cases. Paramount chiefs were thus used by the British as agents of simple social control; they were far from being instruments of colonial oppression... Apart from the obligation which they enforced on behalf of the colonial government, the chiefs could insist on obligations towards themselves. The British made no attempt either to abolish or to restrict the customary rights of chiefs to tribute and labour... By making these rights to labour and tribute legal, the colonial government enabled the chiefs to benefit from their positions.

This quotation makes clear that the negotiations between the British colonial authority and the chiefs not only concerned political authority, but also other interests such as the administration of justice. It was therefore a multiplex relationship in which rules was set in order to regulate authority. In addition to this, there is an internal legitimacy in the form of mutual legitimacy between the British government and the local chiefs.

If we consider the context in which negotiations take place as a social field (of tension), we have to assume that the state as well as the chief are not autonomous in taking decisions concerning the group interests they represent. These interests involve the inhabitants of a (state) territory, who, in the case of the government, must be regarded as citizens, and in the case of the chief, as his followers. This means that the government, although in a formal legal sense it represents the highest political authority, is not autonomous in drawing up rules without showing that it consults with the chief.

But this holds equally for the chief, who bases his authority partly on "tradition" and derives it partly from his formal appointment by that same government with which he has carried on an administrative relationship (von Trotha 1996).

That field in which negotiations take place may be regarded as a "semi-autonomous social field" in the sense used by Moore (1978: 57-58). By this the author means a "social organization that elaborates and enforces rules that govern members of a group". One means by which the government enters upon a "semi-autonomous field" is *law*. The government uses law to exert influence on a "semi-autonomous social field", whether successfully or not[15] (Fisiy 1992: 10-14). The situation of negotiation in which the government and the chiefs find themselves shares one characteristic with a semi-autonomous social field, namely the capacity to lay down norms (van Rouveroy van Nieuwaal 1998). I illustrate this with two examples. The first one concerns Botswana:

> In Botswana, in 1965, a clause was inserted into the Chieftainship Bill by which the government is summoned to recognize chiefs instead of appointing them on the basis of the hereditary claims on which their title is based. It must thus be recognized that chiefs cannot operate independently and autonomously, but are bound by rules of customary law. At the same time, the government has a pratical role, which is to "provide a means by which governmental policy can be more effectively explained and defended... Such an opportunity was particularly valuable in view of the rapid and complex changes which were being made, and increased the likelihood that the chiefs would perform their duties in the districts more efficiently and would work more in harmony with the central government (Proctor 1968: 78).

The quotation demonstrate that the government in Botswana explicitly sought the collaboration of chiefs for the reconstruction of the state which had become independent in 1966, in order to realize a well-founded internal legitimacy between state, citizens and chiefs[16].

I derive my second example from my own field work. It concerns the succession of the "chef supérieur" of the Têm, also known as the Kotokoli (Central-Togo).

---

[15] In many cases, as in that of land tenure, these attempts failted completely (Fisiy, 1992: 12-14; van Rouveroy van Nieuwaal 1995; 1998), or they were used, also by chiefs, to achieve other aims and were transformed in such a way that the law reform promoted their own interests, more than could ever have been the intention of the law reformer.

[16] The situation in Botswana at present is rather different from that in 1966. Recently the Botswanan historian Sekgoma reported: "What remains of the institution of chieftainship in Botswana is nothing but an empty shell whose survival has been critically dependent on the government" (1995: 176).

In June 1980 the chef supérieur of the Têm, Ayéva Issifou, died. Following his death, a fierce struggle over his succession began. Among the seven clans entitled to succession there were numerous candidates. An expensive and exhausting propaganda battle for votes ensued. During a period of six years the struggle for the intensely coveted position ruined many candidates, and others even went bankrupt. Eventually four candidates remained, who, like the others, had been obliged to undergo a painfully thorough "enquête de moralité" by the local judicial and police authorities. From these four candidates the general-president Eyadéma made his choice in 1986. However, after extensive negotiations, the chief's followers succeeded in having the chief granted the title of "chef supérieur" and the corresponding monthly salary, despite the fact that the rights to this title had been explicitly revoked by the Minister for Home Affairs in a 1982 circular.

The following may be said in summary. If we view the negotiations for political authority, and especially the limits to that authority, from a legal anthropological perspective, the contents of negotiation may be regarded as a semi-autonomous field. It is further apparent that both the central government and the chiefs depend on norms from outside that context, or they simply push these norms aside if the situation demands it. Our approach from the concept of semi-autonomous field shows that the negotiations concerning leadership and authority involve a multiplex relationship in which the parties involved may be in a symmetrical or an asymmetrical relation with each other. In the case of the symmetrical multiplex relationship and a stable, regular contact, the negotiations result in a mutual legitimacy. This shows that not only the central government (or its representatives) uses the chiefs to strengthen its own political legitimacy, but also that the chiefs put that collaboration to use to secure their own authority, or to increase it if possible.

Intermediarity

As with the inception of state authority in an agricultural society, colonial authority in Africa was based on different types of government. The concepts of "direct" and "indirect" government are often used in this respect. The distinction between the two is easily made in theory, but because of the great local diversity in the various colonial areas, the systems proved to have many similarities without any noticeable difference. These different forms of colonial government policy have been comprehensively investigated, I do not wish to go into them here, and I refer to the existing literature[17]. Characteristic of any colonial government was furthermore a dire shortage of manpower for implementing its authority, and the fact that this shortage had to be compensated for by using intermediaries ("Mittelmänner", Beck 1989: 27; Spittler 1981: 74-81; von

---

17   See van Rouveroy van Nieuwaal 1987 and the literature references there

Trotha 1988: 324-325; 1993: 432 ff; 1994: passim). The need to institute a local administration not only arose from the lack of administrative personnel, the shortage of financial means and the often very poor infrastructure, it also stemmed from the antagonism between oppressors and oppressed and the divergent interests both these parties represented and pursued. The linkage between colonial government and African population has always been though intermediaries. Eligible for these positions were not only chiefs, but also other persons who were in direct contact with the white government, such as interpreters, soldiers, African clerks, police officers and domestic servants (Groff 1991; Roberts 1991)[18]. It must have been a colourful parade in which the chiefs fulfilled the most important role, even more so because certain legal and administrative measures were put into effect for them, (though only on a modest scale)[19]. Chiefs made it possible for the colonial government to bring immense, often impassable and unknown territories, under their command with few means. This command often consisted more of bluff than of real effective power (Beck 1989: 27).

The intermediarity of which we speak concerns two fields of society. Since the colonial regime, the chief has been integrated into the state administration, and at the same time he belongs, willingly or unwillingly, to the system of the state administration of justice.

The chief formed an "auxiliary" to the colonial administration, necessary for the implementation of that administration or, as the district chief Togbui Kpelly III, explains in our time:

> The chief's main task is to represent his people towards the state. And likewise, to represent the state towards the people. Therefore, the chief is the go-between between his people and the government (van Rouveroy van Nieuwaal 1992).

"Auxiliary" or "go-between": two different terms that express the linking role chiefs play between the state and the people. As a true Janus, the chief turns now towards his people to whom he owes his loyalty, and now towards the state powers who also expect his full loyalty[20]. It is an uncomfortable and unenviable situation in which many a chief has failed to keep his balance. On the one hand this has made the chief the gateway for

---

[18] These were assistants who were used only too readily by the local administrators to become more independent of the chiefs. But because such assistants stay in the same place for long periods of time - much longer than the customary short term of office of the French local administrator - alliances between these assistants and the chiefs were more likely to be formed then they were between chiefs and the white administrator. Such alliances were often even enforced by marital alliances. cf. Spittler 1981: 86

[19] At least in French colonies in Africa

[20] By analogy to Spittler who qualifies the district commissioner as the "Mädchen für alles" (1981:55), von Trotha (1993: 432) considers the chief an "Adressat für alles" to which the district commissioner turns at the smallest occasion.

the central government[21]. On the other hand the chief also becomes the link for mobilizing socio-economic and political sources, both those passed to him from the side of the government as those that he has at his disposition on the side of his own society.

The description used by the district chief Togbui Kpelly III is one every chief in Togo now uses. It refers to a development that started during the colonial era. For it is hardly conceivable that chiefs would have employed such a description for their position at the beginning of colonial government. Of course they were given to understand from the start that they were responsible for enforcing the regulations laid down by the colonial government. But those same chiefs (obviously I cannot know this for sure as I am uncertain whether they have ever asked the question in this way) would not have answered to the question "what is your task?" in the same way as the quoted chief did in 1991. Apparently chiefs in Togo have, in the course of a hundred years of colonial and post-colonial government, conceptualized their role in the following terms: "We are the representatives of the state before our people and we represent the people before the state". This implies that the chiefs have truly accepted the intermediary role imposed on them since the colonial era. In the present predicament, however, it becomes something 'imagined' by themselves. Or, in other words: after more than a hundred years of state formation the administrative intermediarity of chiefs is no longer regarded as a structural necessity. Their intermediary position rather becomes a politico-administrative concept. This means that the distance between the central administrative institutions and the chiefs has grown smaller in the course of time. Hence I interpret the description quoted as a development of their intermediary role in the sense that chiefs are better integrated into the national administrative organization than ever before. One could even argue that this integration was "completed" during the Eyadéma administration, when the confederation of chiefs was accepted into the institutions of the One Party, the Rassemblement du Peuple Togolais (= R.P.T.). The quotation of Togbui Kpelly III shows unmistakably that chiefs feel part of national government and, during the Eyadéma administration, of the political organization.

Intermediarity in this context is characterized by a movement between two extremes. On the one hand, the chiefs, caught as they are between the state and the people, can transform themselves into stooges[22], opportunistically making use of the state

---

[21] A slightly one-sided representation, as the government nowadays has several other means of access to the people, such as city councils, agricultural organizations, etc.

[22] It is only with caution that I use the term "stooge", which I feel is too deterministic. For numerous chiefs have of economic, political and social means at their disposal which permit them to act within certain limits. They also know very well how to use these resources to their own advantage. I may cite the example of Nana Quam Dessou XIV, chief of the city of Aného (South Togo). As a former industrialist, he has vast financial resources which have permitted him to build a palace (van Rouveroy van Nieuwaal 1992). He is not at all dependent on the state. Other chiefs, mostly farmers, possess vast agricultural lands. These chiefs are not intimidated by cutbacks on their income from the state, generally only a modest salary. And they are certainly not willing to act as instruments of that state.

administration. They are then nothing more than state functionaries adorned with a bit of folklore (van Rouveroy van Nieuwaal 1987; von Trotha 1994 a). On the other hand there are chiefs who will not have their leg pulled. They go their own way, though respecting certain limits. For instance, they may withdraw into their position of dispute settlement and, through this position, acquire new power which they use against the administration as it tries to impose a new task on them.

The literature on this subject describes frequent cases of chiefs placed between these two poles. But, this situation is in fact, inherent to the chief's intermediary position. It is all the more delicate in that processes of this type (or the phases of the process) can take on diverse orientations and give rise to diverse explanations. Various factors may play a role here: the personalities involved, the political situation, the divergency of the chiefs resources, kinship ties to other influential, responsible politicians, etc. However, if chiefs are incapable of adequately putting their resources to use at the right time, they risk being caught between the devil and the deep blue sea. Their survival as political beings therefore depends on political processes and their skills at a diplomatic level.

The distinctive characteristic of intermediarity is that the go-between must have independent economic resources at his disposal in order to secure his intermediary position. Without these, he has no room to manoeuvre and becomes a mere tool. But the chief does not have such in every case. For, as Togbui Kpelly III chief also remarks: "If Eyadéma says kill, you have to kill." If he were to refuse certain assignments from the state, he would immediately suffer the consequences in the form of dismissal, or even worse, detention. The reactions of chiefs to state actions cannot easily be lumped together; they are, as stated before, quite diverse. And that is precisely the remarkable feature of intermediarity. It leaves open a range of possibilities to react: the assistant/opportunist option; the option to obey no one; and all varieties in between. This also demonstrates the equivocality of intermediarity. In theoretical considerations of their intermediary role, the chiefs' varying and often opposite reactions to sudden socio-political changes can also give rise to wholly different interpretations of the chiefs' position. But this, too, is inherent to the go-between's role.

Another aspect of intermediarity has far-reaching consequences not only for the chiefs' administrative role, but also for their role as dispute settlers. It is the principle of devolution. This principle is binding for every central government and it implies that the central state authority dismantles the traditional practices concerning appointments, in this case concerning the appointment of chiefs. As the devolution principle was mainly in the hands of district officers during the colonial period, they were once referred to by Delavignette (1939) as "the true chiefs of the empire". Government control over the appointment of chiefs has only increased during the post-colonial period (van Rouveroy van Nieuwaal 1991; 1992). The devolution-principle consists not only of the right to appoint chiefs, but also of the right to dismiss them. This right was and is frequently made use of, because in the colonial era as well as in post-colonial times there have always been plenty of reasons for dismissing chiefs[23]. During Eyadéma's united party rule, a chief could be deposed if there was only the slightest doubt about his loyalty to the regime. Numerous cases can be quoted as an example:

> In December 1987 I met the district chief of Guérin-Koukou (préfecture of Bassar) in Lama-Kara, during the annual meeting of the bureau of the *Union Nationale des Chefs Traditionnels*. He is a dynamic chief whose legal career was crowned with success by his appointment as district chief. However, one mere indiscretion, consisting of not applying for a hunting permit, meant the end of his career as chief, following on a personal decision by the head of state.

Another example involves Essò Erateï, chief in the Bafilo district (North-Togo), who was discharged from office when he, during a public meeting presided over by the prefect, constantly interrupted his administrative superior and, for no apparent reason, publicly urinated. Both actions were deemed unworthy of a chief and formed adequate reason for Eyadéma to intervene and temporarily suspend the chief[24].

The examples show that the head of state, being the embodiment of the central despotic state power, will mercilessly make use of the rule of devolution if it so suits him. The similarity to the colonial past - to the German period at any rate (von Trotha 1994 a) - is striking, although there are also differences. For when in 1986 in Sokodé (Central-Togo, capital of the Tchaoudjo district)[25] the succession to chief Ayéva Issifou, deceased in 1980, eventually came down to four candidates from which Eyadéma made his choice, the head of state used not only political reasons to justify his choice[26]. The state influence in all phases of the competition between the dozens of candidates vying for the position was completely obscured. At least to the outside world.

It is fear for the head of state's unpredictable behaviour which clearly leaves its mark on the chiefs' conduct. In my field observations I cannot find any example to indicate that any chief ever successfully dared to oppose the head of state and his local representatives (among them the regional party bosses of the One Party) without risking his career. A quotation from the speech delivered by the *chef de canton* of Mission Tové

---

[23] Sebald (1988: 288) describes how during the long term of office of "Bezirksamtmann" (district officer) Gruner of the district Misahöhe (German South-Togo) nearly all 544 chiefs in the district were dismissed or replaced for one reason or the other in the course of almost twenty years.

[24] The prefect had a close personal bond with the chief, on account of the affair previously referred to concerning the owls (see p. 31) which had kept the prefect awake but were eventually silenced by the chief. After the prefect's intercession, who had discovered that the chief suffered from a prostate oilment, the chief was able to resume his position as *chef de canton*.

[25] district = préfecture in Togo

[26] The chosen candidate had far earlier been accepted into the One Party, in which he held the position of "regional secretary" (in this case préfecture Tchaoudjo) of the R.P.T.

(South-Togo, Zio préfecture) during a meeting of the Conférence Nationale Souveraine on the 27 July 1991 it clarifies much:

> If the authority of the chief has been ridiculed by governments, it has been the Eyadéma regime that has reduced it to nothing. The chief is under strict orders of the prefect, of the prefect's adjunct, of the under-prefect and especially of the regional secretary of the R.P.T. One order from one of the representatives of the R.P.T. with the slogan "R.P.T. above all: Discipline!", suffices to make the chief sink on his knees.[27]

The devolution-principle has great importance for the institution of chiefs and for the overall government under which the African population lives. By intervening in the appointment (and dismissal) of chiefs through new regulations, the central government puts its mark on the local balances of power. In acephalous societies the colonial government introduced chiefs and in so doing it created new balances of power that had never before existed. It also restricted folk law to the administration of justice by the (new) "chiefs"[28] in their dispute settlement. The present developments show a remarkable similarity to the colonial past on this point as well. When in 1981 a legislated revision of the administrative division of Togo was carried out, several new positions for chiefs were created in new districts that had never existed before. Appointments to the positions that had come into being were completely controlled by the central government, and the appointment of chiefs was eventually to be confirmed by the head of state himself. The people's influence on these decisions, especially that of the family elders, was by-passed or scarcely recognized.

The systematic application of the devolution principle, coupled with a hierarchization of chiefs and the development of administrative units, has contributed substantially to a certain unification of the traditional chiefs. Following others (see Beck 1989: 27-29; von Trotha 1994a: 1-2) this has acquired an administrative character. As a consequence, chiefs have become subaltern local administrators, who as successors of the colonial district officer, are subordinated to the local representative of the central government. Moreover, they have become instruments of political control in the hands of a the head of state and his ruling party. In this way an organisation of traditional chiefs has come into being which, during the Eyadéma administration, became largely loyal to that government. Many chiefs have compromised themselves to a government that had long been hated. This can be deduced, at any rate, from the answer of one of the actors

---

[27] *Journal Courrier du Golfe*, No. 97, 29 July 1991, p. 7

[28] In March 1990 I asked Togbui Kodzo Atsou Glégledzi, *chef de canton* of Agoe-Nyivé (five kilometres north of Lomé) whether he considered himself a chief, knowing that he did not come from a chief family and that his election and appointment in 1981 had been merely a political affair. He answered indignantly : "What? I have been a chief from the moment I was appointed one!". He had been officially designated by electoral vote as *chef de canton* of Agoe-Nyivé by Decree No. 81-172 of 18 November 1981 of the President of the Republic "à l'issue de la consulation populaire du 13 Octobre 1981". See van Rouveroy van Nieuwaal, n.d. ch. VIII

figuring in my documentary *Democratic Daybreak in Togo* (1992) to my question what he thinks of the chiefs' position in the tempestuous nineties:

> Yes, there are some who have helped us. There have been some who have lived with the General for a long time. They have not had the courage to help the people. It is now that one can see them evolve into democracy. It is now that they also seek to do something... There are some who have helped us in our fight. There are some, who have only helped us a little. But there are also those who are hypocritical.

The answer reveals the great disparity between the chiefs' reactions to acute and often intense and fundamental changes. There have been chiefs, though few in number according to the quotation, who supported the democratisation process; others prostituted themselves, even on television, to the ruling government; some watched from the sideline and kept well away, not wanting to risk their skin. By analogy with the chiefs' reactions to the invading colonial authority, we should not be surprised. In those days, too, chiefs displayed a wide variety of reactions to that new authority: some collaborated with it in order to eliminate their local enemies (van Rouveroy van Nieuwaal 1976: 75), others enlarged their power through colonial military government; and then there were some who were simply liquidated or deported because they opposed colonial government. That wide range of reactions stems from the intermediary role chiefs have fulfilled right up to the present day.

But in the long run the acceptance of chiefs into the political organisation, their extensive integration into the administration, will not be without danger. In a different context (van Rouveroy van Nieuwaal 1987) I have warned against a reduction of the chief's role to that of an echo of the past, to folklore. Indeed they have been assigned the role of "guardians of our traditions" in and out of season, accompanied by much ado from the head of state Eyadéma. On such occasions he did not hesitate to adorn himself, like many other African heads of state, with regalia belonging to chiefs. But chiefs were also forced to make an appearance at Lomé airport for the reception of foreign guests, to adorn local meetings of the R.P.T. and to do many other such things. Absence could result in reprisals in the form of a temporary or permanent disposition. Those attending this kind of events could not avoid feeling they were witnessing a political instrumentalization and orchestration of chiefs which not only exposed a gap between the field of state power and the field of "tradition". They furthermore felt tradition was perfidiously being put to use to further legitimize state power (von Trotha 1994 a).

The devolution principle, however, resulted not only in the development of an intermediary administration of chiefs. It was also the origin of an intermediary legal order, which, as von Trotha (1993: 433) has put it, came into being at the intersecton of law introduced by the colonial lawmakers and the judicial and administrative institutions and the normative legal order of the African people. At first the colonial government had acted on the premise of "leaving everything as it is" and not intervening in prevailing folk law. Such was the point of departure at least. The Europeans were convinced that in the field of material substantive law the great diversity could not easily be formed into a unity, even in a small area such as Togo with its innumerable different ethnic groupings. Unity of law was then, as now, an utter utopia as theoretical tract on legal pluralism have showned us (Griffiths 1978; Vanderlinden 1989). This, however, did not mean that there was no intervention on the various fields of justice. The colonial government soon introduced measures against regulations that were considered contrary to the "mission civilisatrice". Such measures were contained in the "repugnancy clause", or in French terminology the "ordre public"[29]. Chiefs were given by the German colonial government to understand that traditional practices that were considered unwelcome, such as holding "oracle verdicts", threatening with supernatural sanctions and other views conflicting with the German (legal) culture, should be left out of dispute settlement (van Rouveroy van Nieuwaal 1980). In this fashion, the German colonial government attempted to utilize the chief as a key figure in the legal order and to make use of his jurisprudence in their pursuit of unity of law. However, it should be noted here that the German colonial policies concerning chiefs - if policies is the right word here - were characterized by remarkable incongruities. Whereas the "Bezirksamtsmann" in one district drew up regulations which accurately demarcated the chief's jurisdiction and even specified which punishments and penalties the chiefs were authorized to impose, chiefs in other regions were left with no authority to administer justice at all (von Trotha 1993: 437 and 449-453). Such was the case for the Konkomba in North-Togo who had chiefs imposed on them as they had no chiefs themselves.

The chiefs' customary law thus became a "constructed folk law" under pressure from the German regulations. It now conformed to what von Trotha (1993: 443) describes in inimitable German as "Fremdtraditionalisierung"[30]. Furthermore, this did indeed also fit in with the unspoken thought of unity of law, but it had nothing to do with a free customary law development in society.

The French colonial government broke with these policies insofar as they uniformly regulated the chiefs' dispute settlement positions by various legal measures (van Rouveroy van Nieuwaal 1976: 35 ff). The main point was that the chiefs' dispute settlement position was strictly limited to "conciliation in civil and commercial matters". Contrary to the German aspiration, the French lawmakers wished to reduce the chiefs' dispute settlement position ever further. Authority in the field of criminal justice,

---

[29] Fournier (1955: 166) expressed this as follows:

It will eventually be necessary that custom is no longer conceived as ultimate reason. The French public order has to be followed, and folk law should not interfere with the field of superior interests of the subjects; interests, of course, as they are considered from the point of view of our Western conceptions of social justice.

[30] Characteristic of "Fremdtraditionalisierung" is that it becomes one of the most important sources for the "legitimatorischen Umgang der Herrschenden mit den normativen Ordnung der Beherrschten". In: von Trotha 1993: 444

still allowed under the Germans was taken from them from the beginning. According to the letter of the law, the administration of justice became fully controlled by state institutions. Thus, a dualistic judicial organization came into being, with law courts where French (colonial) justice was administered for certain groups of justiciables, *Tribunaux Coutumiers* where (in theory) folk law was to be administered. But here, too, based on the thinking of the "mission civilisatrice", legal regulations introduced via the French "ordre public" caused folk law to degenerate to a level of existence such as the French government had in mind (van Rouveroy van Nieuwaal & Baerends 1982).

The Togolese lawmakers adopted this point of view initially. The dual judicial organization was maintained until the Togolese legislator, as one of the last in Africa, decided in 1978 to unify the judicial organization. The French point of view on the subject of the chiefs' position in dispute settlement was maintained as the chiefs remained authorized to "reconcile" parties "in civil and commercial matters". However, as I have shown in several publications and films, legal practice reveals that chiefs, in the judicial realm in particular, are still fully functioning in local judicial matters, even if their role is somewhat scornfully and condescendingly denounced as "conciliation" and "palavers" by the prevailing legal elite. Due to this legal reality, the edifice of the judicial organization has become badly corroded. In some cases the corrosion has even proceeded that the state judge has apparently been shoved aside by the chiefs' active role. This is true, for example, of land law and witchcraft cases - matters which often deeply affect society. In other African countries the situation seems similar (Chaïbou 1994; Ladley 1991).

Summary

I summarize: African chiefs have become since the colonial era caught up in a process of political and administrative unification. In this process they are supported by the principle of devolution introduced by the colonial government, by the firm structure of a hierarchical organization of traditional chiefs and by an increasingly refined governmental administrative division. The tentative end of the latter - at least as far as Togo is concerned is the Territorial Administrative Redivision Act[31]. These aspects together have fostered the development of an "administrative chieftaincy", still bearing the characteristics of intermediarity which were so clearly articulated during the revolutionary period of the so-called "democratization process". Moreover one of the most important other characteristics remains the chiefs' active behaviour in dispute settlement, in spite of efforts by both the colonial and post-colonial governments to reduce and marginalize this traditional position.

---

[31] Act No. 81/9 of 23 June 1981 concerning the Organization of the Togolese Territory.

Apart from this, respect and regard for the chiefs have been seriously endangered by a despotic politicalization of the chiefs' role. From a political viewpoint the chiefs became part of an oppressive system of political control, while their administrative duties in name of the state eventually rendered them lowly-placed office holders. In the long run this process may seriously affect the chiefs' role as representatives of a local cosmological order, even to the extent of becoming mere folklore (van Rouveroy van Nieuwaal 1987 and van Binsbergen, in this volume), just one attraction travel agencies put on their programme for Western tourists. In the process, the chief's intermediary position (of power), acquired in the colonial era, will eventually be undermined as well.

References

ANNOR, Kwame P.
1985   Cultural and Social Identities in Africa: Chieftaincy and Political Change in Ghana. In: 18 Jhrg. *Verfassung und Recht in Übersee*. 2 Quartal: 153-159

BECK, Karl
1989   Stämme im Schatten des Staats: Zur Entstehung administrativer Häuptlingstümer im nördlichen Sudan. Pp. 19-35. In: *Sociologus, Zeitschrift für empirische Soziologie*, 39

BENDA-BECKMANN, Franz von
1979   Modernes Recht und traditionelle Gesellschaften. Pp. 337-351 In: *Verfassung und Recht in Übersee*, 12

BIENEN, Henry
1970   One Party-System in Africa. Pp. 99-127. In: *Authoritarian Politics in Modern Societies, the dynamics of established one party-systems*. S.P. Huntington and C.H. Moore (eds.). London: Basic Books

BLAU, Paul M.
1963   Critical Remarks on Weber's Theory of 1963 Authority. Pp. 305-316. In: *The American Political Science Review*. vol. 62, no. 2, June

BUKURURA, Sufian
1994   The maintenance of order in rural Tanzania: the case of 'sungusugu'. Pp.1-29. In: *Journal of Legal Pluralism*, no.34

CLAESSEN, Henry
1988   *Over de politiek denkende en handelende Mens; een inleiding in de politieke antropologie*. Van Gorkum: Assen

CHAÏBOU, El Hadji Omorou
1994   Marriage, tradition, and womanhood in Hausa society: Women's perspectives. Pp. 63-76. In: *Ufamu*, vol. 22, no.3

DELAVIGNETTE, Robert
1939 *Les vrais chefs de l'Empire*. Paris: Gaillimard

FALLERS, Lloyd A.
1955 The predicament of the modern African chief. Pp. 423-429. In: *American Anthropologist*, 57

FISIY, Cyprian F.
1992 *Power and Privilege in the Aministration of Law: Land Law Reforms and Social Differentation in Cameroon*. Research Report, no. 48. Leiden: Afrika Studiecentrum

FOURNIER, François
1955 Aspects politiques du problème des chefferies au Soudan présahélien. Pp. 147-163. In: *Revue Juridique, Politique et de l'Union Française*, tomé IX

GAYIBOR, Nicole L.
1991 Histoire du Petit-Popo et du Royaume Guin. Paris: Karthala et Lomé: Editions Haho

GRIFFITHS, John
1978 Legal Reasoning from the external and the internal perspectives. Pp. 1124-1149. In: *New York University Review*, 53

GROFF, David H.
1991 The dynamics of collaboration and the rule of law in French West Africa: the case of Kawma of Assikasso (Ivory Coast), 1898-1922. Pp. 145-166. In: *Law in Colonial Africa*. K. Mann and R. Roberts (eds.). London: James Currey

HAAR, Bernhard ter
1939 *Beginselen en Stelsel van het Adatrecht*. Groningen & Batavia: Wolters

HESSELING, Gerti
1992 *Pratiques foncières à l'ombre du droit: l'application du droit foncier urbain à Ziguinchor (Sénégal)*. Research Report, no. 49 Leiden: Afrika-Studiecentrum

HOLLEMAN, Hans F.
1969 *Chief, Council and Commissioner. Some Problems of Government in Rhodesia*. Assen: van Gorkum

KURCZEWSKI, Jacek & Karl FRIESKE
1977 Some Problems in the Legal Regulation of the Activities of Economic institutions. Pp. 489-505. In: *Law and Society Review*, 11, Winter.

LADLEY, Andrew
1991 Just Spirits ? In search of tradition in the customary law courts in Zimbabwe. Pp. 584-605. In: *Proceedings* of the VIth International Symposium of the Commission on Folk law and Legal pluralism. Ottawa (Canada). August 14-18, 1990

LAAR, Elly van
1991 Volkshoofd en Overheid in Afrika - analyse van hun verhouding. Unpublished M.A. thesis. University of Leiden

MILLER, Norman N.
1968   The political survival of traditional leadership. Pp. 183-201. In: *Journal of Modern African Studies*, 6

MOORE, Sally F.
1978   *Law as Process - an anthropological approach.* London: Routledge & Kegan Paul

PELS, Peter
1996   The pidgninization of Luguru politics: administrative ethnography and the paradoxis of indirect rule. Pp. 1-24. In: *American Ethnologist*, 24 (4)

PROCTOR, Jack M.
1968   The House of Chiefs and the political development in Botswana. Pp. 59-79. In: *Journal of Modern African Studies*, 6

ROBERTS, Richard
1991   The case of Faama Mademba Sy and the ambiguities of legal jurisdiction in early colonial French Soudan. Pp. 185-204. In: *Law in Colonial Africa.* K. Mann and R. Roberts (eds.). London: James Currey

ROUVEROY VAN NIEUWAAL, E. Adriaan B. van
1976   *A la recherche de la justice; quelques aspects du droit matrimonial et de la justice du Juge de Paix et du Chef Supérieur des Anufom à Mango dans le Nord du Togo.* Leiden/Hasselt: Afrika-Studiecentrum

1980   Bases juridiques du droit coutumier au Togo dans l'époque coloniale allemande: 1884-1914. Pp. 27-35. In: *Verfassung und Recht in Ubersee.* 1980, 13 Jhrg, no. 1

1987   Modern States and Chieftaincy in Afrika. Pp. 1-41. In: *Journal of Legal Pluralism*, nos. 25 & 26

1991   The Togolese Chief: caught between the Scylla and Charibdis. Pp. 121-152. In: *Afrika Focus.* vol. 7, no. 2 (reprinted in: *Journal of Legal*, no. 32: 19-46)

1992   Aventure démocratique au Togo: le chef traditionnel: pris entre l'état et son peuple. *documentary film*; 22 min. Leiden: Afrika-Studiecentrum

1995   La pauvreté judiciaire au Togo: une question à suivre. *Report for the World Bank.* February 1995; 58 pp.

1996   States and Chiefs: Are Chiefs Mere Puppets ? Pp. 39-78. In: *Journal of Legal Pluralism*, nos. 37 & 38

1998   Law and protest in Africa. Resistence to legal innovation. Pp. 70-119. In: *Sovereignty, Legitimacy and Power in West African Societies - Perspectives of Legal Anthropology.* E.A.B. van Rouveroy van Nieuwaal & W. Zips. (eds.). LIT Verlag: Hamburg

n.d.   *L'Etat moderne au Togo et sa contrepartie le chef traditionnel: un mariage de raison?* forthcoming (Karthala: Paris)

1982   (with BAERENDS, Elza A.)

La parcelle du gendre complotteur - manières coutumières et modernes d'acquérir des droits sur la terre à N'zara (=Sansanné-Mango), Nord-Togo. Pp. 49-71. In: *Droit et Cultures*. no. 4

ROUVEROY VAN NIEUWAAL, E. Adriaan B. & Donald I. RAY (eds.)

1996   Introduction. The new Relevance of Traditional Autorities in Africa. Pp. 1-38. In: *Journal of Legal Pluralism, nos. 37 & 38*

SEBALD, Peter

1988   *Togo 1884-1914. Eine Geschichte der deutschen "Musterkolonie" auf Grundlage amtlicher Quellen*. Akademie: Berlin

SEKGOMA, G. A.

1995   The Nature, Structure and Functions of Chiefship in Contemporary Botswana: Possibilities for Democratization. Pp. 175-203. In: *Proceedings* of the Conference on the Contribution of Traditional authority to Development, Human Rights and Environmental Protection: Strategies for Africa. Nana Arhin Brempong, Donald I. Ray & E. Adriaan van Rouveroy van Nieuwaal (eds.) Africa Studies Centre: Leiden

SKINNER, Edward P.

1968   The 'paradox' of rural leadership: a comment. Pp. 11-38. In: *Journal of Modern African Studies,* vol. 9, no. 2

SPITTLER, Gerd

1981   *Verwaltung in einem afrikanischen Bauernstaat. Das koloniale Französich- West-Afrika, 1919-1939*. Freiburg/Zürich: Atlantis

TANGRI, Roger

1980   Paramount Chiefs and central government in Sierra Leone. Pp. 183-195. In: *African Studies,* 39

TROTHA, Trutz von

1988   Zur Entstehung von Recht. Deutsche Kolonialherrschaft und Recht im 'Schutzgebiet Togo', 1884-1914. Pp. 317-346. In: *Rechtshistorisches Journal* , 7

1993   Intermediäre Rechtsordnung. Zur Organisation der Häuptlingsgerichtbarkeit in der deutschen Kolonie Togo, 1884-1914. Pp. 431-453. In: *Sprache, Symbole und Symbolverwendungen in Ethnologie, Kulturanthropologie, Religion und Recht*. Festschrift für Rüdiger Schott zum 65. Geburtstag. W. Krawietz, L. Pospisil and S. Steinbrich (eds.). Berlin: Duncker & Humblot.

1994a   *Koloniale Herrschaft. Zur soziologischen Theorie der Staatsentstehung am Beispiel des 'Schutzgebietes Togo'*. Tübingen: Mohr

1994b Streng, aber gerecht, -'hart, aber tüchtig'. Über Formen von Basislegitimität und ihre Ausprägungen am Beginn staatlicher Herrschaft". Pp. 69-90. In: *Legitimation von Herrschaft*. W.J.G. Möhlig and T.von Trotha (eds.). Köln: Köppe

1996 From Administrative to Civil Chieftaincy: Some Problems and Prospects of African Chieftaincy. Pp. 79-108. In: *Journal of Legal Pluralism*, nos. 37 & 38

VANDERLINDEN, Jacques

1989 Return to Legal Pluralism: Twenty years later. Pp. 149-158. In: *Journal of legal Pluralism*, no.28

VAUGHN, Olufemi

1988 Les chefs traditionnels face au pouvoir politique. Pp. 44-56. In: *Politique Africaine*, 32

THE ELUSIVE CHIEF: AUTHORITY AND LEADERSHIP IN SURMA SOCIETY, (ETHIOPIA[1])

Jan Abbink

Introduction

This chapter makes the point that for an understanding of the social reproduction of authority and hegemony of state structures, an analysis of local mechanisms of politics, governing and control is necessary. In a process of social reproduction one notes the mediation and articulation of the national and the local, where chiefs, as joints of authority and policy, may play an important role, but in very different shapes (see Fisiy 1995): chiefs and local leaders may be elusive in more than one respect.

From recent scholarly discussions it is evident that a study of local forms of authority and chieftaincy in Africa has renewed theoretical and practical relevance. In the search to discover short-cuts to development, the interest of governments, NGOs and the development community in local chiefs is also growing due to their being perceived as new focal points to enhance legitimacy ('democratisation') and as mediums of social change in African societies.

Processes of political and social change in the African post-colonial polity are, however, problematic and contradictory. On the one hand we see efforts at

---

[1] I acknowledge with gratitude the support for fieldwork and further research provided by the Netherlands Organisation for Scientific Research in the Tropics (WOTRO, WR 52-610), and the African Studies Centre (Leiden). I also express my thanks to the Editors of *Africa* (Istituto Italo-Africano, Roma) for permission to use a similar article which I published in their journal in 1997 (vol. 52: 317-342)

'democratisation' and popular participation in politics, but on the other, a delegitimization or breakdown of central state power, often followed by simply an adaptive transformation of autocratic elite rule. The first development was often followed by the second. Within both these processes, there has indeed been a resurgence of these local traditions of "chieftaincy" in its many forms. Local chiefs (who often have historical and cultural referents, which does not necessarily mean that they are always 'legitimate' because of these referents) have often taken the chance to secure a role within the new political space, or have stepped into a vacuum of power left behind by a retreating central government. The administrative competence and local acceptance of these newly emerging chiefs is, nevertheless, disputed. In the local arena, instead of being hereditary or chosen standard-bearers of cultural traditions and democratic ideals, they are often political agents in their own right and act with a degree of opportunism, geared to their own contemporary interests[2]. In the intersecting domains of the local and the wider national or transnational setting, they are contested because many of them are new civil servants appointed by the central government to bypass 'traditional' or customary chiefs, and act often as power brokers and political entrepreneurs.

The diversity of local leadership in Africa is great, but its wider potential seems limited: a comparative study would suggest that the resurgence of chiefs, e.g., as 'democratic counterpoints', is most likely a temporary phenomenon. The resurgence may only be an adaptive transformation, and does not in itself reflect an ongoing democratisation. It can also easily relapse into new forms of local despotism.

I will discuss recent developments of local authority and 'leadership' in a society in southern Ethiopia where any form of hierarchical chieftaincy proper was not present. The intention is not another effort to explain the 'survival' of chiefs in the post-colonial state structure, or to gauge the potential of chiefs to become focal points of 'democratisation'. It is primarily to examine the nature of 'authority' in a non-state social formation and to highlight aspects of the transformation in patterns of local leadership in twentieth-century Ethiopia. There are several small-scale societies or social formations in this country that defy cherished models of political authority and chieftaincy. They nominally pose a challenge for the central government and its effort to redefine state-society relations in the aftermath of a period of dictatorial state-communist government from 1975 to 1991, although as relatively autonomous political structures they will most likely face co-optation or demise. A comparison with other forms of local authority and chieftaincy from various areas of Eastern Africa may help to assess the specificities of the Surma and Ethiopian case.

The nature of local authority and the scope and range of local government with and through 'chiefs' is also widely misunderstood in the global game of development

---

[2] Some after indepencence retained a new 'chiefly' position which was instituted by the colonial state.

undertaken by foreign donor-countries, due to the institutional and ideological constraints inherent in the effort itself. While this state of affairs cannot be easily remedied, it might at least be advisable to develop and stimulate a critical sense of what the local views and aims are, and to find out at what point external meddling should stop to let the local society develop its own path of change.

Ethiopia, while being a country of great diversity in ethno-cultural groups and customary political-legal traditions, has not figured prominently in scholarly discussions on African chieftaincy. This may be due to various factors, but a very important one is the absence of a colonial legacy in politics and law. This has prevented the problematic of 'indirect rule', etc. which has been the issue of a voluminous literature on West and Central Africa, and has also retarded and significantly modified the impact and pace of globalising forces on this country. Ethiopia also had an old indigenous state with its own legal and political traditions of, and solutions for, local governance. There is, nevertheless, potential comparative relevance to a study of chiefs and political authority in Ethiopia. The ethnographic literature on the dynamics of chieftaincy and local leaders in Ethiopia is fairly rich, although theoretical reflection is scarce: there are no systematic comparative studies of transformations of local authority and leadership in Ethiopia as there are for the ex-colonial regions of Southern and Eastern Africa.[3]

This chapter takes one case for special consideration: the Surma (also known as Suri) of south-western Ethiopia, a society where 'chiefs' in the proper sense of the word are lacking,[4] but where the nature of the polity and of its ritual leaders can be compared to that in other areas. It should be noted that the Surma area has been one of instability and violence in the past eight years, with hundreds of people killed in either inter-ethnic conflicts or government punitive action. An analysis of the local constructions and dynamics of authority, leadership and state power may reveal some of the reasons.

Ethiopia's multi-ethnic polity

Ethiopia is a country of growing importance, with the third largest population in Africa. For historical reasons, Ethiopia was and is often considered as 'not quite Africa', both in the West and in Africa itself (see Teshale 1996). The image goes back to the medieval European representation of Ethiopia/Abyssinia as a legendary Christian state 'surrounded by Muslims' (The Muslim expansion in the early Middle Ages had cut off contacts with the West from the tenth until the early fifteenth century). In colonial

---

[3] Donham & James' pioneering book (1986) is an outstanding exception, but has not led to many follow-up studies.

[4] This chapter is based on fieldwork among the Surma, Me'en and Dizi peoples done in the years 1990-1995.

Africa, the country retained its prestige as one of the oldest independent sources of African culture. Partly, these views were based on the ancient independent state tradition of Ethiopia. At least since the first century BCE, a central state was known the Ethiopian highlands (Aksum). It was centred on a monarchy buttressed by a universal religion (Orthodox Christianity, since about 340) and on a politico-religious literary and juridical tradition (in the Ge'ez language). The presence of an indigenous state is indeed important in comparing patterns of chieftaincy and leadership in Ethiopia with those of other areas. The Ethiopian monarchical state was long confined only to the central highlands, some 45% of the present state territory. In the areas incorporated since the late nineteenth century - mostly low-lying pastoral areas - other forms of governance and authority were dominant. There were, for instance, segmentary societies (Somali), age-grade societies in the east and south (Oromo, Konso, Darasa, Sidama), small-scale 'divine kingdoms' as well as democratic assembly-societies (in the Omotic-speaking areas, see for instance Abélès 1983, Bureau 1981), and hierarchical chiefdoms in the central and southern regions (See Todd 1978, Haberland 1993). The diversity was staggering and posed a challenge for the centralising empire-state of Ethiopia and its socio-cultural order in the first half of the twentieth century.

In the pre-modern era, central state rule (either in direct or in tributary form) was already contested, even in the various core regions of Ethiopia like Tigray and Begemdir, without, however, losing its organising and normative force. On the southern periphery, elite-strata of the Oromo people, which had substantially expanded into the highland areas since the mid-sixteenth century, were partly incorporated into the state elite, whereby ethnic identity as such was not a prime criterion. In addition, several Oromo kingdoms emerged in the eighteenth and early nineteenth century, inspired by elements from that central highland state tradition. Northern monarchical traditions may also have had a defining influence on the smaller kingdoms in the Omotic-speaking areas in the South (see Haberland 1965; 1981).

Ethiopia was never colonised - it was only occupied for five years by Fascist Italy in the 1930s - and thus did not receive the direct impact of colonial judicial and political administration[5]. But the imperial-type government under Haile Sellassie (r. 1930-1974) showed some structural similarities with a 'colonial' government, imposing alien rule and a tributary economic system on subject groups, not least in the southern, recently incorporated, areas. The imperial regime could, in a radical view, be labelled as a form of internal colonialism. Many ethnic groups in Ethiopia saw significant, often dramatic, transformations under the Empire state. Nevertheless, core elements of their traditional ideas of authority and local governance were often maintained, in ideology and collective memory, if not in actual form then often in dormant state.

---

[5] The case of Eritrea is different: there the Italians established a colony in 1890 which lasted up to 1941. Colonial administration and thinking made a deep imprint in Eritrean society, still noticeable today.

The period after imperial conquest of southern Ethiopia since the 1880s created new patterns of local leadership, often in the form of a combination of direct rule (the state appointment of military chiefs as governors), and a version of indirect rule (naming local chiefs from an ethnic or regional group as government liaison men). If the indigenous structure did not have an institution that could be called 'chieftaincy', one was imposed from above. Often, local people with a feeble prestige or power basis in their own society were appointed, which led to predictable problems of representativeness and manipulation, known from the Western colonial systems elsewhere in Africa. Hence, the *cultural articulation* of these two traditions of authority and leadership - the central and the local - was complex and varied across groups. Seen from a political-anthropological perspective, Ethiopia was a social 'laboratory' for political-legal experimentation. It yielded continuities in local leadership where elites were maintained, though co-opted or where neo-traditional chiefs emerged from the local society. But it yielded also ruptures where imposed state administrators and non-indigenous rule were introduced.

From the late nineteenth century up to the present, Ethiopia, though with an underlying political culture of authoritarianism, moved through three fundamentally different political systems (apart from the Italian intermezzo of 1936-1941): feudalist monarchy (up to 1974), state-communist centralist republic (1974-1991), and an ethno-regional federal republic (since 1991). In the present study, the question is to what extent these different types of governance and authority structure have had a transformative impact on traditional forms of chieftaincy and local leadership. This question has great relevance, because the local appropriation and re-creation of ideas and practices of national governance and state 'legitimacy' can prove decisive for the social basis and political stability of a regime.

As the Surma, like the dozens of other ethnic groups in Ethiopia, form part of a larger whole, we first sketch the Ethiopian administrative context.

Ethiopian local administration

Under the Ethiopian imperial system until 1974, one principle was paramount: loyalty to the emperor, as the unifying political figure and source of divinely ordained power. The personal bond was important: primarily, *people* had to be controlled. There was some measure of administrative decentralisation and delegation of power but this never significantly affected the hierarchical power structure ultimately controlled by the emperor (see Aberra 1968). Over the years, the structure became increasingly autocratic. Emperor Haile Sellassie had initially been a moderniser, intent on bringing modern education, economic development, a nation-state and an efficient central-state bureaucracy to a country where the regional nobility and provincial war-lords and settler-communities in the conquered south were traditionally strong. Their position was based on hegemonic land-tenure, buttressed by hereditary rights or resulting from confiscation. In the South there was also that of free-holds. The possession of (claims to) land provided the economic pillar of the 'Amharised' gentry in the pre-revolutionary system. Haile Sellassie, as long as he could not or did not carry out a fundamental land reform, had to leave the elites in the core regions of the empire (like Tigray, Gojjam, Begemdir, Jimma and Wollo) a substantial amount of autonomy, as long as they recognised him as the sovereign. This highly patrimonial structure was characterised by a very slow rate of change, and a continued subjugation of the peasantry in a crippling tributary system.

Another feature of the imperial policy was that national integration and socio-cultural assimilation of the many ethno-cultural groups and religious communities came only in second place (Clapham 1975: 77), after the overriding aim of political-economic control. The different cultural commitments of these local populations were to a large extent respected, or just ignored. Only when entry into the *national* echelons of power was aimed at, an assimilation to the dominant Amhara cultural style was necessary (language, religion, manners). In the southern provinces, which had only been part of the empire since the late nineteenth century, there were many smaller decentralised societies, but few powerfully entrenched provincial elites of nobles which the monarch had to reckon with.[6] In these areas, often seriously disorganised after the destructive conquest, a new structure of authority was instituted. As the hereditary chiefs or kings were often initially removed, representatives of the new stratum of the military and settler groups[7] were appointed as administrators. Their rule was based on the control of resources and local labour power. This was the infamous *gäbbar*-system: every northern soldier, settler or administrator received a number of local people as his *gäbbar*s or tributary retainers, who had to work on his land, fetch fuel wood, do maintenance work, deliver tribute in kind, etc. This system was a heavy burden on the local population, undermining their own productive capacity. It led to abuse, over-exploitation and impoverishment. Its abolishment in 1941 did not give an immediate improvement of the lot of rural people, because most land in the South remained in the hands of a minority of big landlords.

Alongside this first layer of political-economic control, the second one was allowed to exist: that of local, indigenous representatives. These people were of lower rank, placed under the governor or district administrator and acted a liaison-men for their own

---

[6] The case of Eritrea is different: there the Italians established a colony in 1890 which lasted up to 1941. Colonial administration and thinking made a deep imprint in Eritrean society, still noticeable today.

[7] Now well-known by the term *neft'ennya* (i.e., gun-bearing settlers), although here was a wider assortment of people like traders, craftsmen, shopkeepers, farmers, bar-keepers, etc. which came in their wake. In recent years, the term *neft'ennya* has become an unspecified term of abuse used in all kinds of contexts.

society. Under the *ancien régime* (up to 1974) there were several of such positions, two of which are important in the region to be discussed: the *balabbat* and the *chiqa-shum*.[8]

The *balabbat* (literal meaning: 'one who has a father', i.e., a recognised genealogy indicating his status as a 'big man') was the legitimate claimant or owner of a certain territory, and confirmed in his position by the administrators. He could be a clan elder, a spirit-healer, a ritual leader, or a traditional chief or king of a certain ethnic group.[9] Later the word simply came to mean 'big man' or leading, wealthy figure in the local community, i.e. also outside the ethnic group in question. In the Maji area there were even several Amhara *balabbat*s, who had assimilated to local society, although they stood above it in rank or cultural prestige. In the government structure, the *balabbat* had no legally well-defined administrative tasks, although he was held responsible for order and for the political compliance of the local community. He often became more dependent on the central authorities than on his own community.

The *chiqa-shum* (literally: 'mud chief') was a government-appointed chief of a certain rural area or a village (nominally under the *balabbat*). Although the incumbents got this position either by inheritance, by nomination or by election within the local community (Berhane 1969: 36), the *balabbat*-appointment was not always a logical extension of the local leadership pattern based on indigenous socio-cultural ranking. Among the Me'en people, for instance[10], none of the five traditional *komoruts* (headmen, see below) ever took up the position of government chief; only some of their subordinate 'chiefs' did so. The mud-chiefs, while having no military or judicial powers, were to keep law and order, organise collective works and allocation of land, and communicate government laws and directives to the rural populace (Berhane 1969: 38).

For more *nomadic* people like the Surma, however, the *balabbat* and the *chiqa-shum*-positions were largely irrelevant. The government never succeeded in involving the nomadic groups in the administration. It contented itself with maintaining contacts with what it saw as 'traditional leaders' necessary to keep local peace, start mediation in disputes with farmers, and get the taxes (ibid., p. 39) . In most nomadic-pastoral areas,

---

[8] The other two were *melkegna* and g^wult-*gejj*, both military administrators in conquered or expropriated areas (see Berhane 1969: 40-41).
The political system of the Ethiopian empire also knew a complex range of *honorific* political titles, but these did not have any relation to political functions actually exercised. They were only evidence of a recognition of a person by the Emperor for past achievements or loyalty. Such titles, like *dejazmach, gerazmach, kenyazmach, balambaras,* or *fitawrari,* were derived from ranks in the old imperial army and were given to people of all ethnic groups throughout Haile Sellassie's reign. It does not predict an actual power position. Even among the Me'en and Surma in remote southern Ethiopia one came across a few persons with such titles.

[9] For instance, the Dizi paramount chiefs and the kings of the Maale, Dime or Gofa peoples were called *balabbat*.

[10] A group of ca. 60,000 shifting cultivators living north of Maji town who linguistically and culturally have much in common with the Surma.

police or army posts were established, but these had virtually no impact on the structures of daily life.

In the days of the military socialist regime from 1974 to 1991, called the *Dergue*, the political structure changed significantly, with more direct influence from the state. First, the *balabbat*s, *chiqa-shum*s and religious leaders were thoroughly delegitimized, stripped of power and prestige, banned or executed. Local organisations called peasant associations took their place (see below). Within this new organisational structure, a pervasive politicisation of the countryside was achieved.

Under the ethno-federal structure after 1991, the political framework of peasant associations was maintained but reorganised along ethnic lines. Preferably (young) people from the dominant local ethnic community could be appointed as chairmen. In addition, ethno-political parties were set up for virtually every ethnic group in the South (i.e., dozens of them) under the guidance of the governing national party, and all appointments on the district and regional level (recruited from all the ethnic groups, and not primarily on the basis of educational achievement or experience) were channelled through them. Thus, state hegemony was, so to speak, defined and established *through* a discourse of ethnicity, stimulated and controlled by the central government.[11] (In this, it adhered to the view that a defusing of ethnic problems and domination of one group could only be achieved by explicitly recognising ethnicity, not suppressing it). In what follows, we describe the Surma political system and look at how the Surma moved though these three phases of political regime in modern Ethiopia.

The Surma polity and the Surma area

The Surma (some 26,000 people) are agro-pastoralists in Ethiopia's Southern Region, near the border with Sudan. Since 1898 they are formally part of Ethiopia, although they also lived in Sudan, where they had most of their grazing land. But the Surma have largely remained outside the political dynamics of twentieth-century Ethiopia, and could in fact remain a self-governing group, like before 1898. This was partly due to their perceived 'marginality' (see Donham & James 1986): they spoke a Nilo-Saharan (Surmic) language and not a Semitic or Cushitic one like the central highlanders; they were a non-literate, small-scale society, politically without a recognised, strong executive leadership stratum. They were also seen, by sedentary farmers and people in the villages, as "uncivilised nomads" in a remote borderland. Nevertheless, their area was not unimportant economically. Since the founding of villages in the Maji area since 1898, a profitable trade in ivory, cattle and slaves emerged, especially in the early

---

[11] Dominated by one party, the Ethiopian Peoples' Revolutionary Democratic Front, the former guerrilla movement that replaced the Mengistu-regime in May 1991. Its core is the Tigray People's Liberation Front, which has played a leading role in the reshaping of post-Communist Ethiopia.

1900s. Surma sold ivory and some other big game products (rhino horn, leopard skins, giraffe-tail hair) to northern Ethiopian settler-traders. They were themselves also raided by these village people, for cattle and for slaves, especially when the decrease of elephant herds caused a crisis in the ivory trade in the 1920s (see Garretson 1986: 206, 210). However, the Surma - being perceived as roaming nomads living in a border area - were never subjected to the *gäbbar*-system. They were pastoralists with transhumance routes going deep into Sudan and had a tactic of retreat every time a government patrol came along.

Under restored Ethiopian domination after 1941, the Surma nominally fell under the district administration in Maji village. Markets and market participation of Surma increased but remained biased and underdeveloped. As a source of ivory, cattle, or labour power (slaves before the war), the entire Maji area had dried up. The lack of economic integration of the Surma in the wider Ethiopian society is a major factor accounting for their continued political marginality until the 1990s.

The structure of 'authority' among the Surma

The Surma are a segmentary society, based on strong ideas of equality and balance between individuals and territorial sections. They do not know the chieftaincy as an institution of hierarchical political authority. Surma have no persons with executive functions, redistribution rights and judicial authority. But they are not 'leaderless'. Authority among them is not a question of 'governing', but of debate, of 'coming to terms with each other' in dialogue. Through this, the right course of action and a balance between diverging interests are negotiated. The unifying institutions whereby this authority is constructed are two: a 'reigning' age-grade of elders, and a ritual leader or figurehead, called *komoru*.

- The age-grade system is well-known from many other East African pastoral societies: a division of men in formally distinguished grades to which access is given by ritual means.[12] The Surma distinguish four grades: the first two, of the children and the youngsters (or 'warriors'), the other two, the grades of the 'junior' and 'senior elders'. The third grade of the junior elders, called *rora*, is the one with active political authority. This grade is initiated roughly every 20-25 years and bears a collective name. In public debates - the assemblies of collective decision-making - the members of this age-grade are dominant. In a strict political sense - e.g., decisions taken for the

---

[12] Political-public functions are a domain of males. Women had no separate age-grading system, but derived status from their husbands' position. There is no historical record of female *komoru*s either. For an exhaustive discussion of the age-grade system among the Nyangatom, an agro-pastoral people neighbouring the Surma, see Tornay 1986 and 1989. These works also contain very fruitful theoretical reflections on the importance of age-grading as an alternative political system.

'common good' of the people - the age-grade might be said to have the dominant political influence. The second element in the political system - and the more important one for the purpose of this chapter - is the *komoru*. There are at present three *komoru*s among the Surma. The word *komoru* has an elusive character and challenges any translation. 'Chief' is not really the right word, because the person with this role has no executive, enforceable power over others. Although he is seen as being *barari*, i.e. having a certain supernatural power, or charisma in its most basic form, he is not a hierarchical authority figure with executive powers. He does not distribute land, dispense justice, or impose sanctions. The translation given by Turton (1973: 328) as 'priest' comes close but has some unintended connotations: there is no well-defined supernatural belief structure of which the *komoru* is a custodian, and he is not officiating in institutionalised religious services. The *komoru*-position has perhaps more elements from that of the 'earth chief' among several Central African peoples (see below). He is not allowed to leave the territory that is nominally his. One might also call him a 'headman'.[13])

The actual function of the Surma *komoru*[14] comprises several things:

* rain control,
* acting as ritual 'war leader': giving orders to start it (auspices) or giving advice (and blessings) on raiding and battles with enemies,
* initiate mediation and reconciliation among Surma groups,
* act as 'sacrificer' at certain social and ritual occasions (although never at funerals),
* ritually initiate fields for cultivation,
* participate in intestine divination,
* give ritual and protective blessings for cattle and people,
* sum up public debates and articulate the consensus reached.

We see that in all this the komoru is both a guardian or role-model in the social order of the Surma, and a 'ritual conductor' of supernatural force coming from the Sky-God (*Tumo*) through and to beneficial forces like rain and fertility, directing it to people and cattle (see Turton 1975: 180). Once the Chai-Surma *komoru*[15] briefly summed up his 'job' in the following manner: "Do you see the sky, with God, up there?" he asked, raising his hand towards the sky. "Do you also see the earth here, with the village, the people? I am between them, I must take care that they come together." The *komoru* is a normative figure, and as such universally respected. A *komoru* gets his position by a combination of ascriptive and achieved criteria: he comes from one of the old Surma

---

[13] In the definition of Harris (1988: 356). In his work on the Anuak, Evans-Pritchard (1940: 47-48) used the term 'headman' to describe the *kwai ngom*, the 'father of the land', although these people had the Anuak nobles (*nyiye*) above them as leaders.

[14] Having explained it here, in what follows I will use the word *komoru* as the untranslated noun.

[15] The Surma have two sub-groups, called Tirma (with two *komoru*s) and Chai (with one). The *komoru* of the latter, known as Dolloté V, was one of my key informants.

clans, he must have intelligence and charisma, be a good public speaker and should not show an impatient or aggressive character. He is selected by elders of the reigning age-grade, confirmed or elected by the people, and then ritually installed. After this, his position is unassailable, and he cannot be 'voted out of office' or deposed (except in case of mental illness or violent behaviour). It is important to note that the *komoru* is not a spirit medium and not an 'earth cult' priest', how much we might have liked to interpret him as such for comparative purposes. Both Turton and I consider him in a sense as belonging to a unique class of ritual headmen.

If specifically compared to the leaders of territorial or earth and fertility 'cults' of Central or West Africa, on which there is an important literature (see Werbner 1977, Schoffeleers 1978, 1992, Tengan 1990, Zimón 1995), we see points of similarity but also of divergence. Similarity is found in the idea of 'fertility' as the leading metaphor; also in the ethno-territorial connection, i.e., the activity of the *komoru* on behalf of the Surma polity located in a specific territory. Third, the nature of authority in societies with an 'earth cult' is more ritual than 'secular' political, although it has political aspects in that the life of the local polity is regulated by it. All this holds, obviously, for the Surma *komoru*. Fourth, there may be an element of 'scape-goating' in the attitude of the Surma toward the *komoru*, which is a familiar trait also found in earth cults in central Africa, which show that the 'king' or the chief had to sacrifice himself for the benefit of the community (see Simonse 1992). As mentioned in a forthcoming article (Abbink 1998), the Surma know a 'blessing ritual' where they face the *komoru* in a threatening way as if to attack him. But actual death or injury is never inflicted on him. Perhaps it is a ritual act to challenge the *komoru*'s blessing and to divert the power which he has (via the connection with the Sky-God).[16]

The divergences between *komoru* and territorial cult leaders are more significant:

* Among Surma, there is no real 'cult' or veneration of the earth or of any supernatural powers/spirits belonging to the earth or of beings personified as guardians of the land (contrast Tengan 1990: 3; Simón 1995). There is only the Sky God Tumo, an abstract and remote divine force. There are *no shrines* of any kind.
* It is the guarding of a social order within Surma society, fostered and ritually controlled by the *komoru*, which is important, i.e. the behaviour of people living now, not of the ancestors or spirits of the land. It should also be noted that the Surma at present live in an area which is not originally their own; and although there is a cultural nostalgia for the place of origin which features as a topos in their collective memory (original land-right myths, burial places of the *komoru*s and clan ancestors), their adaptation to the new area of settlement has shown that they are not completely dependent on the earth or territory per sé but more on the social and ritual order kept among the humans who inhabit it.

---

[16] The neighbouring Mursi people have a very similar ritual called 'spearing the priest', described by Turton 1973 and in his later works.

* The Surma do not have a form of cult which can win 'adherents' outside the Surma community, and it is neither meant to deal with personal nor collective crises. The *komoru* is a mediator with divine/cosmic force on behalf of the Surma and other people who make their living *in that area*. Though this does not exclude the inclusion of new people into Surma society, this only happens in rare cases.
* *Komoru*-activity does not cover the complete 'flow of fertility'. For the enhancing of fertility through the flow of rain, the Surma are, interestingly, dependent on the neighbouring Dizi people, who may perform such rites for them in case of drought (though this bond has deteriorated in the past recent decade).

A more obvious comparison than with the 'territorial cults' of Central and Southern Africa would be that of the *komoru* with the 'spear-masters' and 'masters of the earth' among the Dinka, Nuer, Atuot, and other Nilotic peoples. These have, in critical historical junctures, assumed certain political-military roles, or at least provided inspiration for armed action. Examples are the prophet Ngundeng among the Nuer against the British colonialists in the beginning of this century (Johnson 1994: 199, 329), and the prophet Wutnyang Gatakek in the present Sudanese civil war (Hutchinson 1996: 340-341): but their authority is based on indigenous acceptance of their roles as spiritual, as providing the reference point for cultural core-values of the society. The same is true for the *komoru* among the Surma.

Local authority should also be seen in a regional context, as the various ethnic groups in southern Ethiopia are partly dependent on each other. There is a striking difference between Surma *komoru*s and the 'sacred' chiefs of the neighbouring Dizi people. These chiefs, although they are also guardians of fertility and have priest-like functions, are well-defined political office holders, with their own ritual and administrative retainers, and have also a complex system of behavioural and food taboos separating them from the commoners (see Haberland 1993: 273-293).

Among the Surma there is also a more secular type of 'headman': the *gulsa*, who is a territorial or village leader. Although he is not 'appointed' by the *komoru* but elected by the local people, he derives his authority from the *komoru*, who gives him his blessing. A *gulsa* has no supernatural aura, and cannot perform all the above functions of a *komoru*, but he must maintain law and order in his name. If he transgresses his authority or rules by force he will sooner or later be removed, often by violent means.[17]

In sum, authority among the Surma is constructed on the basis of certain inherent qualities deemed present in an hereditary clan line and of a ritual division of labour (between age grades, and *komoru* and commoners). The nature of *komoru*-authority keeps him *out of* direct sphere of 'politics' and the fight over material interests. Within Surma society we thus find a balanced system of indigenous *consensus politics,* based

---

[17] This happened in late 1996 with an extremely violent local tyrant in a village in the Tirma area: he was shot dead in a brawl by some opponents, who were residents of his own village.

on a fusion of sacred and profane elements, and geared to maintain order in the cosmos (rain, fertility) and in the social domain (especially relations between the generations, clan-groups, and territorial groups).

It was inevitable that the northern settlers and the administration would take the *komoru* as the 'chief' of the Surma, and they tried to enlist them as government *balabbat*s with administrative and representative functions. But as the political role of the *komoru* was always overestimated by the state administrators the *komoru*s could never be relied upon as effective local leaders.

The Haile Sellassie era: administration at a distance

The Haile Sellassie era from 1930 to 1974 was marked by indirect rule over peripheral regions such as southern Käfa, home to smaller ethnic groups like Me'en, Surma, Dassanetch and Dizi. The town of Maji, the administrative centre of the region under discussion, was located in the Dizi country. In the years after the conquest of 1898, the Dizi people, a sedentary agricultural group, were strictly controlled under the *gäbbar*-system of forced labour corvées, tribute payment and slavery. Haberland has estimated (Haberland 1993: 11) that in the period 1898 and 1936 the Dizi were reduced to perhaps a tenth of their original strength. The northern settlers were centred in the handful of new villages in the highlands, from where they administered the surrounding countryside and the lowlands (cf. Garretson 1986).

The state was concerned with affirming its authority through the nation-wide establishment of the monopoly on the use of armed force and the imposition of tribute or taxes, the local northern settlers were to execute these twin aims. The contradictory aspects of this venture were obvious: the state needed the northerners - mostly Amhara - who had come as conqueror-settlers who nominally shared the Christian religion and the hierarchical political ideology of the state elite, but was keen to check their predatory use of force and their build-up of an autonomous provincial power-base. Before the Italian occupation, the local settlers always kept the upper hand in the exploitation of the Maji area.

In the Italian period (1937-1941), the old leadership structure dominated by northerners was replaced, and raiding for slaves and cattle was contained. Four army border posts were established in the Surma area to guard the frontier of *Africa Orientale Italiana* with British East Africa and the Anglo-Egyptian Sudan. Contacts between Italians and Surma were superficial, although at least in one incident the Italians carried out a violent punitive action against them.

After 1941, the Ethiopian central government reasserted its authority, taking over the four Italian army posts and trying to improve the administration of one of the most exploited and ravaged areas of the empire. Emperor Haile Sellassie made the Maji district an area to be directly ruled under the Crown (called a *mad-bet*), a kind of personal domain where he could bypass local settler-interests and experiment with administrative innovations. The emperor tried to get a picture of local concerns of the various communities beyond the northern settler-population. In 1951 for instance, he convened a big meeting of Käfa local leaders (especially the *balabbat*s) in the regional capital Jimma. Although the Surma people did not participate, several Me'en leaders did.

Apart from the enforcing of law and order, the second core element of state hegemony was introduced: taxation. This was to replace the tribute extracted, often by force, by the village settlers in the days of old. From 1942 to 1968, the Surma indeed paid taxes in kind (a monetary value converted into heads of cattle), and for co-ordinating this, the Chai-Surma *komoru* Dollote IV (Wolekorro) had been appointed as a *balabbat*, although for practical purposes the government tax collectors worked through the village[18] headmen. Haile Sellassie also tried (unsuccessfully) to start a 'civilisational offensive' among the Surma, by providing them with clothes, tools, improved seeds, and urging them to start plough agriculture.

Some trade posts had also been set up in the Surma area, settled by northerners. Trade (barter) of livestock and grain was the only meaningful contact they had with these settlers. The Surma were never involved in local administration. Three main reasons can be identified. First, administration was virtually absent: there were no government institutions or agents in the Surma domain. But second, and much more important, was the total lack of interest both of the settlers in involving them in it, and of Surma for dealings with an administration that did not bring them visible advantages. The Surma saw themselves as a separate political unit. This self-conscious attitude was maintained until this day. In terms of their segmentary political ideology, they differentiate themselves not only from their neighbour-peoples like the Nyangatom, Anywa, Toposa or Dizi, but also from the highland Ethiopians in general, whom they collectively call *Golach*. They see their own *komoru* as structurally equivalent to the emperor, or nowadays the prime minister (most powerful), of Ethiopia as a whole. This was illustrated in an incident of 1993, when, during a stalemate in conflict-resolution talks with soldiers of the new Ethiopian government, one Surma *komoru* broke off the discussion and said: "From now on I, as the one who talks for the Surma, cannot and will not deal any longer with small-time soldiers, but will only speak to Meles [the then Ethiopian president, J.A.] himself!" Finally, the political economy of land and labour exploitation after 1941, while not feudalist like the pre-war *gäbbar*-system, remained predatory and hierarchical; traders and district officials illicitly 'augmenting their income' dominated the scene. Surma were left alone and militarily kept in check if necessary. In cases of disputes or occasional violent incidents (such as cattle-raiding)

---

[18] It has to be noted that the Surma are not identified primarily on the basis of village residence but on that of membership in a herding unit, but I refrain from elaborating this here.

between Surma and non-Surma, mediation talks were held under the auspices of the government with village chiefs. But the indigenous and state political traditions were not confronted head-on, and the Surma traditional leaders were not captured in a state structure, only repressively controlled.

The Surma and the Dergue: efforts at incorporation and transformation

In the era of the *Dergue*, the revolutionary government that came to power after 1974, things changed radically. In the emerging revolutionary discourse of socialist-communist Ethiopia, the Surma were a 'primitive-communalist' society, the lowest stage on the evolutionary ladder, and as such presented an ideological and developmental challenge to a regime committed to the 'overthrow of the ruling classes' and to socialist-collectivist development.This paragraph is partly based on Abbink 1994a, where the case of the Me'en people is discussed in more detail.[19]

Compared to the *ancien régime* of Haile Sellassie, the Ethiopian revolution brought a policy of recognition of the existence of ethnic groups or 'nationalities' (the old Stalinist term). This was, among other things, the reason for the founding of the "Institute for the Study of Ethiopian Nationalities" in 1983, a political research bureau directly responsible to the government. Also, in some speeches and declarations of the leader of the *Dergue*, the 'right to self-determination' was rhetorically granted. But the underlying aim was always unity at all cost, and the development of the nationalities should be in terms of a 'progression toward socialism'. This implied a ruthless attack on traditional elites based on the control of land.

In 1975, after the Proclamation on the 'public ownership of rural lands' of March that year (which slashed away the power-base of the land-owners and the Church by declaring all land state property), the first 'development through co-operation' campaign (*zämächa*) started. 'Cadres', urban students and other leftist officials came to the countryside to 'lead and instruct' the population about 'socialist reform and reversal of oppressive structures', and to institute new local administrations. For these revolutionary cadres - young people freshly trained in Marxist thinking - all the *balabbat*s, kings, land-owners and hereditary leaders of any kind were the oppressive ruling classes, which should be neutralised. This campaign reached the Me'en and Surma areas in 1976. But among the Surma, and among similar groups such as the Me'en (see Abbink 1994b) these cadres met with problems.

The first recorded contact (in 1976) of the cadres and students with the Surma was immediately after they disembarked from the aeroplane after landing on the bush

---

19 This paragraph is partly based on Abbink 1994a, where the case of the Me'en people is discussed in more detail.

airstrip in the Surma territory. At the first meeting convened (with some Tirma and Chai), there was total misunderstanding. The cadres had difficulty in explaining their mission, and not only because of language problems. There were no land-owners or identifiable 'chiefs': they could not trace private property (because land was common free-hold based on actual use), and they could not maintain that the 'producers were divorced from their means of production'. An oppressive land-owning stratum could not be identified; there were no classes in Surma society - except age-classes, but that was not what the cadres meant. Surma elders and *komorus* were not ostensibly different from average Surma, and the cadre question as to "who were the *balabbats*" was initially not understood by the Surma.

The revolutionary officials then chose for a developmental and 'ideological' offensive, e.g., by ordering the Surma 'to start wearing clothes', to settle in one place and practise plough-agriculture, to tone down their ceremonial duelling contests, and to stop wearing the characteristic big Surma female lip-plates and ear-discs. The response was one of incomprehension. One Surma elder said that they "... would give up their own customs when the visitors would give up circumcision, or writing down everything in their notebooks." A few subsequent meetings were held but were largely fruitless. The cadres left, and, also for practical reasons (no food, no facilities, the threat of malaria), did not return. Interestingly, the Surma also did not take the visitors very serious. They knew that Haile Sellassie had been deposed, but saw that in the subsequent turmoil no new, legitimate leadership of Ethiopia had been formed. In the group of young cadres, they did not see a worthy equivalent to their own *rora* elders and *komorus* with which to deal on an equal basis. This scepticism remained vis-à-vis all subsequent local administrators.

More than had ever been the case in the Haile Sellassie era, the local administrators and Ministry officials in the period of the *Dergue* were people coming from outside, trained in Marxism-Leninism. They organised the peasantry in 'peasant-associations', a new form of collectivist units of rural producers, instituted nation-wide. Its chairmen were local people, often scions of important local families. They made *balabbats* and *chiqashums* redundant. In addition, it was not uncommon for *sons* of the traditional rural elite, whether 'Amhara' or of indigenous ethnic groups, to become a cadre for the government.

For minority ethnic groups, especially when a part of their traditional authority structure was still intact on the eve of the revolution (as among the various ethnic groups in the Maji area, like Surma, Dizi, Me'en, or Bench), the most radical change after 1974 was the utter delegitimisation and attempted elimination of hereditary chiefs and ritual specialists by the government. Some were killed, some were dispossessed, and their ritual paraphernalia, insignia, and objects were confiscated and destroyed. Among the Me'en and Dizi, there is a tragic record of devastation and public humiliation of such chiefs. They had to give up their age-old cultural artefacts, which now are irretrievably lost, and were forced to break traditional chiefly taboos (e.g., concerning food). Among the Me'en, Dizi and Bench people, the traditional leaders and chiefs, however, did not die out; they simply went underground. In some areas they could even continue their practices (of mediation, performance of ritual, spirit-healing, divination) in covert fashion. Nevertheless, the Surma elders and *komoru*s, institutionally and geographically elusive, were not seriously affected by this revolutionary drive. They did not lose their land-base because they never had one. As we saw, their authority was constructed in non-material domains.

In the years after the cadre-campaign, a few peasant-associations for the Surma were designed (although the Surma were not 'peasants' and loathed what they saw as the highland farming culture of toil and poverty). These remained constructions on paper only. In two locations in the Surma area primary schools were set up, as well as a mobile veterinary service for Surma cattle that served for a few years. Local officials attempted to re-instate tax-collection which had been discontinued in 1968, but were not successful, due to non-co-operation of the Surma elders and *komoru*s and persistent difficulties in pinning down the 'responsible people'. Administration of the Surma area went through the officials in Maji village, and through the local police and army chiefs of the three contingents stationed in the Surma area. Their most important job was to organise periodical reconciliation between Surma, Dizi, Anywa and Nyangatom, after large-scale cattle-raiding and homicides.

Until 1989, the government still had the 'monopoly on the means of violence' in the area. But after that year it was gone, due to the self-arming of the Surma with contraband rifles. In 1990 the soldier posts were abandoned, due to threats for their security. This sudden influx of modern rifles was a factor that unexpectedly changed the entire political setting in the Maji area. It not only undermined government authority and local peace with neighbouring groups, but also threatened the Surma political system itself (see section 7). This incidentally illustrates that the process of political reform or incipient 'democratisation' can be thwarted by unexpected factors.

The general *Dergue*-policy toward ethno-cultural traditions in the South had been paradoxical. Totalitarian, hard-line socialism was the dominant ideology, but in various documents (the 1976 Program of the National Democratic Revolution), as well as in the work of the Institute for the Study of Ethiopian Nationalities, the regime appeared to want at least to pay lip-service to ethnic diversity and pluralism in the country (cf. Solomon 1993: 154). However, the stratum of traditional leaders who expressed this ethnic diversity and its concomitant cultural resources was largely neutralised. In its radical modernisation drive, the *Dergue* succeeded, more than Haile Sellassie ever did, in removing these traditional chiefs from the political arena, replacing them with peasant-association chairmen, a new style of politicised and dependent local leadership. Headmen and chiefs retreated to the cultural domain, where their survival was deemed harmless.

Incorporation of the Surma polity into a post-Communist state structure: in search of 'leaders'

Since the 1991 change from a state-Communist unitary system to a federalised ethnicity-based system of government, the Ethiopian political landscape has changed dramatically, also in remote regions like Maji. Ethiopian national identity is being redefined as a unity in diversity, with the emphasis on ethnic groups as the constituting elements. The new ruling party, the EPRDF (see note 13), came to power after a guerrilla struggle conducted in the name of ethno-national liberation. The 'national question' was seen as the problem which had generated perpetual violent conflict in Ethiopia. In the view of the leading party, the various 'nationalities'[20] of Ethiopia should receive autonomy and administer their own affairs, 'without any one ethnic group dominating'. In this line, ethnicity has been declared as the basis for new regional organisation (in zones, i.e., districts largely along 'ethnic boundaries'), for the staffing of local administrations (by local ethnic candidates only, excluding the northerners), and for education and justice (to be conducted in the vernacular languages).

Before the impact of such post-Communist change was felt in Surma society, there had been an *internal dynamic* in the Surma polity, not directly caused by state imposition but by the above-mentioned problem of the 'democratisation' of violence: the wide availability of automatic rifles. The internal dynamic revealed the specific nature but also the vulnerability of leadership and authority in Surma society. Two things were central here: a devaluation of the role of the *komoru* and a crisis in the age-grade system. Both were triggered by the sudden militarisation of the young generation: the influx of large numbers of automatic rifles and ammunition allowed every male to have at least one Kalashnikov. Its availability and fire-power (for a generation that had only known spears and slow three-bullet reloading rifles of at least 50 years ago) led to a youthful fascination with the exercise of violence (in raiding, ambushing neighbouring groups, and in 'conflict settlement' within their own society).

The *first* aspect of internal change was an erosion of the role of the *komoru*. The sphere of ritual-religious activity in Surma life has become less important in the eyes of young people. Several of the village headmen (the *gulsa*), were able to play a much more active role. Another element is that at present only one of the traditional three *komoru*s of the Surma is active. One has been killed about fourteen years ago by the *Dergue* and his designated successor died at the hands by another Surma five years ago (which was unprecedented). He has not yet officially been replaced. The third one has recently died, without a successor being installed yet. Although this lapse in the prominence of the *komoru*s might only be momentary, there was definitely a crisis in that the *necessity* or relevance of *komoru*s was questioned. As we will see below, their diminished role is also related to the new political situation among the Surma.

---

20   The official Ethiopian term (in Amharic: *behéreseb*) for 'ethnic group'.

The *second* aspect of crisis was the gradual shift in the balance of power between the generations. The youths (mainly of the second age-grade, called *tegay*) dissociated itself from the elders. They no longer heeded to the advice of the *rora*-elders, went on independent robbing and killing expeditions, and evaded ritual obligations (elaborated in Abbink 1994a and 1998). These young people hence gained a much more independent position than the traditional authority system could cope with. Organising values of the age-grade system were eroding. This deteriorating relationship between the generations (or better, between the age-grades, their formal expression) led to an all-out crisis that lasted for eight years and is still not solved satisfactorily (1997). The youngsters for years refused to be initiated in the grade of junior elders (*rora*) because they would not part with their 'free life-style'. Because of it, the Surma clashed with neighbouring ethnic groups. Many people were killed in violent incidents. Economic relations also worsened and internal rivalry between Surma increased. Also with government forces the tension grew, because Surma were impervious to appeals to stop violence and register their weapons. The critical point was reached when some Surma of the *tegay* age-grade (the 'rebellious grade') made an attack on a Dizi village and also killed some EPRDF soldiers. This sparked a punitive action in late 1993 in which several hundred Surma (many women and children) were killed in a two-day battle.[21] This destructive violence gave the elders and the *komoru* the possibility to reassert themselves - as 'political agents' - and to press for the initiation-ceremony of the *tegay* to make them *rora*, social adults (see Abbink forthcoming) Thus, after a delay of more than a decade, a new *rora*-initiation ceremony of the Chai Surma was held in November 1994. However, it was not done according to the rules: many young Surma 'just took' the *rora*-title even if they were not qualified for it in either a biological or psychological sense. They entered *en masse*, apparently with the aim to stay together as a group. This led to the social anomaly of 'children' becoming 'elders', and to a corresponding decline in the authority and moral integrity of the *rora*-group. The present new *rora* cannot be said to have any 'example-function' for the rest of society, like the elders of past generations (claimed to have) had.[22] Thus, the crisis in the Surma political system is not over.

The programme of the new government was, in a sense, to 'recapture' this ethnic community, which due to its strategic position along 80 kilometres of Sudanese borderland and its increased economic relevance (the gold-trade, in which hundreds of Surma were active, and game resources), became more important. One of the strategies was to elicit a new indigenous but loyal leadership stratum. This was an ideological

---

[21]   In the almost six years of post-1991 government, more Surma have died in violent encounters (apart from this battle, dozens in violent inter-ethnic incidents) than in the Haile Sellassie and *Dergue* periods combined. Surma violence was probably also at its worst level ever in the years 1990-1996.

[22]   It is remarkable that among the Nyangatom agro-pastoralists (the Surma's southern neighbours), a similar process of militarization of the youth has seemingly *not* led to a breakdown in authority structures.

point corresponding to the conception of ethnicity as the new basis for a definition of group and democratic rights, and was declared relevant for all the southern ethnic communities. Ethnic groups *had* to be represented through their own ethnic party (founded under the auspices of the EPRDF) and their own people in the reorganised local administrations (in the Zones and the Regional-State governments) and in the national parliament (the House of People's Representatives). In the Surma area itself, a new institution, the 'Surma Council' (in Amharic: the *Surma Mikir Bet*) was installed in 1994 - a local council (of eleven people), set up at the instigation of the zonal administration. It was supposed to administer the newly created 'Surma *woreda*' (sub-district), which, like the other *woreda*s in the Zone, was created on an ethnic basis. The members of the council are mostly young Surma, with knowledge of the Amharic language, necessary for communication on the regional and national level. The installation of this Council was done with substantial pecuniary incentive (Loyalty appeared to have been bought: the new office-holders rose from scratch to positions of authority and relative wealth - i.e., a monthly government salary, fringe benefits - and were thus tied to the government).

The new administrative system imposed by the central government[23] has not considered a role for the generation of senior elders and the *komoru* among the Surma, although they were recognised as having some influence. In late 1995, the Surma Council, at the instigation of the district administration, enlisted the only active *komoru* (at that time) as a 'work manager'[24] with a government salary. Such a position contradicted his traditional role of neutral or emblematic figurehead 'above the parties', and would lead to a decisive weakening of his position and role-model function. However, after hardly eight months, in June 1996, this *komoru* resigned from this position. If he would have stayed on, he would have encouraged the process of making himself redundant, and most likely he saw that danger. His decision to keep aloof may also be interpreted as a move against state co-optation and cultural dominance. This may indicate an emerging counter-discourse among Surma - which is also evident among elders and some youngsters outside the Surma Council - about the relation between Surma group identity and Ethiopian identity, whereby the issue of cultural values and local autonomy vis-à-vis the encroaching state will be the defining elements.

The Surma Council, as a would-be political-administrative institution, has had great trouble in establishing itself as a representative or legitimate body among the Surma. Local people see it as to much external-dominated, and membership in it has become a contested resource: members get a good salary, and can augment their income by various other means (e.g., the money demanded from foreign tourists who visited the

---

23   There are now also representatives of the Ministries of Finance, Education and Agriculture present in the Surma region, all of non-Surma origin.

24   In Amharic called *sira-asfets'ami*, a position created within the context of the peasant associations of the *Dergue* period. In Amharic called *sira-asfets'ami*, a position created within the context of the peasant associations of the *Dergue* period.

Surma area).[25] The Council members are confirmed in their position in a process only vaguely resembling elections and have thus only a precarious legitimacy, also to local Surma standards.

The work that the Surma Council is expected to do may bypass the traditional arena of political decision-making, which is done in the Surma assemblies or public debates (called *mezi*) held under the auspices of elders and the *komoru*. The state has its own program to be implemented, and in its view 'democratisation' primarily means 'ethnic representation' and working through ethnic elites, and not grass-roots decision-making. This ethnic model *may* work: even though they are co-opted into a state structure where they have little influence, the Surma do have a voice. They are now also formally represented in the national parliament (in the House of Peoples' Representatives they have one seat), and in the local zonal and regional administration on the basis of the ethnic quota-system. But the Surma have an engrained perception of the encroaching Ethiopian state - whatever its nature - as an imposition, with few advantages. Indeed, if participatory local administration is not established, and if public debate, consensus-building, and ritual confirmation of decisions is neglected, the Surma will remain a dissatisfied and unstable element. This partly depends on which people are going to fill the position of chairmen in the peasant-associations, which the zonal government intends to install among the Surma. If the elders are barred form doing this, another field of tension will be built up. The new stratum of young Surma leaders[26] will not be able to enforce government policy. Explaining and getting acceptance for government policy in the ethnic community itself cannot be tackled without the support of the community leaders, such as the *komoru* and the age-grade elders, and possibly of the members of the emerging new age-grade of youngsters, who are going to be potential competitors of the new Surma politicians.

Prospects and conclusion

Southern Ethiopian local administration always knew an uneasy alliance of two types of leaders: imported highland rulers and local, indigenous chiefs or ritual leaders who represented the ethnic polities. The latter have never been the carriers of real authority. Since Haile Sellassie's reforms of the system of regional and local administration in the late 1940s, the appointed local chiefs (*balabbat*s and *chiqa-shum*s) were basically government liaison men, who had neither decisive, autonomous power nor full

---

25 Its record so far (late 1996) has been rather dismal. There are reports of a lack of activities, alcohol abuse and frequent infighting. Barely one year after its establishment, there was a great conflict about the illicit appropriation of tourist money (in May 1996). This split the council and required the intervention of the zonal and regional governments.

26 Towards December 1996, most of the Surma council members had passed a three-month training-course for local administrators in the regional capital Awasa. For them it was the first trip ever outside their home area.

legitimacy among the populace. The only sphere in which they were tolerated to function was in that of adjudication and customary law, as far as the transgression or crimes did not involve homicide or serious 'trans-ethnic' criminal cases. Nevertheless, the local leaders had more leverage and prestige among Haile Sellassie's administration than under either of its successor regimes. In the era of the emperor, the Surma had one *komoru* named as *balabbat,* although he could not be said to carry out administrative tasks. The Surma were basically ruled (which in practice meant 'taxed') directly from Maji.

Under the *Dergue*, a centralisation drive was reasserted again after a period of leniency in the first years of the Revolution era. In the Ethiopian South as a whole, what remained of the old local leadership structure was ideologically and materially destroyed, and replaced by the heads of peasants' associations and co-operatives, set up according to socialist-collectivist ideology. These leaders became the conduits of government policy, inevitable collaborators in dubious and deeply unpopular government schemes (like forceful army recruitment, villagization and collectivisation of production). The countryside was thus politicised to a degree never seen before. Although younger collateral members of local leading families were often able to secure such new local leadership positions, the former chiefs or ritual leaders themselves were not tolerated by the regime as office holders, e.g. as chairmen of peasant associations. In addition, their relatives who were appointed did often not follow the advice or policy line of their seniors, but tried to exploit the new niche of local power for their own ends. The Surma were able to 'escape' any pervasive state rule because of their geographical and cultural remoteness, the limited economic value of their area, and the lack of available 'leaders'.

Under the new federal government since 1991, a new phase of 'remote-control administration' was instituted, based on the state's selection of younger, relatively uneducated and inexperienced local people, mostly youngsters and ex-Army soldiers who know Amharic.[27] But their effective power or room for manoeuvre was kept extremely limited. In the case of the Me'en and the Surma - both relatively 'traditional' polities in the Ethiopian context - we could see that their leaders or assigned representatives were either co-opted or replaced by a new stratum of carefully chosen, more malleable persons (few of them with any recognised authority). Although the new 'leaders' occasionally consult with the elders and the *komoru,* they tend to bypass them in trying to introduce the ideas or carry out the policy instructions of the zonal or regional administration.

In the particular case of the Surma[28], we have seen that the nature and structure of 'authority', of 'leadership' in their political ideology was culturally specific and not

---

[27] Apart from the ex-soldiers (in the army of the previous government), virtually all Surma are monolingual.

[28] The same case could be made for the Me'en, Dizi and other groups in the South.

congruent with the image and expectation that the new EPRDF-government had of local leaders. In the near future, the force of political pressure and financial incentives emanating from the central authorities will keep the new group of 'ethnic leaders' in place. Whether the activities of this new stratum will lead to an erosion of the socio-cultural referents of 'traditional leadership' in societies like the Surma is unclear. In cultural terms, the Surma (and Me'en) *komoru*s derive their position not primarily from secular power defined in the political arena, but from the religious-ritual domain. Hence, they are not real competitors of the state. They remain outside 'politics', delegating it to others. In this sense, they are elusive, but this characteristic also allows for their adaptive persistence, as long as the material basis and ideological value-system of their society are not fundamentally changed.[29]

Even though the Surma *komoru*s - the most respected figureheads and reference points of internal peace and social order for the Surma - will continue to act as authoritative ritual intermediaries in their own polity, they cannot but lose their prestige and role even further as the new leadership gains a foothold. Although the strengthening of the 'cultural identity' of minority groups or 'nationalities' like the Surma was proclaimed to be a central aim of the new federal policy of Ethiopia, the perhaps inevitable tendency to bypass the stratum of traditional authority and core cultural values as expressed in the age-grade system and the *komoru*-institution, obviates that aim. It is ironic that the process of incorporation of local leaders and ethnic polities in Ethiopia is being implemented through a discourse of culture and ethnicity - denied in the days of the emperor and ignored in those of the *Dergue* -, while at the same time political practice and the administrative context make the actual content of that ethno-cultural tradition almost superfluous. In post-Communist Ethiopia, the political co-optation of ethnicity and local chieftaincy is thus complete, with the state - perhaps rather unique in contemporary Africa - in a stronger position than ever to realise its reformist and hegemonic ambitions. The question of how this process unfolds, thereby not only challenging local forms of authority and leadership but also transforming their scope, integrity and cultural valuation, might set the agenda of future research.

References

ABBINK, Jan G.
1994a   Changing patterns of 'ethnic' violence: peasant - pastoralist confrontation in southern Ethiopia and its implications for a theory of violence. Pp. 66-78. In: *Sociologus*, 44

---

[29]   Unlike in some other countries in Africa (cf. Fisiy 1995: 59), however, the control over *land* will not be an item in the competition between state and leaders in this part of Ethiopia.

1994b   Refractions of revolution in Ethiopian 'Surmic' societies: an analysis of cultural response. Pp. 734-755. In: *New Trends in Ethiopian Studies,* vol. 2. H.G. Marcus (ed.). Lawrenceville, N.J.: Red Sea Press

1998   Violence and political discourse among the Chai Suri. In: *Surmic Languages and Cultures.* G.J. Dimmendaal (ed.). Cologne (forthcoming)

ABELES, Marc
1983   *Le Lieu du Politique.* Paris: Société d'Etnographie

ABERRA, Jemberre
1968   The prerogative of the Emperor to determine powers of administrative agencies. Pp. 528-541. In: *Journal of Ethiopian Law* 5

BAHRU, Zewde
1991   *A History of Modern Ethiopia 1855-1974.* London: James Currey

BERHANE, Ghebray
1969   *L'Organisation de l'Administration Locale en Ethiopie.* Addis Ababa: Addis Ababa University, Faculty of Law

BUREAU, Jacques 1981
1981   *Les Gamo d'Ethiopie. Etude du Système Politique.* Paris: Société d'Etnographie

CLAPHAM, Christopher
1975   Centralisation and local response in Southern Ethiopia. Pp. 72-81. *African Affairs,* 74

DONHAM, Donald, L.
1992   Revolution and modernity in Maale: Ethiopia, 1974 to 1987. Pp. 28-57. In: *Comparative Studies in Society and History,* 34

1994   *Work and Power in Maale, Ethiopia.* New York: Columbia University Press (second edition)

DONHAM, Donald L. & James L. WENDY (eds.)
1986   *The Southern Marches of Imperial Ethiopia. Essays in History and Social Anthropology.* Cambridge: Cambridge University Press

EVANS-PRITCHARD, Edward E.
1945   *The Political System of the Anuak of the Anglo-Egyptian Sudan.* London: Percy Lund, Humphries & Co., for London School of Economics and Political Science

FISIY, Cyprian F.
1995   Chieftaincy in the modern state: an institution at the crossroads of democratic change. Pp. 49-62. In: *Paideuma,* 41

GARRETSON, Peter P.
1986   Vicious cycles: ivory, slaves and arms on the new Maji frontier. Pp. 196-218. In: *The Southern Marches of Imperial Ethiopia. Essays in History and Social Anthropology.* D.L. Donham & W.James (eds.). Cambridge: Cambridge University Press

HABERLAND, Eike
1965 *Untersuchungen zum äthiopischen Königstum.* Wiesbaden: F. Steiner Verlag
1981 Notes on the history of Konta: a recent state formation in southern Ethiopia. Pp. 735-749. In: *2000 Ans d'Histoire Africaine. Le Sol, la Parole et l'Ecrit - Mélanges en Hommage à Raymond Mauny.* Paris: Société Française d'Histoire d'Outre-Mer
1993 *Hierarchie und Kaste. Zur Geschichte und politischen Struktur der Dizi in Südwest-Äthiopien.* Stuttgart: F. Steiner Verlag

HARRIS, Marvin W.
1988 *Culture, People, Nature. A Introduction to General Anthropology.* New York: Holt, Rinehart & Winston

HUTCHINSON, Sharon E.
1996 *Nuer Dilemmas. Coping with Money, War and the State.* Berkeley - Los Angeles - London: University of California Press

JOHNSON, Douglas W.
1994 *Nuer Prophets. A History of Prophecy from the Upper Nile.* Oxford: Clarendon Press

McCLELLAN, Charles W.
1988 *State Transformation and National Integration: Gedeo and the Ethiopia Empire, 1895-1935.* East Lansing: Michigan State University, African Studies Center

SCHOFFELEERS, J. Matthew
1992 *River of Blood. The Genesis of a Martyr Cult in Southern Malawi, c. AD 1600.* Madison: University of Wisconsin Press

SCHOFFELEERS, J. Matthew (ed.)
1978 *Guardians of the Land. Essays on Central African Territorial Cults.* Gwelo - Salisbury: Mambo Press

SIMÓN, Henryk
1995 Earth priests and earth shrines among the Konkomba people of Northern Ghana. Pp. 77-86. In: *Hemispheres* (Warsaw), 10

SIMONSE, Simon
1992 *Kings of Disaster: Dualism, Centralism and the Scapegoat King in Southeastern Sudan.* Leiden: E.J. Brill

SOLOMON, Gashaw
1993 Nationalism and ethnic conflict in Ethiopia. Pp. 138-157. In: *The Rising Tide of Cultural Pluralism - The Nation State at Bay?* Crawford Young (ed.). Madison: University of Wisconsin Press

TENGAN, Edward B.
1990   The Sisala universe: its composition and structure (an essay in cosmology). Pp. 2-19. In: *Journal of Religion in Africa*, 20(1)

1991   *The Land as Being and Cosmos. The Institution of the Earth Cult among the Sisala of Northwestern Ghana*. Frankfurt - Bern - New York - Paris: Peter Lang

TESHALE, Tibebu
1996   Ethiopia - the 'anomaly' and 'paradox' of Africa. Pp. 414-430. In: *Journal of Black Studies*, 26

TODD, Dave
1978   Aspects of chiefship in Dimam, South-west Ethiopia. Pp. 311-332. In: *Cahiers d'Etudes Africaines*, 18

TORNAY, Serge
1986   Une Afrique démasquée. Initiation et sacrifice chez les pasteurs d'Afrique Orientale. Pp. 69-92. In: *Les Rites de Passage Aujourd'hui. Actes du Colloque de Neuchâtel*. P. Centlivres & J. Hinard (eds.). Lausanne: Editions L'Age d'Homme

1989   *Un Système Générationnel. Les Nyangatom de l'Éthiopie du Sudouest et les Peuples Apparentées*. Paris: Labethno, Université de Paris X (Thèse d'Etat), 2 volumes

TURTON, David
1973   *The Social Organisation of the Mursi, a Pastoral Tribe of the Lower Omo, Southwest Ethiopia*. London: London School of Economics and Political Science (Ph.D. thesis)

1975   The relationship between oratory and the exercise of influence among the Mursi. Pp. 163-183. In: *Political Language and Oratory in Traditional Societies*. M.Bloch (ed). London: Academic Press

1992   How to make a speech in Mursi. Pp. 159-175. In: *Ethnographic Film Aesthetics and Narrative Traditions*. P.I. Crawford & Jan K. Simonsen (eds.). Åarhus: Intervention Press

WERBNER, Richard P. (ed.)
1997   *Regional Cults*. London - New York - San Francisco: Academic Press

MODERN LOCAL ADMINISTRATION AND TRADITIONAL AUTHORITY IN ZAIRE. DUALITY OR UNITY? AN INQUIRY IN THE KIVU

Dirk Beke

Introduction

This study will first examine the evolution and the current role of chieftaincy and traditional local institutions in their relation to Zairean government, and more specifically their position in various formal and de facto processes of decentralisation. I will be asking whether we can still speak of a duality – traditional versus modern – and whether any such duality would still equate 'small-scale rural' with 'traditional', and 'larger-scale rural' and 'urban' with 'modern'.

The second part of the article will begin with a brief outline of the factors that governed decentralisation in Zaire. I will analyse the situation in the tumultuous Kivu region in late 1995 and early 1996, after the resident Rwandan-speaking population had been joined by a flood of refugees from Rwanda.[1] The focus here will be on the relations between modern local administrative institutions and chieftaincy in this complex political and ethnic melting pot. I will explore what role chieftaincy plays in current local conflicts, with special attention to the struggle for land.

---

[1] Field data were collected by Dirk Beke and Dirk Verboven in a study done for the Belgian Ministry of Cooperation in the Northern and Southern Kivu Provinces in April 1995. The full report and the interviews were published in Dutch (Beke et al. 1995). This article was written before the events of 1997.

I will further investigate the extent to which aspects of modern administration and modernity are present in rural areas, and whether significant traditional elements play a part in urban areas.

Belgian Colonial administration

Belgian rule in the Congo was founded on two different types of local administration, both of which had tight structural links. The first type consisted of entities organised according to a European (French or continental) model of modern administrative law, including provinces, districts, regions, towns and municipalities. The second type was based on entities called indigenous or native *circonscriptions*. The latter were distinctly subdivided according to their rural or urban nature. Rural *circonscriptions* were referred to as 'customary milieux' and included *chefferies* and *secteurs*,[2] while urbanised *circonscriptions* were called 'extra-customary milieux' and included 'extra-customary centres'[3] and 'native towns'.[4]

The customary milieux were governed by traditional African law, provided that the 'customs' were not in conflict with the colonial rules of public order. The *chefferies*, under a local chief, were small entities, most of them ethnically homogeneous. The *secteurs* were larger entities, which either corresponded roughly to the ancient kingdoms with an original paramount chief, or assembled several small ethnic groups under a neo-traditional chief. The paramount chief was recognised by the colonial governor as the *chef de secteur*. The colonial administration continued to recognise the village chiefs but dealt with them only through the *chef de secteur*. Many recognised chieftaincies in the Belgian Congo, however, no longer encompassed the original ethnic groups; in other cases the colonially recognised chief enjoyed no traditional authority. Like other colonial regimes, the Belgians frequently appointed chiefs over groups that had no tradition of chieftaincy. Such chiefs often operated as mouthpieces for the colonial administration (Buell 1928 / 1965 (2): 479 - 488).

The extra-customary milieux were urban areas where Congolese people of different ethnic origins lived together and were believed to be 'detached from all forms of customary organisation' (Organisation of the Native Administration 1957: 89). Such centres were administered by a chief, assisted by an assistant chief and an advisory council. The chief and the assistant were appointed by the European district

---

[2] The Native Areas Decree of 1933 confirmed previous legislation and continued in force until 1957.

[3] This type of municipal status was regulated by three decrees dated 23 November 1931, 6 June 1934 and 22 June 1934, which were consolidated by the Royal Decree of 6 July 1934 pertaining to extra-customary centres.

[4] This type of districts were established after World War II; the basic legislation was the Act of 20 July 1945.

commissioner, who also appointed the members of the council 'in accordance with the wishes of the local inhabitants'. Contrary to the name, the inhabitants of the 'extra-customary centres' were subject to their own customary law, although new legal rules gradually emerged on the basis of case precedents established by the native tribunals of these centres (Organisation of the Native Administration 1957: 92).

From 1945, 'extra-tribal concentrations' could be constituted by the provincial governors in native towns. Such towns were administered not by traditional authorities but by the European administration, sometimes assisted by a Congolese 'town chief', an assistant chief, a ward chief and a council, all appointed by the district commissioner (Organisation of the Native Administration 1957: 93).

With the exception of the *chefferies* and *secteurs*, territorial administration was seldom if ever decentralised. It was not until the end of the colonial period that some sort of standardisation was proposed which could offer sufficient flexibility. In the speech of Governor-General Pétillon to the Belgian Congo Advisory Council we can read:

> One must conclude ... that it would be harmful to the advancement of certain rural communities to define too closely and to over-emphasise the differences that we have discovered between them and the town-people. Our system of administration must be sufficiently elastic to be adaptable to any circumstances and to dispense with such arbitrary classifications, which only obscure the real situation and leave the intermediate cases without a suitable solution.
>
> The best way to achieve this was to condense certain fundamental principles into a single decree that would apply to all communities, from the most 'backward' to the most 'advanced', and then specify how and on what occasions the 'guardianship' of the local representative of the central authority should be exercised (New Institutions 1957: 81).

An attempt to reform and unify the urban areas, and to afford the Congolese with a modest degree of political participation, came in 1957 (Décret du 26 mars 1957), only three years before independence (Wallis 1958: 88-93). The same year, new legislation (Décret du 10 mai 1957) was promulgated for the territorial organisation of rural areas. It reconfirmed almost entirely the existing dual structure, with its distinction in administrative structure between rural and urban areas, as well as its distinction between the smaller *chefferies* (with their full recognition of chieftaincy) and the larger *secteurs* (with their chief appointed by the district commissioner). The sole traditional element in the latter was the rule that decisions should be taken 'if possible in accordance with the wishes of the local inhabitants' (Art. 20). Later it was argued that this also allowed for popular consultations in the form of elections (Paulus 1959: 224).

Decentralisation and the place of chieftaincy in Congo/Zaire: characteristics of decentralisation since independence

After independence, public administration first remained largely similar to that under colonial rule. The young government fell heir to the Belgian *dossier-administration*, but it proved grossly inapplicable in the newly established republic (Mpinga-Kasenda 1973: 212). The indivisibility of the power structure explicitly coincided with the centralism and unwieldiness of the colonial system (Willame 1992: 54). Decentralising measures propagated by the Zairean regime since 1977 have created, on paper, ten administrative levels. In practice, though, this structure has never functioned as a decentralised administration, due both to political neglect by the regime and to measures continuously imposed by the hierarchy above (Kanynda Lusanga 1984: 71-77).

The first period after independence (1960-1967): continuation of colonial duality of local administration

During the first period after independence, the colonial Décret sur les circonscriptions indigènes of May 1957 remained in force for the indigenous *circonscriptions*. Above and alongside this traditional system, a modern administrative apparatus was maintained; it was characterised by internal diversity. The first constitution, the *Loi fondamentale* (1960), allowed the provinces a high degree of autonomy. Each could organise its own form of local government. As a result we encounter a great diversity of administrative entities at the various levels of government: some provinces were divided into traditional *circonscriptions*, districts and territories, in addition to their (urban and rural) towns and municipalities; others were divided into districts or into prefectures (Mpinga-Kasenda 1973: 50-51). Notwithstanding this diversity, one common characteristic persisted almost everywhere in local government: the previous colonial duality, with its modern system alongside a traditional system.

Mobutu regime creates a centralised state in an attempt to abolish traditional local power (1967-1977)

One consequence of Mobutu's coup in 1965 was the abolition of provincial autonomy. The Act of 10 April 1967 (Ordonnance-Loi no. 67-177)[5] changed the structure of the state to one characterised by strong centralisation and standardisation. The provinces were deprived of their legal autonomy and legislative powers. Local governmental structures were made similar in all provinces. Districts and territories lost their autonomous powers and, similarly to the provinces, became purely administrative entities in a highly centralised state. Only the towns and the extra-customary centres retained a decentralised status; the municipalities became ordinary administrative entities (O.L. no. 68-024 & 68-025). Provincial governors were no longer to be elected by the local citizenry; they became civil servants appointed by the central authorities.

---

[5] abbreviates as "L.O."

In 1969, the regime tried to establish direct control over the local governments. A new law in March 1969 (O.L. no. 69-012) drastically altered the administration of the local *collectivités*. Although customary legal rules applying to the administration of villages, *secteurs* and certain *chefferies* remained intact, central authority intervened in these structures by abolishing the *collèges permanents* (executive assemblies) and by appointing chiefs through the interior ministry. The purpose of this reform was to acknowledge political structures founded on customary law, while integrating them into a centralist state administration.

A law promulgated in January 1973 ushered in a thorough shake-up of the administrative system. It divided Zaire into regions, subregions, zones, *collectivités* and localities, none of which was legally autonomous (Loi no. 73-015, Art. 5). Important in this context is that this law abolished the distinction between the traditionally administered *chefferie* and the semi-modern *secteur;* similarly to the former 'centres', these become identical units called *collectivités*, formerly known as *collectivités locales*.

The 1973 law also did away with provincial councils and the councils of the *collectivités locales* and rescinded the autonomous status of all decentralised units. It ended formal rights of intervention by rural collectivities in the nomination of local chiefs (Art. 24). Not only were the chiefs of the new *collectivités* to be appointed by the interior minister, they were deprived of any power based on customary law. This meant the formal abolition of the *chefferies,* a measure obviously aimed at undermining chiefly authority by placing it outside the scope of formal administration.

Instead of its power being neutralised, however, chieftaincy continued to be a crucial factor, precisely because of its specifically local tasks. The survival of chieftaincy was directly counter to the political aims of Mobutu's *Mouvement Populaire Révolutionaire* (MPR) regime, which was obviously jealous of that power. In practice, chiefs were not radically excluded, as that would have created a total administrative vacuum in rural areas. It was even reported that chiefs were curbing the power of the commissaire de zone. Ultimately the Zairean state began using party ideology and political propaganda to turn this traditional legitimacy to its own advantage, for instance by appointing chiefs to the post of commissaire de zone (Gould & Mushi-Mugumorhagerwa 1977: 274). A modest adjustment was made in 1977, when the 1973 law was supplemented by an act applying to zones and urban subregions.

Restoration of modest decentralisation (1977-1982)

To gain more legitimacy for the regime and to consolidate MPR rule, firmly controlled one-party elections were held in 1977, both at the central level – for the National Legislative Council and the MPR Politburo – and for the town councils. This process of legitimation also resulted in the granting of some limited autonomy to urban entities (Loi no. 77-028, 19 November 1977) and the rural entities (Loi no. 78-008, 20 January

1978). This modest decentralisation was not a general process, however, for no real autonomy was given to other administrative levels like regions and zones. In 1981, the MPR Central Committee decided to create regional assemblies, zone councils and collectivity councils as deliberative assemblies (State decision no. 05/CC/81). They were empowered to review and improve action plans made by local authorities and to oversee their implementation. This reform became law in 1982.

Further formal decentralisation and reinstatement of 'indigenous' local government (1982-1995)

The Act of 25 February 1982 (Ordonnance-Loi no. 82-006) divided Zairean territory into a range of administrative levels: regions, towns, urban zones, rural zones and *collectivités*. Although some observers saw this law as a cautious return to effective local democracy (Dhedonga 1984: 258), its actual implementation showed it to be nothing more than a façade to conceal the central authorities' grip on the so-called decentralised entities (Djelo 1990: 103).

The authorities in all these territorial units might be called semilocal authorities, meaning they are to act partly as local governments and partly as organs of the central administration (Cour & Taborga 1988: 56). All units are to have their own elected council, empowered to adopt a local budget funded by local revenues.

The head of a region, which the new legislation referred to as a decentralised unit with legal autonomy, is called a governor. The governor is appointed by the president after nomination by the minister of territorial administration. This official has the same typically dual function as in the classical continental or French administrative system, representing the national government in the region, while at the same time functioning as the regional authority. He is assisted by a vice-governor, likewise appointed by the president.

The subregions, the *cités* (the 'centres' in previous legislation), the *groupements*, *localités* and *quartiers* are not decentralised entities. *Cités* do appear to have a proper budget, but no elected council. The *quartiers*, subdivisions of an urban zone or centre, are headed by a *chef de quartier*, an appointed civil servant. Notably, most of the urban centres in the Kivu region (and probably also in the rest of Zaire) possess no cité statute and are therefore not towns which would make them decentralised entities. Where towns do have a proper statute, the division of powers between them and the urban zones is not clearly defined (ACDI 1992: 97).

At the level of *collectivités* (the lowest governmental unit) it is worth noting that the 1982 law has largely reinstated the provisions of the 1957 colonial decree, once again creating a distinction between *collectivités-secteur* and *collectivités-chefferie*. As stipulated in the earlier legislation, the *chefferie* is to be ruled by custom, the *secteur* by law (Dhedonga 1984 259). Both types of *collectivités* are to be headed by a *chef de collectivité*, acting under the supervision of the commissaire de zone. He is assisted by an *chef-adjoint de collectivité*, who has no autonomous authority but who acts on behalf of the chief in his absence. By law, the former chairs the council of the *collectivité*, making him both the traditional and the governmental leader.

Every *collectivité* also has an elected local council. Prior to the 1982 reforms, this *conseil de collectivité* was formed by the village chief and earth priests, who since 1977 have again been formally appointed according to traditional law. As such, these dignitaries have both worldly (political and economic) and religious functions. They adjudicate on matters of customary law in the traditional *circonscriptions;* they designate the successor to a deceased chief; they evoke the spirits to secure the fertility of the land or the abundance of hunting or fishing. With the exception of the chief of the *collectivité* and the different subchiefs of the *groupements*, the members of the Conseil de Collectivité have since 1982 been elected by universal suffrage, two members for every unit *(groupement).* Despite this formal modernisation, traditional authority is still exercised ex officio within the council.

With regard to the role of traditional power, I have pointed out that a clear distinction should be made between the *collectivités-secteur* and the *collectivités-chefferie*. As in the former *secteur*, the *collectivités-secteur* encompass more than one ethnic group group on the basis of ethnic kinship. Its formal governmental structure betrays a modern type of local organisation, although the chief is regarded as representing traditional authority as well. The *collectivités-secteur* are drawn together governmentally when different ethnic groups are presumed too small for 'harmonic development' on their own. Under MPR one-party rule, the *collectivité-secteur* consisted of three institutions: the people's committee, the council and the chief of the *collectivité*. The chief presided over both the council and the MPR people's committee within the *collectivité* (Kanynda Lusanga 1984: 41-42). He thus had not a dual but a triple function: he represented the state within his *collectivité*, he represented the local authority, and he was the local party representative. He was designated by the MPR, who chose him on the criteria of 'militancy and competence'. His mandate lasted five years. In the one-party context, the government of the *collectivité* was subordinated to MPR directives. Since the installation of a multiparty system in 1990 (Art. 8, Constitutional Act of 18 July 1990, and government declaration of 6 October 1990), the role of the local dignitaries within the single party has ceased to exist, and only two institutions remain within the *collectivité-secteur*.

The *collectivités-chefferie* are, like the former *chefferies*, organised by and based on 'custom', which consists of traditional law and ethnicity. This type of entity harks back to ancient kingdoms such as Congo, Lunda and Kuba. The *collectivité-chefferie* is headed by a traditional chief appointed by a council of elders in accordance with traditional law. After approval by the minister of territorial administration (*Commissaire d'état à l'Administration du Territoire*) and confirmation by the Commissaire Sous-Régional, he is mandated for life.

The legitimacy of local chiefs in the *collectivités (secteur* and *chefferie)*, as derived from traditional power, has been increasingly questioned. Since they are modern officials too, they have important non-traditional powers. It has been rumoured further that many chiefs have obtained their power as a result of intrigues between politicians and local administrators. This is a source of numerous conflicts over the reliability of traditional power (Rapport 1992). Moreover, many local political dignitaries were criticised in the 1980s for using revenues from farmers and taxes to their own benefit (*Hebdo JUA*, January 1991).

The *collectivité-chefferie* has a further governmental subunit, the village (*localité*), headed by a chief appointed according to local customs. He is recognised in this function by the chief of the *collectivité* and by the Commissaire Sous-Régional, the head of the subregion.

With the attempts at political democratisation and the strong self-reliance movements that proliferated after 1990, NGOs are reported to have frequently supported popular leaders within village structures to mobilise the population against authoritarian and corrupt *chefs de collectivité* or *chefs de groupements* (Beke et al. 1995: 34). The latent political turmoil, the virtual lack of communication infrastructures (passable roads, postal services), and the indistinct limits of competence and powers between modern formal administration, the military, local business elites and traditional power structures have meanwhile given rise to a wide variety of informal models of local government in Zaire.

An example of a compromise between modern and traditional local government at Kaziba (Southern Kivu)

An April 1995 inquiry in the Bushi region (Southern Kivu province) brought to light an interesting example of a compromise between modern and traditional government in the Kingdom of Kaziba.[6] The *mwami* or paramount chief, was currently assisted in his government by two councils: one traditionally appointed and empowered for traditional problems (dispute settlement) and general matters of policy; and a modern, elected council concerned especially with problems of an administrative nature, such as infrastructure and development projects. Their division of tasks does not keep the councils from meeting together to discuss major problems in the *chefferie*.

A typical example of a problem belonging to the domain of the traditional council is the allocation of land. The chief normally allocates land rights within his territory, assisted by his dignitaries in the different areas. Various systems are possible, from limited tenancy to full, unrestricted ownership (with payment of an ownership duty known as *kalizi*). This title does not, however, entitle the individual owner to sell the land – land

---

6   Interview with Mwami Chimaye II Nakaziba, Kaziba, 9 April 1995, (video). See also Beke et al. 1995, interview annexe.

remains the social property of the community, under supervision of the chief (see also van Rouveroy van Nieuwaal 1998). If the landowner permanently leaves the *chefferie*, the land automatically reverts to the local community.

The Mwami of Kaziba has admitted that, under the influence of modernisation, new systems of ownership have developed, not only in urban areas but also in his region. This means that 'extra-customary lands', over which traditional authority no longer has a say, exist in rural areas too. The traditional community is thereby threatened with dispossession. Consequently, to place lands under this arrangement in Kaziba, local government approval is still required, granted at a plenary meeting of the two councils.

Proposals by the National Conference for local government in the Third Republic

According to the Draft Constitution proposed to the National Conference in 1993, Zaire was to become a federal republic. As in 1960-1973, regions would again be called provinces.[7] The number of provinces could be changed only after agreement with the inhabitants concerned; provinces would possess legal and governmental autonomy (similar to that in federal states) and would be represented in the bicameral system in the senate. The division of powers between the federal state and the provinces was set out clearly in the draft, which was intended to put a resolute end to the long-standing interference from Kinshasa. The question may be raised, however, whether this federalism (which was supported by a majority in the National Conference) did not merely serve to mask the current political ethnicisation (Willame 1994: 136).

Notably, the draft explicitly acknowledged the authority of traditional law (Art. 161); every province was to promulgate an organic law organising such authority.[8] This still seems to have reflected no more than a moderate shift in attitude concerning the place of traditional power and the preservation of duality in the decentralisation process. Customary power was to be confined to the very lowest governmental bodies.

The special report on decentralisation issued by the Administrative and Territorial Commission of the National Conference in August 1992 argued that 'the *localité*, the *groupement* and the *collectivité-chefferie* are the lower rungs of the governmental structure whose foundations rest on tradition' (Rapport 1992: 83). However, the commission went on to propose the 'progressive modernisation of customary power to adapt it to the needs of development and democratisation' (Rapport 1992: 85). It argues

---

7 Title I of the Transitional Act of 14 August 1992 refers explicitly to the 1964 constitutional referendum to change the name of the country, the names of certain regions, the national flag and the national anthem.

8 This draft constitution was never adopted.

that although customary power is recognised at the very lowest levels *(localité* and *groupement)*, mayoral elections should still be held both in the *collectivités-secteur* and the *collectivités-chefferie* (under a new name, *communes rurales*) – thereby opening the possibility that someone from outside the traditional ruling family will be elected. The report also insists on a 'clear-cut separation of the governmental function of the traditional chief in cases where the person elected is the customary chief' (Rapport 1992: 87-88).

The situation in Zaire in early 1996: informal decentralisation and ethnicisation

Viewing all the decentralising measures taken since independence, one perceives that such reforms have failed to bring real autonomy for regional and local authorities, except in one brief period. My analysis shows that persistent inappropriate use of formal measures of decentralisation has actually served to reinforce centralisation in Zaire.

The erosion of both centralised state power and the communication infrastructure have, on the other hand, fostered true regional and local authority and spontaneous informal decentralisation. This development undeniably has many positive consequences: NGOs and other civic organisations have provided local populations with an incentive to self-reliance, and many people have exhibited a sense of inventive entrepreneurship. Even within previously disbanded regional and local governments, people have made ambitious attempts to take government into their own hands. Nonetheless I should point to negative effects in some areas, where local rulers, often in conjunction with the military, have misused this de facto autonomy for their own benefit. Furthermore, mainly as a result of general scarcity, the ethnicisation of many areas of the country has led to outright ethnic cleansing in local government, education and even in commerce and trade.

Such dangers, together with the appalling images of the Rwandan genocide, gave President Mobutu convincing arguments, especially abroad, for a restoration and relegitimisation of his power. This strengthened the myth of Mobutu's indispensability. The image of a strong central authority as the only viable alternative was a welcome political trump card for him and the Kengo government, and we even saw the opposition in Kinshasa emphasising the importance of Zairean unity and taking a somewhat retreating stance on expanded local autonomy.

Decentralisation and the struggle for land in the Kivu

So far I have been discussing formal lines of organization in which chiefs were enlisted by law. In the Kivu, a second form of decentralisation occurred which was rather based on popular incentives and not so much on formal state.

Rwandan-speaking Zaireans and Rwandan refugees in the Kivu

The present Northern and Southern Kivu provinces are inhabited by a great variety of ethnic groups, some more closely linked than others. A number of these groups stand out because they are Rwandan-speaking. In the situation before the massive influx of refugees in 1994, these groups lived dispersed across both Southern and Northern Kivu. Important concentrations were found in the zones of Rutshuru and Massisi to the north of Lake Kivu and the Virunga volcanoes. The proportion of the Rwandan-speaking population in Northern Kivu presently ranges from 40% to 60%. In 1988, the World Bank had put it at around 22% of the total population of Northern and Southern Kivu combined; in absolute numbers this would mean 1.5 to 2 million people (ACDI 1992: 50).

In early 1996, the total Rwandan-speaking population, including population growth and the estimated 1.2 million refugees from 1994, was probably between 3.5 and 4 million. Different groups are commonly distinguished:

- Rwandan-speaking Hutus and Tutsis that already lived in the area in the pre-colonial period, including the group presently called the Banyamulenge (Rwandan-speaking Tutsis);
- Rwandan immigrants that arrived in the Congo in the period 1936-1954;
- the first wave of political refugees after 1959, mostly Rwandan Tutsis;
- those who infiltrated Zaire clandestinely, the so-called economic refugees;
- the enormous mass of Hutu refugees that fled Rwanda following the 1994 genocide;
- a limited group of Hutu refugees that fled Burundi since 1994 (their language Kirundi is similar to Kinyarwanda, the Rwandan language).

In Southern Kivu, around Bukavu, there appears to have been little or no ethnic tension up to early 1996 between Hutu refugees and the major local groups such as the Bushi, who are closely related to the Rwandans. Further south, around Uvira, some tensions were reported involving the Banyamulenge.

In Northern Kivu, relations have long been tense. Even before the recent mass arrival of refugees, severe ethnic conflicts existed. Scarcity of land was the primary cause of disturbance between the 'indigenous' and the Rwandan-speaking populations; in some areas (such as Walikali and Rutshuru), Rwandan speakers formed up to 60% of the total. It was reported that in September and October 1994, newly formed Hunde and Nyanga militias, fearing the massive arrival of Rwandan refugees, attacked and killed about 150 Rwandan-speaking people (Muholongu 1995).

Most of the Tutsis living in Northern Kivu, refugees from 1959, returned to Rwanda in 1994. As we shall see, their right to Zairean nationality forms a delicate question, as they tended to be seen as Mobutu supporters by other ethnic groups in Kivu. In Northern

Kivu such groups appear extremely concerned about their social and political situation, given their minority position vis-à-vis the mass of Rwandan-speaking inhabitants and refugees.

Since independence, the Zairean authorities have never succeeded in drawing a clear distinction between these various categories of people of 'Rwandan descent' (*Zairois de souche rwandaise*, naturalised Rwandans, illegal immigrants, and refugees). In reality, people from these different administrative categories are often related to one another. Moreover, registry archives are unreliable. Rwandan-speaking families and individuals have also spread to towns and cities in the rest of Zaire, some of them now holding important political or administrative functions or pursuing successful business and commercial activities. It is known that some have obtained Zairean passports in exchange for loyalty to Mobutu.

The confusion between the different categories of Rwandan-speaking people has been a source of constant uncertainty about their right to Zairean nationality. According to treaties signed at independence, all Banyarwanda and Barundi (literally 'people from Rwanda' and 'people from Burundi') resident in the Belgian Congo before 1950 were to be regarded as Zairean nationals, whereas later immigrants would not be. The Act of 26 March 1971 (Ordonnance-Loi no. 71-020) stated that 'the people native to Rwanda-Urundi and living in the Congo on 30 June 1960 are deemed to have acquired Congolese nationality on that date.' In 1981, however, a new law (Loi no. 81-002, 29 June 1981) severely curtailed the granting of Zairean nationality to Rwandan-speaking inhabitants: they now had to prove their ancestors had lived in Zaire before 1885 (when the area was partitioned by the Berlin Congress). The retroactive force of this law nullified the existing nationality rights of Rwandan-speaking communities and required new individual applications for naturalisation. Obviously this provoked considerable legal insecurity and frustration (Muholongu 1995).

Tensions between 'Zaireans' and the 'non-naturalised' escalated in 1991 when an official investigation was launched into the origin of the 'non-Zairean' population (in Kivu these were mainly Rwandan speakers). The prescribed procedure was a review of naturalisation proceedings and of identity cards specifying 'locality' of origin. In reality, and with the support of other local ethnic groups, the inspectors began investigating even the etymology of names and the grammar of language; traditional dignitaries and even the governor were called upon to trace their familial origins when doubts arose (Braeckman 1992: 39). One consequence was that many young Tutsis left Zaire to join the ranks of the armed Rwandan opposition, the FPR, in Uganda.

It should be noted that many Rwandan-speaking people in Zaire have acquired privileged economic and social positions, and this success is one reason for the ethnic tensions. Their presence in the densely populated region of Kivu has also given rise to many disputes about the use of land.

As to their political influence in the region, it is likewise important to know that a demographic explosion of Hutus and Tutsis of Rwandan descent meanwhile threatens to gain them an electoral majority in Northern Kivu.

Since independence, and particularly under the rule of Mobutu's state party the MPR, we see that many Rwandan-speaking Zaireans in Kivu have regularly appealed to the modern state administration and to official tribunals to defend their interests. This frequently brings them into conflict with traditional ethnic government, which stands up for the interests of its own 'indigenous' group. The authority of chiefs has become a key means for various other ethnic groups to defend their interests against the Rwandan-speaking population – and often against the modern (Mobutu) government.

The decline of the one-party state and the emergence of opposition groups and of the *société civile* since 1990 has profoundly shaken the balance of power. In Kivu, de facto decentralisation has spawned new alliances between local populations, chiefs, NGOs, *mutuelles* (see below) and some segments of modern government and the local police.

In response, some Rwandan-speaking, mainly Hutu farmers, have created parallel power institutions, out of distrust for both the official and the traditional institutions (Braeckman 1992: 23). Many now view the local gendarmerie – and with some good reason – as an instrument of the chiefs (Pabanel 1993: 134). Some local societies have instituted a sort of defence system, whereby gendarmes act as local police to protect the population and its possessions. Rwandan-speaking inhabitants were even refused admission to transitional institutions such as the National Election Commission and the Regional Council. In the sovereign National Conference, too, many Rwandan-speaking Zaireans were deemed to be immigrants and were thus stripped of their right to representation.

Ethnic conflicts and the use of modern and traditional authority in the struggle for land - vague and inadequate Zairean land legislation

The Zairean Land Act of 20 July 1973 (Loi no. 73-021), as amended in 1980, indirectly exacerbated the ethnic conflicts by nationalising all land, including the 'indigenous lands' controlled by the chiefs and the earth priests. The traditional authorities were thus robbed of their centuries-old authority to dispose of lands. According to this law, land could be given in concession by the state. Zairean nationals could acquire a 'right of perpetual concession', whilst non-Zaireans could receive a 'normal concession' for a maximum of 25 years. A concession could include several rights, from use, usufruct, lease or tenureship, but the ownership rights themselves belonged to the state.
The new land law thus not only attempted to regulate the use of the lands covered by the modern (written) legal system, but also those falling under the system of traditional law. Furthermore, it created considerable uncertainty about how such traditional land titles

were to be managed. No further rules were laid down, even though that was explicitly required by Article 389 of the act. The consequence of this void in the legislation is that chiefs now invoke traditional law to allocate 'indigenous' lands.

Manipulations in land concessions

The procedure for granting land titles in rural areas required the government to carry out a preliminary investigation. Such investigations, which date from the colonial era, were to ascertain whether traditional rights of local populations were being respected (Beke 1994). They were carried out in principle by regional authorities, but the commissaire sous-régional and the commissaire de zone were charged with verifying the information. After land was allocated to a concessionaire, the latter had a number of obligations: to pay an annual fee, to effectively occupy the land, and to manage it as stipulated in the concession contract.

Given the weakness or outright absence of a public administrative structure, such judicial safeguards have been largely meaningless to the farmer. In addition, the regional authorities charged with land titles have sometimes been long distances away from the people residing in the countryside. Furthermore, due to widespread corruption, excessive informal costs are involved in obtaining a legal land tenure title from the authorities (Tsongo 1994: 5).

Ethnic conflicts and confrontation between traditional and modern land law in the Kivu

Another direct consequence of the imprecise legislation is that people in Kivu has remained loyal to the chiefs in land matters. These are usually the local paramount chief or *mwami*. According to traditional law, the *mwami* retains within his jurisdiction all rights to the lands belonging to the traditional system.

In Kivu many conflicts have arisen when 'immigrants' and foreigners, using their knowledge of modern land legislation, have established large ranches through concessions. Parts of the indigenous population living according to traditional norms have seen themselves dispossessed of lands essential to their livelihood (Tsongo 1994: 17; MacGaffey 1982: 101-103). Such conflicts also exist on a smaller scale. Rwandan-speaking inhabitants tend to appeal to modern legislation whilst indigenous Zaireans act upon traditional land law.

Many Zairean citizens do not realise that their own society can lose the land of its ancestors through the application of modern law and manipulations with the concession procedures. Such manipulations have been facilitated by the statutory provisions that invest all land ownership in the state.

The lacunas in the legislation applying to traditional lands are also a source of considerable uncertainty to many judges. They face major difficulties in applying modern law when it conflicts with the traditional law they believe is more just (MacGaffey 1982: 102-103). As we have seen, the struggle for land, particularly in Northern Kivu, has opposed Rwandan-speaking people, who often invoke modern land law, to 'indigenous' groups who appeal to traditional law.

Proliferation of neo-traditional institutions in towns:
the mutuelles tribalo-régionales

The *mutuelles* set up in North and South Kivu since 1990 (Kabungulu Kibembi 1995) show many similarities to the well-known *tontines*, the voluntary associations for mutual financial help existing in many African countries. There are also some significant differences, however. *Mutuelles* are wholly urban associations led by modern elites, and though they may have significant links with traditional authorities, they are not controlled by them in any effective way. While *tontines* fulfil an exclusively socioeconomic function, providing mutual financial support based on certain criteria (such as ethnicity, profession, friendship, or traditional organisational structures), *mutuelles* have a political function, too, based solely on ethnic and/or regional standards. The *mutuelles* fall clearly into the pattern designated as 'urban tribalism' (Samba Kaputo 1982: 16-22; Young 1965), from which the urban voluntary organisations also originated (Wallerstein 1964: 83-85).

It is reported that *mutuelles* in Kivu have secured guaranteed representation in NGO frameworks. When political opportunities arise, these ethnically and regionally based groups have also formed coalitions with one another.[9] *Mutuelles* in Kivu are fulfilling an important surrogate function in the virtual absence of financial institutions and modern formal governmental structures. Modern formal institutions in the towns have been superseded to a significant degree by such neo-traditional, ethnically based institutions. These now also play a key role in conflict resolution through the use of the palaver, the tradition of long discussions (Batabiha 1994: 46).

Growing ethnicisation in the Kivu

More recently, the *mutuelles* have clearly joined in the general process of ethnicisation of non-governmental institutions in Kivu. This process has resurged since the influx of the Rwandan refugees in 1994. It has even made significant inroads into the new institutions of civil society. The strong hope of political liberalisation that arose after 1990 had led to the robust emergence of a *société civile*, and the creation of political parties, of numerous NGOs (many of them church-linked), and even of several local universities. Initially, most such new civic organisations were multi-ethnic, or ethnicity was not a primary organising principle, at least. They began taking over many tasks

---

[9] Interview with Batabiha Bushoki (Goma, 12 April 1995); see also Batabiha 1994

from the failing and corrupt official institutions, and they became instrumental in the formation of political consciousness. The collapsing Mobutu regime's virtual lack of control over faraway Kivu opened further opportunities for social self-reliance through the civic organisations. Lack of funds, experience and trained staff, however, fostered rivalries between and within many of the young NGOs. Many such rivalries developed into ethnic frictions.

With the arrival of the refugees in 1994, Kivu felt threatened by what we might call a Mobutu restoration, which was accompanied by repression from newly arrived Zairean troops. Many reports have indicated that the insecurity in Kivu was due not so much to the refugees as to presence of the powerful Zairean military. Popular, ethnic unrest was regularly incited by the Mobutu regime as an pretext to neutralise, intimidate or even liquidate local branches of opposition parties, as well as the burgeoning civil society and its organisations.

The fresh political and social unrest transformed some ethnic tensions into real ethnic conflicts, both between 'indigenous Zairean' ethnic groups and between them and Rwandan-speaking groups. Moreover, the presence of the newly arrived Hutu refugees, the former Rwandan (Hutu) army and the Interahamwe militia became a serious threat to the local Zairean Tutsi minorities in Kivu. The predominantly pastoralist Tutsis in Northern Kivu suffered persecution at the hands of local 'indigenous' Zairean ethnic groups, aided and abetted by armed Rwandan Hutu refugees.

The result is that, from 1995 onwards, the more or less traditionally regulated, pluralistic organisations became transmuted into clearly politically inspired pressure groups based on the single precept of ethnicity or region. This warning by a critical Zairean journalist of the risk of social implosion in the region well characterises the atmosphere:

> Les troubles entre les tribus Tutsi et Hunde, Hunde et Nande, Nande et Hutu, Nyanga et Hutu, Hutu et Tutsi, au Nord-Kivu, Tutsi-Bembe et Tutsi-Fuliro au Sud-Kivu prouvent de l'absence de toute adhésion à un projet commun de cohabitation pacifique; les guerres interethniques au Rwanda et au Burundi ... sont des évènements qui pourraient se produire ailleurs (Kabungulu Kimbembi 1995: 5).

Not surprisingly, the menace of ethnicisation has fallen on fertile ground in relatively well-organised local traditional communities. It has stimulated or compelled the chiefs to exercise their role as leader and defender of their ethnic group or subgroup. The chiefs have gained new legitimacy as 'genuine' representatives of 'indigenous' Zairean people opposing 'foreign' (Rwandan) encroachment. In early 1996, when thousands of Hunde and Nyanga in Northern Kivu were driven from their lands and villages by armed Hutus, their chiefs issued desperate calls for help and protection from the Zairean government and the international community.

In considering the process of ethnicisation and the revival of chieftaincy, we must not forget that, in the governmental power vacuum, many local communities in Kivu's rural areas seized upon the opportunity to organise under the leadership of their chiefs. Links were laid between traditional structures and customs and elements of 'modern' government and development. Within the territory of the Kingdom of Kaziba, for instance, local roads were maintained by the population and users were required to pay tolls, agricultural projects were set up with the help of NGOs, and even a small-scale hydropower plant was operated to produce electricity for local consumption.

The political unrest and spiralling ethnic conflicts have transformed self-reliance into self-defence. Unfortunately, the local 'indigenous' groups have proved no match for the well-armed Hutus nor, as we would see later in 1996, for the Tutsi rebels of Zairean origin who returned from Uganda to join their Banyamulenge Tutsi communities in Southern Kivu.

Conclusions

It is very remarkable indeed that the colonial notion of a dually structured local government was embraced by the Congolese (Zairean) authorities after independence almost with no questions asked. Small-scale local government in rural areas could be performed by chieftaincy, while in the larger *circonscriptions,* the *secteurs,* the chief became a modern administrator, appointed by modern authorities for a 10-year term 'if possible in accordance with the wishes of the local inhabitants'. Although this may reflect some measure of toleration towards chieftaincy, all aspects of chieftaincy were banned at higher state levels, as well as from local government structures in urban areas. Modern government was considered the only possibility there. Beginning in 1969, and more radically with the new local government legislation of 1973, a full standardisation of modern local administration was carried out under the control of the MPR, doing away with all formal structures into which chieftaincy was integrated. In actual practice, however, the traditional institutions continued to show strong resistance. With its 1982 reforms, Mobutu's MPR regime later shrank back from the standardised, purely modern administration, and reinstated in large measure the colonial arrangements applying to the *collectivités.* Again a distinction was made between the *collectivité-secteur* and *collectivité-chefferie* – the *chefferie* ruled by custom, the *secteur* by law. The same duality was reflected in the designation or appointment of chiefs and in the composition and role of local councils. The urban areas continued to be administered entirely by modern structures.

In the past decade, the gradual deterioration of the Zairean state administration has begun to generate some genuine regional and local autonomy, a sort of spontaneous, informal decentralisation. The capacity for self-reliance within local populations has been revealed by the emergence of a large number of NGOs and by the revival of chieftaincy in rural areas. At the same time, the *mutuelles tribalo-régionales* developed in the urban areas. Although traditional ethnicity has become a basic element in the *mutuelles*, they do not seem to have incorporated chieftaincy to any great degree.

The state of affairs in Kivu local government is determined in part by factors that also apply to the rest of Zaire (social and economic misery, lack of basic infrastructure, ethnicisation). There are also factors specific to the Kivu: the presence of Rwandan-speaking communities and Rwandan refugees, the political role of the NGOs and the strong position of *mutuelles tribalo-régionales* in the urban centres.

With respect to land law, officially only one system has existed in Zaire since 1973, based on codified law. In legal practice, however, a dual system of modern law and traditional law is functioning. The confrontation between modern and traditional land law is accompanied by, and often even results from, the escalating ethnic conflicts (as in recent years in the Kivu). Strong arguments have been raised for new land legislation that recognises the duality. Incorporating the modern and the traditional system into one set of legislation could create more legal safeguards.

Regarding decentralisation, it must be observed that lawmakers and even the Conférence Nationale have persistently adhered to the claim of strict duality – that small-scale rural government should be traditional, whilst urban and larger-scale rural government should be modern. Actual practice, however, presents a very different picture, both in the Kivu and in the whole of Zaire. The debate at present not so much about whether to recognise chieftaincy as about the level up to which its power should extend. When the need for standardisation in local government is argued, it is always in terms of the notion of administrative modernisation, including democratisation in the form of elections. Although practice reveals the existence and the revival of strong traditional governmental structures even in urban areas, current discussions on governmental reforms in Zaire seem to allow no reference whatever to a form of standardisation that could incorporate traditional solidarity and chieftaincy into higher levels of the state and into urban government.

A realistic governmental system will require those involved to acknowledge modernity even at the lowest levels, but at the same time they will have to accept traditional elements in the urban areas, such as the *mutuelles*, the organisations for mutual solidarity and assistance based on ethnicity. Chiefs should possibly also be given an official position on urban councils, even if not a dominant one.

What this study of the Kivu has especially demonstrated is that a reform of local government should do far more to address local hostilities between ethnic groups, including Rwandan-speaking groups. A form of decentralisation based on a distinction between mono-ethnic and multi-ethnic units could be more suitable than one distinguishing between the traditional and the modern. It would have guarantees built in for a fair representation of all ethnic groups, even small local minorities. It would mean that any governmental entity at any level in areas inhabited by significant numbers[10] of people from more than one ethnic group – as is the case in most of the Kivu, as well as in the country as a whole – each should have a guaranteed minimum representation in local assemblies and executive institutions. Local chieftaincy, for its part, should be included in an adapted form of so-called 'endogenous decentralisation' (Huynh Cao Trí 1988), combining a selection of traditional and modern methods in governmental decentralisation.

References

A.C.D.I. (Agence Canadienne de Développement International)
1992   Schéma régional d'aménagement Maniema-Nord-Kivu-Sud-Kivu. Document préliminaire, n.p.

BATABIHA, Bushoki
1994   Pour une identité ethnique source de dynamisme... Pp. 37-47. In: *Cultures entre elles: dynamique ou dynamite? Vivre en paix dans un monde de diversité.* T. Verhelst & E. Sizoo (eds.). Paris: Réseau Sud-Nord

BEKE, Dirk
1994   Land-law in Belgian Central Africa. Pp. 57-67. In: *Our Laws, Their Lands. Land Laws and Land Use in Modern Colonial Societies.* J. de Moor & D. Rothermund (eds.). Münster/Hamburg: LIT Verlag

BEKE, Dirk & Ivo CARLENS & Dirk VERBOVEN
1995   *Lokale en regionale bestuursvormen als politieke stabilisering van etniciteit in Afrika. Deelrapport Kivu (Zaïre),* Ghent/ Antwerp: RUG / RUCA

BRAECKMAN, Colette
1992   Le Zaïre et ses régions. Pp. 33-41. In: *Enjeux nationaux et dynamique régionales dans l'Afrique des Grands Lacs.* Lille: URA

BUELL, Raymond L.
1928/
1965   *The Native Problem in Africa.* Vol II, London

COUR, Jean-Marie & Paul TABORGA
1988   *Regional Development of Kivu, Document of The World Bank, Zaïre Urban Sector Mission Report.* March 15, Vol. 7 of 8, Annexe VII

---

10   The defining point for a 'significant number' could be 10% in towns, *localités* and *collectivités*, and 5% for the higher administrative levels.

DHEDONGA DHEBA CHELE
1984   L'administration des collectivités locales au Zaïre. Pp. 255-262. In: *Annuaire du Tiers Monde*, vol. 8

DJELO, Empenge-Osako
1990   *L'impact de la coutume sur l'exercice du pouvoir en Afrique noire. Le cas du Zaïre.* Louvain-la-Neuve: Le bel élan

MacGAFFEY, William
1982   The Policy of National Integration in Zaire. Pp. 87-106. In: *Journal of Modern African Studies*, vol. 20, no. 1

GOULD, David & MUSHI-MUGUMORHAGERWA
1977   La multirationalité et le sous-développement: écologie du processus décisionel dans l'administration local zaïroise. Pp. 261-285. In: *Canadian Journal of Political Science / Revue canadienne de science politique*, vol. X, no. 2, June

HUYNH CAO TRÍ
1988   *Participative Administration and Endogenous Development*. Brussels / Paris: IIAS / UNESCO

KABUNGULU KIBEMBI, Pascal
1995   Mutuelles tribalo-régionales: risque d'implosion sociale. p. 5. In: *Haki Yetu*, vol.1 no. 10 (January)

KANYNDA LUSANGA
1984   *La décentralisation territoriale zaïroise à l'épreuve de la théorie et des faits.* Les Cahiers du CEDAF / ASDOC-Studies, no. 2, April

MAFIKIRI TSONGO
1996   Pratiques foncières, phénomènes informels et problèmes ethniques au Kivu (Zaïre). Pp. 46-63. In: Phénomènes informels et dynamiques culturelles en Afrique (dir. G. de Villers). *Afrika Studies/Cahiers Africains*, no. 19-20, April

MUGOLONGU, Apolinaire
1995   Déconfiture de l'état, poussées identitaires, violence et politique au Zaire. Pp. 1-12. In: *Les racines de la violence dans la région des grands-lacs*. Brussels: Les Verts au Parlement européen

MPINGA-KASENDA
1973   *L'administration publique du Zaïre.* Paris: Ed. A. Pedone.

1957   New Institutions of Local Government in the Belgian Congo. Pp. 79-84. In: *Journal of African Administration*, Vol. IX, nos. 1 & 4

PABANEL, Jean-Pierre
1991   La question de la nationalité au Kivu. Pp. 32-40. In: *Politique Africaine*, no. 41

1993   Conflits locaux et stratégies de tension au Nord-Kivu. Pp. 132-135. In: *Politique Africaine*, no. 52

PAULUS, Jean-Pierre
1959 *Droit public du Congo belge*. Brussels: ULB Institut de Sociologie Solvay

ROUVEROY VAN NIEUWAAL, E. Adriaan B. van
1998 Law and Protest in Africa: Resistance to Legal Innovation, Pp. 70-118. In: *Sovereignty Legitimacy, and Power in West African Societies*. E.A.B. van Rouveroy van Nieuwaal & W. Zips (eds.). Hamburg: LIT Verlag

RAPPORT *de la Commission administrative et Territoriale*. Kinshasa: Conférence
1992 nationale souveraine (CNS)

SAMBA KAPUTO
1982 *Phenomène d'etnicité et conflits etno-politiques en Afrique noire post-coloniale*. Kinshasa: Presses Universitaires du Zaïre

WALLERSTEIN, Isaak
1964 *The Road to Independence: Ghana and Ivory Coast*. Paris / The Hague: Mouton

WALLIS, C.A.G.
1958 The Administration of Towns in the Belgian Congo. Pp. 88-94. In: *Journal of African Administration*, no. 2, April

WILLAME, Jean-Claude
1994 Gouvernance et Pouvoir. Essai sur trois trajectoires africaines. In: *Afrika Studies/Cahiers africains*. no. 7 - 8, Brussels, CEDAF/ASDOC

YOUNG, Crawford
1965 *Introduction à la politique congolaise*. Kinshasa: Ed. Univ. du Congo

NKOYA ROYAL CHIEFS AND THE KAZANGA CULTURAL ASSOCIATION IN WESTERN CENTRAL ZAMBIA TODAY
resilience, decline, or folklorisation? [1]

Wim van Binsbergen

Introduction [2]

Resilient chieftainship

African traditional leaders, or chiefs, were a showpiece of classic anthropology,[3] and thus revealed the links both chiefs and anthropology have entertained with the colonial project. This may have been an important reason why these chiefs did not feature

---

[1] Earlier versions of this paper were presented at the conference on Chiefs in Africa today, African Studies Centre, Leiden, 7 March, 1996; and at my postgraduate methodology seminar, Free University, Amsterdam, 3rd June, 1997. I am indebted to Wouter van Beek, Albert Trouwborst, Henk Meilink, Gerda Sengers, Thera Rasing, Ferdinand de Jong, and especially to the editors E. Adriaan B. van Rouveroy van Nieuwaal and Rijk van Dijk, for useful comments on earlier versions of this paper.

[2] Anthropological and oral-historical fieldwork was undertaken in Western Zambia and under migrants from this area in Lusaka, in 1972-1974, and during shorter periods in 1977, 1978, 1981, 1988, 1989, 1992 (twice), 1994 (twice), and 1995. I am indebted to the Zambian research participants, to the members of my family who shared in the fieldwork, to the Board of the African Studies Centre for adequate research funds, and to the Netherlands Foundation for the Advancement of Tropical Research (WOTRO) for a writing-up year in 1974-75. For background reading and evidence on specific points, cf. my publications as listed in the bibliography. On Nkoya court culture especially music, also cf. Brown 1984

[3] From the extensive literature I mention: Apter 1961; Apthorpe 1959; Fallers 1955; Fortes & Evans-Pritchard 1969; Mair 1936; Richards 1935, 1960; Schapera 1943, and 1963

prominently in the post-colonial blueprints as worked out by constitutionalists and political scientists in the 1950s-1970s. The emphasis was on the unitary state with a unique source of authority: the people, whose will was expressed through the regular secret ballot. Chiefs have appeared to exist on a different plane, deriving their authority and power from sources outside the post-colonial nation-state, even if they are co-opted into the latter's institutions through subsidies, state control over procedures of appointment, recognition and demotion, membership of governmental bodies of the modern state sometimes including a House of Chiefs (comparable to a House of Lords, or Senate, in North Atlantic parliamentary democracies), and ceremonial respect extended to the chiefs on the part of state officials. Post-colonial African economies and systems of governance may have declined, but chiefs have often risen to new levels of recognition and power. Still their position does not systematically derive from, nor coincide with, the constitutional logic of the post-colonial state.

Chiefs in Africa[4] have managed to maintain for themselves a position of respect, as well as influence and freedom of manoeuvre in the wider national society far exceeding their formal powers as defined by post-independence constitutions. This is obviously related to the legitimation gap of a modern bureaucratically organised state based on mere legal authority (Weber 1969), in a social context where for most citizens the ideological, symbolic and cosmological appeal of such legal authority is partial and limited. Considered to be heirs to pre-colonial kings, the chiefs are co-opted in order to lend, to the central state, some of their own legitimacy and symbolic power. By virtue of occupying a pivotal position in the historic cosmology shared by large numbers of villagers and traditionally-orientated urban migrants, the chiefs represent a force which modernising state elites have found difficult to by-pass or obliterate.

This is only one side of a process of interpenetration of traditional and modern political organisation. It is not only the state which co-opts the chief as an additional power base. On the strength of the respect their traditional position commands, chiefs have also successfully penetrated the state's administrative and representative bodies, thus acquiring de facto power bases in the modern political sector. Of this phenomenon we shall encounter a striking example below, when we examine the many modern offices our protagonist, Chief Kahare of Western Zambia, has held since the 1960s.

Approaches to African chieftainship

Various approaches have tried to interpret the situation of African chiefs.
One of the earliest attempts to make sense of the structure of colonial society was that of *dualism*, which was thought to inform not only the colonial economy for which it was first conceived, but to apply also to the political and legal structure of the colonies; these

---

[4] E.g. van Rouveroy van Nieuwaal 1984, 1987, 1992, 1993, 1994, 1995; Nana Arhin Brempong c.s. 1995; and references cited there.

were thus depicted as *plural societies*, with a hierarchical multitude of ethnically defined socio-political and legal domains, integrated only by the colonial administration.

Later the discipline of legal anthropology was to develop the perspective of *legal pluralism*,[5] in order to add subtlety to the concept of the plural society, trace in greater detail its implications in the legal sphere, and extend the analysis to the postcolonial situation and to North Atlantic society. It is the legal emphasis which has made the concept of legal pluralism has cast much light on the nature of the chief in modern Africa: chiefs are defined at the intersection between modern and traditional systems of constitutional law, and one of their principal spheres of activity is the judiciary.

Another attempt to cope with the chiefs' being situated at the intersection between two apparently independent and autonomous systems, has been the neo-Marxist theory of the *articulation of modes of production*, according to which each mode of production hinges on its specific logic of exploitation underpinned by symbolic and legal institutions while the relationship between modes of production is one of exploitative reproduction; while this approach has also been applied to African chieftainship (Beinart 1985; van Binsbergen & Geschiere 1985: 261-270) and illuminated the economic aspects of chieftainship, it was less successful in tackling its many other sides.

Both the modes of production approach, and the plural society approach, have taken for granted - by the assumption of firm boundaries between fundamentally distinct 'logics' or 'systems - what perhaps needs most be problematised and explained: the nature of constitutional and legal dualism in modern Africa, and the way in which it is socio-culturally produced and reproduced. Are the boundaries between the traditional politics in which chieftainship defines itself, and the modern state, not situational rather than absolute? Much of the practice of African chieftainship consist not in the strict observance but in the manipulation, crossing, even denial of these boundaries. Is the insistence on two different spheres perhaps not so much an analytical fact but an ideological construct of interested actors, waiting to be exploded by scholarly analysis? This leads, as a fourth theoretical variant, to a *transactional approach* to African chieftainship, which traces interactions and relations between the various actors (individual and collective) in the contemporary African states, and beyond the formal features and demarcations of legal systems, traces the actual forms of their material exchanges, power and influence.[6]

---

5   Cf. Bentsi-Enchill 1969; Vanderlinden 1989; Griffiths 1986

6   Here I have to admit to an inconsistency in my earlier work to chieftainship, which perhaps can be taken as an indication of the analytical pitfalls in this field in general: although my comparative study of Zambian chiefs and the state (van Binsbergen 1987) was implicitly conceived along such transactionalist lines, with a wealth of detail on boundary crossing, my specific work on the chiefs of western central Zambia, by contrast — based on much richer data gathered in the course of 25 years in a limited geographic area — has been largely dualistic. I am afraid this inconsistency has not been totally resolved in the present paper, due to my own limitations certainly, but also to the analytical and theoretical difficulties of modern African chieftainship.

My use of the term 'transactional' could create confusion. Broadly, the term is understood to denote at least two somewhat different approaches in modern anthropology:

(a) The departure, as from the 1960s, from rigid structural functionalist models of social organisation in terms of enduring, well-defined and strictly bounded institutions; and their replacement by much more fluid conceptualisations of the social and political process. In the latter, the social order springs not from individuals' blind and slavish copying of institutional patterns, but from these individuals' creative and strategic enactment of such contradictory principles as are available in the normative and symbolic systems at their disposal. The names of Barth, Bailey and Boissevain[7] are traditionally associated with this innovative departure, but there is much to be said for the view that these three authors merely made explicit a development which had already been implicit in much Manchester School work from the 1950s onwards.
(b) A rationalistic narrowing-down of the approach under (a) in such a way that methodological individualism is claimed as anthropology's only analytical stock in trade; the wider - partly unconscious - structural patterning of individual perception and choice is swept under the carpet; the social actors are presented as virtually omniscient, eminently rational; and far from being confronted with a plurality of contradictory cultural and cosmological orientations, these actors' are presented as subject to only one, unitary and consistent orientation.

Clearly my use of the term 'transactionalist' throughout this paper is in terms of variant (a), not of the reductionist variant (b). A transactionalist approach does not make the actors in the field of modern chieftainship any more rational than actors usually are wherever in the modern world; specifically it leaves room for actors aspiring - for local cultural and cosmological reasons defining a man's ideal career pattern - to a historical political role as 'traditional ruler', even if - like in Zambia today - the concrete benefits of such an office in terms of financial remuneration and central state power are minimal.

The main advantage of transactional approaches over structural-functionalist approaches, is that a transactionalist approach does not already take for granted the conceptual boundaries between the so-called 'traditional' and the so-called 'modern' sphere of politics in colonial and post-colonial African states. On the contrary, a transactional approach invites us to study how, concretely, the actual interactions between chiefs and their various interaction partners at the local, regional and national level, in themselves *create and maintain* these boundaries. By implication, much as the distinction between traditional and modern politics permeates the literature on chieftainship in modern Africa and is often considered to be illuminating and inevitable, it is this very distinction which needs to be explained most. A transactional approach may come some way towards such an explanation. It shows chiefs and non-chiefs

---

7   Cf. Boissevain 1968; Bailey 1969; Barth 1966; 1969

constantly moving back and forth in the so-called traditional and the so-called modern domain, in demonstration of the fact that the boundary separating these domains is far more porous and situational than all these actors are prepared to admit in their own official normative and ideological statements. A rigid institutional approach takes the boundary for granted and as such risks begging the question which is at the heart of the analytical problem posed by contemporary African chiefs.

However, the case becomes more complicated, and transactionalism less convincing, when the local actors at least believe in the neat compartmentalisation which their interaction has thus created - like in the Zambian case.

In the 1980s African chiefs were rediscovered as exponents of a domain of legal and political relations where the true, richly complex and contradictory nature of contemporary African states can be confronted with the formal and restrictive models of constitutional legislators and positive political scientists. Here the details of the performance of the African states can be studied, and formal defects as well as informal remedies recognised. This resulted in a limited number of studies of African chieftainship in a transactionalist vein, highlighting the chiefs' continuing and increasing power not only outside but also within postcolonial African states.[8] Such insights also allowed us to reinterpret the position of chiefs under colonialism according to less static models (Chanock 1985; Prins 1980). In the present study the emphasis will likewise be transactionalist, although an underlying theme will be that at the background of such transactions as in fact occur we may yet discern the existence, not of two but of three fairly distinct socio-political domains: the postcolonial state, the indigenous political system, and the civil society.[9]

The present argument

The main purpose of this paper is to confront the thesis of the resilient chief with a limiting case from western central Zambia. After setting the descriptive framework we shall examine in detail the chiefs' power base and their room for manoeuvring. This power base turns out to be declining and the chiefs are desperately experimenting with new strategies in order to survive. They are driven into the arms of new actors on the local scene, against whom they are rather defenceless. One of these new actors is an ethnic voluntary association founded and controlled by the chiefs' most successful urban subjects, often their own kinsmen. This non-governmental organisation has been amazingly successful in bridging indigenous politics and the state in a process of

---

[8] The work of my friend and colleague van Rouveroy van Nieuwaal, as cited in my note 4 above, is an excellent example of this trend.

[9] The literature on chieftainship in Zambia in far more extensive than can be discussed in the scope of this article. In order to save space, I refer to the extensive references in: van Binsbergen 1987 and 1992

ethnicisation; gradually however the revival of chieftainship which this non-governmental organisation has brought about, is turning out to lead not to resilience but to impotent folklorisation if not annihilation of chieftainship, and as a result tensions are mounting between chiefs and the ethnic association.

During much of the argument we shall be guided by a transactionalist orientation. However, towards the end we shall have to admit the limitations of a transactional approach as indicated above. We shall have to concede that the contradictions of modern African chieftainship cannot be fully understood within a transactional framework. The need for further theoretical work in this field will be manifest from my continued inability to convincingly resolve the contradiction between the transactionalist and the structural functionalist perspective. Here the role of the chiefs' urban, elite subjects may be that of a *deus ex machina*, saving our analytical day because, transactionally, their cultural and organisational bricolages around the Kazanga festival and the Kazanga Cultural Association in general, at the same time

• help to construct the dichotomy between the traditional political domain and the modern state, and
• dissolve that dichotomy by involving the chiefs in a process of ethnicisation that essentially bridges these domains in the context of the elites' political and symbolic manipulation.

Traditional rulers in western central Zambia

Today there are no independent states on the fertile, well-watered, only slightly elevated lands on the Zambezi/Kafue watershed: western central Zambia. Around 1850 the several small-scale local states came to be politically and economically incorporated in the expanding state system of the Kololo (militarily organised South African immigrants who had captured the Luyana state of the Lozi or Barotse, whose centre was the Zambezi flood plain between today's towns of Kalabo and Mongu). While the Luyana state was recaptured on the Kololo in 1864, its hold on the local states persisted; it even tightened with the advent, in 1900, of the colonial state, which allowed the indigenous Lozi administration considerable freedom. Only two royal titles in the region managed to survive, as senior royal chiefs, the incorporation into the Lozi state: Mwene ('King') Kahare of the Mashasha people and Mwene Mutondo of the Nkoya Nawiko. The proper name Nkoya originally referred to a stretch of forest near the Zambezi/Kabompo confluence, then became the name of a dynasty associated with that area; the latter in turn gave its name to the Mankoya colonial district, and finally the name became an ethnonym for all non-Lozi original (i.e. pre-1900) inhabitants of Mankoya (as from 1969 Kaoma) district. The many other royal titles were replaced by Lozi representatives. Two other royals who were closely related to the Mutondo dynasty has in time moved their capitals to outside Barotseland (now Zambia's Western Province):

Mwene Kabulwebulwe and Mwene Momba, who from the outset had been recognised by the colonial state in their own right.

A decisive year in the development of 'Nkoya' to a self-assertive ethnic group was 1937, when the Lozi king established, smack in the middle of Mankoya district, a filial branch named[10] Naliele of his own court in order to control the local chiefs, judiciary and district finance. Another such year was 1947, when Mwene Mutondo Muchayila was demoted and exiled for ten years by the Lozi king on grounds of restiveness. Lozi arrogance, limited access to education and to markets, and the evangelical South African General Mission, stimulated a process of ethnic awakening. As from the middle of the twentieth century more and more people in eastern Barotseland and adjacent areas came to identify as 'Nkoya'. The usual pattern of migrant labour and urban-rural migration endowed this identity with an urban component, whose most successful representatives distinguished themselves from their rural Nkoya nationals in terms of education, income and active participation in national politics. While the Lozi continued to be considered as the ethnic enemies, a second major theme in Nkoya ethnicity was to emerge: *the quest for political and economic articulation with the national centre*, by-passing the Lozi whose dominance at the district and provincial level dwindled only slowly.

Since they shared (albeit very modestly) in the Barotse subsidy, in return for which the Lozi king (and his successors, the Lozi Paramount Chiefs) had accepted incorporation in the colonial state in 1900 and in Zambia in 1964 (cf. Agreement 1964), court culture was preserved through much of the twentieth century at the capitals of Mwene Mutondo and Mwene Kahare. The complex historic organisation of their courts has continued to define such offices as the king (*Mwene*, plural *Myene*), his sisters (*Bampanda wa Mwene*), his wives (*Mahano*), princes and princesses (*Bana Mwene*, any offspring born to the incumbent *Mwene* or previous *Myene* while in office), his Prime Minister (*Mwanashihemi*), senior councillors with titled ranks as judicial, protocolary and military officers, priests, executioners, musicians and hunters. In addition the court houses clients, many obliquely reputed to be of slave descent. If court offices have continued to be coveted and contested until today, it is not only because they have offered virtually unique opportunities for salaried employment in the local countryside, but also because the political and symbolic order these offices represent is still vital to the subjects of the Myene. As a distinctive physical structure (marked by a royal fence with pointed poles (*Lilapa*), within which the Mwene's palace, audience/court room,

---

10 Significantly, this name derived from that of the 19th century Lozi capital. The new branch court was originally headed by the Lozi prince Mwanawina; when, following a system of positional succession, he had become Paramount Chief of the Lozi, he was succeeded by prince Mwendaweli, who had been Gluckman's research assistant. This is only one indication of the fact that Gluckman's view of the Lozi indigenous administration including its judicial role was partial to its ruling elite (cf. Brown 1973; Prins 1980). For an understanding of the Nkoya situation this is unfortunate (van Binsbergen 1977); but in all fairness it has to be admitted that such partiality in fieldwork is inevitable (my own work on the Nkoya shows a complementary partiality); nor did it prevent Gluckman from being one of the most impressive anthropologists of his generation.

regalia shelter and royal shrine are situated), with at a conveniently short distance[11] the sacred grove where the graves of earlier *Myene* are administered by the court priests, these capitals (*zinkena*, sing. *lukena*) have constituted the spatial centres of Nkoya political ideas through much of the twentieth century. The main element of court culture which disappeared from the surface of tradition politics in the area is human sacrifice, which played a prominent part in the nineteenth century. The *Kazanga* royal harvest festival, whose falling into disuse during the colonial period is not unrelated to the central role human sacrifice played there, was only reinstated in 1988, in greatly altered form, and not by the chiefs but by an ethnic association enlisting the chiefs' support. Formally, slavery and tribute labour (the two main sources of labour at the *zinkena* in the nineteenth century) lost their legal basis in the 1910s, and in practice they ceased to exist in the 1930s; but the chief can and does still command inputs of free labour time when it comes to such tasks as the maintenance of the royal fence, the construction of shelters at the *lukena*, and similar productive labour undertaken in the context of development activities (erection of schools, clinics, maintenance of roads) concentrated around the *lukena*. Formal tribute (*ntupu*) is no longer levied by the Myene, but in practice the customary greeting of the Mwene by villagers and returning urban migrants tends to be accompanied by gifts (still designated *ntupu*) in the form of cash or manufactured liquor, while in local production by villagers around the *lukena* (e.g. beer brewing, alcohol distilling, hunting, fishing, agriculture) the Mwene's prerogatives are often recognised by a gift of produce. However, even in this cash-starved rural environment these material prestations cannot be considered anything but minimal; they no longer come close to the order of magnitude of court-village exploitation in the nineteenth century. Of the military, political, economic and ideological structure of kingship of that time, it is mainly the ideological elements which have persisted, no longer effectively supported by, nor supporting, material exploitation.

Of course, at present, at the end of the twentieth century, it is virtually impossible for the local villagers to maintain the view — which must have rather well corresponded with the realities of the first half of the nineteenth century — that the *lukena*, in a largely implicit but well developed ritual, political and economic spatial cosmology, is the hub of the universe. The present-day *Myene* have themselves been active in the outside world, usually pursuing salaried careers there before acceding to their royal office; and after accession their involvement with distant state institutions, organised on a very different footing from the *lukena*, make it clear that the *lukena* is now very much only a periphery of the world. Admittedly, most of these royal activities occur outside the gaze of the subjects. The subordination which these outside involvements imply for the Mwene's position is seldom made explicit but usually covered under traditionalist

---

[11] This is only a twentieth-century development, caused by the fact that under the colonial state a royal capital could no longer, as in pre-colonial times, be moved over distances of scores of kilometres after the death of the king. However, pre-colonial royal burial sites surrounded by deserted *zinkena* which have returned to bush, have continued to be venerated even if at great distances from the capitals of later incumbents.

decorum with plenty of respectful squatting and hand-clapping on the part of modern state officials and other visiting outsiders. As late as the 1970s many of Mwene Kahare's subjects could therefore still cherish the illusion that whenever he was summoned to the national capital Lusaka to attend a meeting of the House of Chiefs (an advisory body to the government with hardly any formal powers) he went there 'to rule Zambia'. But the villagers could not fail to notice that preciously little benefits from this 'rule' were coming their way, in the form of improved roads, clinics, produce markets, educational opportunities etc.

According to a stereotype current in South Central Africa, chiefs are the focus and the leaders of an ethnic group, and guide their subjects in ethnic self-articulation. At first glance, such a situation also obtains in western central Zambia. On closer analysis, however, the situation is more complicated. Under the precolonial conditions of the 19th century, kings were often ethnic strangers (cultivating a Lunda identity e.g. by the Lunda language, allegiance to the Lunda king Mwatiyamvo in what is now Zaire, and circumcision; cf. Bustin 1975), heading multi-ethnic, sprawling and shifting local polities based on tribute, military force, and chief-controlled ritual. Only in the 20th century did the emergence of the concept of 'tribe' under the combined efforts of colonial administrators, missionaries, and African Christian intellectuals, produce a situation where the chiefs, as heirs to the precolonial kings, were the administrative and judicial heads of the areas they administered and whose inhabitants came to be conceived as one 'tribe'. The successive incorporation, more or less at minority status, in the wider state systems of the Kololo, Luyana and British, served to blur the cultural and structural distinctions between the 'Nkoya' court and the local villages, since now the court was no longer the exploitative 'other' but, to the contrary, the instance from which the local population derived their ethnic name and their increasingly vocal ethnic identity amidst the inimical and exploiting wider world. Yet the equation of ethnic group and chief was not self-evident and therefore remained capable of being challenged or at least ignored by actors (like the Kazanga Cultural Association, as we shall see below) seeking to capture Nkoya ethnicity as a resource for their own political game. In the 1930s and 1940s, the local struggle against the Lozi was largely concentrated at the royal courts. In the process however, chiefs gradually lost the initiative to church leaders and successful urban migrants — a new elite largely composed of their own junior kinsmen. An ethnic voluntary association, the Kazanga Cultural Association, emerged among successful urban migrants as the latter's main instrument of ethnicisation in the 1980s.

Before we can examine the interaction between chiefs and this non-governmental organisation, and interpret it in terms of the central theme of African chiefs' performance in today's social and political landscape, let us first discuss the chiefs' power base and, in the next section, the details of the ethnic association.

- 105 -

The chiefs' power base today

The social dynamics around Nkoya chieftainship can hardly be characterised in terms of resilience. There are signs of attempts at active adaptation to new political and economic conditions, but these attempts are desperate and largely unsuccessful. Often the chiefs are mere marionettes in a play stages by outsiders. This will be clear from the following detailed examination of the chiefs' power base today; we shall concentrate on the situation of Chief Mwene Kahare. For this purpose I shall discuss, with varying degrees of detail, the following topics:

- the chief among his kinsmen, including royal councillors;
- chief, subjects and land tenure;
- judicial aspects of chieftainship;
- the impact of the existence of another royal chief in the district;
- the Lozi indigenous administration;
- the modern state;
- chiefs strategies for enlarging their scope for manoeuvring, by embarking on new modes of action
- the role of encroaching outsiders

The chief among his kinsmen, including royal councillors

Among other roles, the chief is a kinsmen. His kinship obligations have a double effect: they impose upon the chief, as upon all other heads of families in Zambia today, the burdensome obligation of providing financial resources in a steadily declining economy; but they also remind the chief that as a kinsmen he is only the equal or the junior of many of his kinsmen, and has to be heedful of the advice (*ku longesha*) especially from those of his kinsmen who are senior headmen themselves.

The very fact that the royal successor is not determined by inflexible rules but depends on election (with candidates being chosen by senior headmen from among a pool of half a dozen or so serious contenders, all of them — not necessarily very close — bilateral consanguineal kin of previous incumbents; cf. diagram 2) makes the power base of these chiefs in traditional constitutional law relatively weak, and liable to factional machinations from defeated candidates. This is, incidentally, a major reason why the chiefs of this region have individually welcomed the protection from a superior political power (be it the Lozi king, Paramount Chief, and the colonial and postcolonial state) as from the second half of the nineteenth century.

Membership of the royal council (only its two or three most senior members are remunerated and recognised by the district secretary) is a prerogative of certain village headmanships; incumbents of any village headmanship are selected by the village's secret council of elders, subject to recognition of a village headman by the chief as holder of the communal land.

Chiefs have always been very much aware of the dangers they are under at their own court, and it is the chief's sister's obligation to act as cup bearer, tasting all food and beer and ensuring that it is not poisoned. Nor are the stories of regicide entirely a thing of the past:

> *Mwene Mutondo Chipimbi's autocratic nature.* The new chief's failure to accept such criticism and to stick to court protocol within a few months created such disenchantment between Mwene Mutondo Chipimbi (elected in 1991) and his councillors, that his own and his wife's death within a year after his accession was readily attributed to these courtier's aggression, either through sorcery or through poisoning.

Chief, subjects and land tenure

In the eyes of his subjects, the chief's most obvious characteristic is his hereditary status as legitimate, elected successor to (in fact, the incarnation of) the Kahare title, which is at least 200 years old; this ensures him of the unconditional support of his subjects in so far as they have no aspirations for the throne themselves. His royal status has a direct implication for his subjects' access to land as the principal agricultural resource. Despite the reform of land tenure in Zambia in the 1970s, the chief has retained the right to issue land to individuals, regardless of ethnic affiliation, residence or citizenship. This makes him the benefactor (and beneficiary of the usual, irregular, and usually very small tribute in money and alcoholic beverages), not only of his own local people identifying today as Nkoya, but also of a considerable number of Lozi immigrants who since the 1970s built their village in one of the valleys under chief Kahare's authority. He was also a key figure in the creation of the massive Nkeyema Agricultural Scheme in 1970. In Kaoma district, agriculture is not just subsistence agriculture; already around 1970 the transition to producing hybrid maize for the market was made on a very small scale, with a few bags per household, but due to the poor performance of the marketing organisation which never pays up in time, market agriculture has become very unattractive.

The need to provide cash as the head of the extended family of royal kinsmen (especially classificatory sisters) converging on the palace, coupled to the state's failure of providing a stable and sufficient income, may bring the chief to abuse his powers in desperate egoistic acts such as large-scale issuing of land to ethnic strangers, of which we shall see a striking example below.

Judicial aspects

Shortly after independence, Kahare's customary law court was moved dozens of kilometres away from his palace and (like all other chief's courts) put directly under the supervision of the Ministry of Justice; officially the chief merely retained the right to endorse the appointment of the members of what was henceforth called the Local Court.[12] In the late 1980s a customary court was reinstated at the palace; its members are senior councillors (the chief only acts as a distant advisor not present during the sessions) and although its jurisdiction is limited and shady, the court enjoys great popularity and authority.

The other royal chief in the district

Besides the Lozi chief of Naliele, Kaoma has two royal chiefs identifying as Nkoya. The competitive nature of these two royal chiefs' relations means that — in a typical zero-sum game situation — one's chief ascendance implies the other chief's decline, and even if it does not (specifically, when ascendance is due to new, national-level political resources opening up, outside the district level, so that the zero-sum game situation no longer applies) it is still interpreted in these terms by either chief's subjects. This severely limits the possibility of enlarging the chief's power bases by inter-chief alliances.

The Lozi indigenous administration

Gwyn Prins (1980) made a name for himself in African history by proposing a transactional model of active strategy on the last independent Lozi king, Lubosi Lewanika (1878-1916), in order to supplant the image of passive and impotent submission to the imposition of colonial rule, at the turn of the twentieth century. At present, almost a century later, and encapsulated in the postcolonial state, Lewanika's successor the Lozi Paramount Chief is a prominent member of the Seventh Day Adventist Church, and in all respects an example of the resilient chief found elsewhere in Africa today.

The constraints from the part of the Lozi traditional administration upon the chieftainship of Mwene Kahare and Mwene Mutondo are clear from the fact that as from 1994 (when new incumbents acceded to both titles) both royal chiefs and their courts have been without remuneration from the state for lack of recognition by the Lozi Paramount chief: they had refused to go and prostrate themselves before him in the traditional manner. This reflected unprecedented escalation of the Lozi-Nkoya conflict

---

[12] Cf. Hoover c.s. 1970a, 1970b; Spalding 1970

(including a war of newspaper articles, occasional ethnic violence, the construction of the major royal drums by the new Mwene Mutondo - denied to the Nkoya chiefs such drums since the mid-19th century! - and the death of chief Litia attributed to Nkoya sorcery). Lack of recognition by the Lozi Paramount Chief made it impossible for the Kaoma district secretary to confirm the new appointments and to pay out the salaries. At the Kahare capital, the musicians are no longer paid and (disrupting a virtually unbroken tradition of at least two centuries)[13] they have allowed the royal drums to remain silent, — except for a few occasions when a prominent visitor manages to bribe the unemployed and absent musicians to once more go through the motions, for a few minutes, of what used to be a honourable and coveted profession. This stands in sharp contrast with the situation in the early 1970s, when half an hour of ceremonial drumming and singing by the chief's orchestra, every sunrise and every sunset, was the reassuring signs that the king was alive and well. Meanwhile, the Paramount Chief's court, and the Naliele court, continues to function as an appeal court in traditional constitutional matters and as the only court where royals can be tried (even in cases involving traditional family law); ethnic and regionalist defiance of Lozi overlordship is not enough to terminate this situation, and even if it did it would leave a legal vacuum of the very sort which instigated the colonial administration to create the Naliele court in the first place, in the 1930s.

The modern state

Once recognised by the Lozi Paramount chief, the incumbent of the Kahare title further requires the recognition from the President of the Republic, who has the new incumbent gazetted as a condition for his remuneration through the district secretary's office. That office also recognises and pays all other court officials eligible for remuneration. With his virtual monopoly over state motor transport in the district, the district secretary also regulates the chief's access to governmental bodies and to the outside world at large. In fact, the chief is not allowed to leave his area without formal permission from the district secretary.

In exchange for this massive dependence the chief receives a remuneration far lower than the legal minimum wage in formal sector employment. Moreover, payment of salaries has been dependent upon the availability, at the distant district capital, of cash and transport for the paymaster arrears of several months have not been unusual. This irregularity, added to the fact that not the chief himself but the district secretary controls remunerated court appointments, has left the chief with little practical power over his

---

[13] Near the turn of the twentieth century, Mwene Kahare Shamamano killed his drummers on the suspicion of adultery with the royal wives; as punishment the Lozi king Lewanika deprived Shamamano from the right to a royal orchestra; Shamamano — one of Lewanika's military officers — had owed his accession since he was of the wrong lineage. Only in the 1930s were the Kahare royal rums reinstated.

courtiers and their ceremonial and judicial activities. As a result, the chief is in an incessant financial crisis. His main source of cash for the upkeep of himself and considerable numbers of royal kin is from irregular tribute. In the 1970s chiefs were still heavily involved in hunting and the ivory trade — a remnant of their extensive precolonial rights over natural resources and natural species. By 1990 this source of income had entirely disappeared, due to the extermination of game in the 1980s (not only by poaching locals but also by ethnic strangers using machine guns), and by the tightening control of the ivory trade under the CITES international treaty.

However, dependence of the chief upon the state at district level used to be only one side of the medal. Between 1960 and the 1980s Chief Kahare held the following impressive modern offices, all of them for many years in succession: he was a Trustee of the United National Independence Party (UNIP, which ruled Zambia between 1963 and 1991), a member of the House of Chiefs, a non-elected member of the Kaoma Rural Council, and a member of the Provincial Development Committee of Western Province. Unfortunately, this substantial power base in the modern state did not survive into the 1990s. The link with UNIP ceased to be an asset when this party lost out to Mr Chiluba's Movement for Multi-Party Democracy (MMD) in 1991. The resignation from other modern offices reflect not only the ageing chief's gradual retreat from public life but also the effect of Lozi and Mbunda/Luvale political mobilisation against the Nkoya at the district and provincial level, despite the considerable overall political success of Nkoya ethnic politics since the late 1970s.

Chiefs desperately seeking to enlarge their scope for manoeuvring, by embarking on new modes of action

All this suggests that the chief's power base is fairly limited, and declining. He does not have many options for the execution of their own authority. it is remarkable that such attempts as the Nkoya chiefs have shown in recent years to enlarge the scope of their options have all been in the field of nostalgic symbolic production. Principally this includes responses triggered by the successful emergence of the Kazanga Cultural Association; these we shall discuss below. But there have been other responses in a similar vein in the course of the 1990s.

The initially eager adoption of the format for self-assertion which the Kazanga Cultural Association accorded them, suggested that outside the domain of nostalgic symbolic production the chiefs had little option for manoeuvring. This is also clear from the other nostalgic initiatives which they showed in the mid-1990s and which shall be summarised below: the construction of new kettledrums, the sending of a punitive expedition, and the appropriation of the Kazanga festival premises by an enterprising chief's son.

Mwene Mutondo's new kettledrums (1994). In 1994 Mwene Mutondo, only acceded one year previously, for the first time since ca. 1850 defied the prohibition from the part of the Lozi indigenous administration and its Kololo predecessor, and ordered major royal kettledrums (*maoma*) to be made. Following the surviving traditions to the letter (van Binsbergen 1992: *passim*), the drums were sculptured with the images of a lizard and a python, in a very crude fashion because woodcarving as a craft disappeared when witchcraft eradication movements in the interbellum cleared the region almost entirely and permanently from all wooden effigies (the only exception known to me being the Mutondo royal shrine). In making the drums, the historic pattern was emulated even to the extent that two small children were sacrificed to the new drum. While other, minor royal drums are played by court musicians with client status, Mwene Mutondo took it upon himself to beat this central symbol of chieftainship. Significantly, the new drums were kept at the palace for over a year before being exposed to the public gaze at the Kazanga annual festival which the ethnic association of the same name has organised in the district since 1988.

Mwene Kahare Kubama sends a punitive expedition (1994). The year 1994 again saw a similar emulation of a precolonial historic pattern. Mwene Kahare Kubama, a few months after his accession, was confronted with the usurpation of one of his sub-chieftainships, that of Mwene Kakumba, by a Lozi incumbent who had simply ousted the original incumbent during his life. When protests from Mwene Kahare's Ngambela (Prime Minister) were not heeded, Mwene Kahare told young men from around his palace to arm themselves, travel to Kakumba's village across a distance of 35 km, and remove the Lozi impostor from the subchief's palace by force: a punitive expedition (Nkoya: *nzita*; the Sotho/Lozi word *impi* is more familiar) to issue from the palace, for the first time since the 19th century. This was also the first time that ethnic tension in the district actually led to bloodshed. The desperate and unrealistic nature of the attempt is clear from the fact that the dozens of Nkoya men involved in this violent action were arrested, and that a year later they were still awaiting trial. Clearly the chief can still rely on his subjects as a power base, but to little strategic avail. Yet the move was not totally rejected by the state: the Kaoma district secretary, who as a Lunda entertains a felling a ethnic affinity with the Nkoya chiefs, issued a decree to the district's Lozi chiefs (apart from the Naliele royal chief) to the effect that they had to obey the Nkoya chiefs as their overlords — in itself a unique triumph for Nkoya anti-Lozi militancy.

That the backward-looking, nostalgic nature of these moves is not incidental but reflects the general orientation of Nkoya traditional politics today is further brought out by the following case, even if this one involves not a ruling chief but his son.

- 111 -

An enterprising prince. Mr Daniel Muchayila, in his late thirties, is a son of Mwene Mutondo Muchayila; as we have seen above, the latter was one of the main heroes of Nkoya identity. Daniel is merely a *Mwana Mwene*, i.e. a prince, and on two occasions (1991, 1993) he failed to succeed to his father's throne. This did not prevent him from taking up residence at the new festival grounds which had been created for the Kazanga annual festival, and specifically in the branch court building reserved there for the Mutondo chief and his staff. Here Daniel even tried cases for the benefit of the surrounding villagers, charging fees and fines and keeping the proceeds for himself. Not being a chief, by such action he polluted the sacred quality of the Mutondo chief's court at the festival grounds, even if this constituted a totally new situation unforeseen by traditional rules. Although the prince's action had tacitly been condoned by the Mutondo court, the building had to be relinquished. During the Kazanga festival of 1994 Chief Mutondo had to make use of either of the buildings erected for Mwene Momba or Mwene Kabulwebulwe, who had not been able to attend. It is as if the traditional outside forms of the imitation royal courts at the festival grounds demand being filled with traditional forms of socio-political behaviour (such as holding court), endowing such forms with a deceptive appearance of reality. And against the background of 20th century Nkoya history the episode reminds one inevitably of the founding, in the 1930s, of the Naliele court - the most hated symbol of Lozi suppression, a branch of the distant Lozi Paramount Chief's court over which Yeta III appointed his son as branch manager.[14]

Encroaching outsiders

In addition to nostalgic and ineffective ways of responding to the changing political landscape of today, the chieftainship of western central Zambia is becoming the toy of other categories of actors representing different fields of socio-political organisation than the indigenous political system. The most conspicuous actors in this connexion are: expatriate commercial farmers, and the Seventh Day Adventist Church, besides of course the Kazanga Cultural Association.

---

[14] This is not the only example in the context of Nkoya-Lozi relations that proclaimed ethnic antagonism is contradicted by actual rapprochement. Other examples in the context of the present argument are Mr Kalaluka's Lozi ancestry although he was for decades the highest-ranking Nkoya politician; and Mr Mayowe's functioning as the district representative of the Lozi-dominated National Party, while he was running for the chieftainship of Mwene Kahare. Many more such examples could be quoted. This highlights the manipulative, strategic element in ethnicisation (cf. van Binsbergen, in press), and will only puzzle those who have not understood that the emphasis on ethnic identity - in the Nkoya case and in general - as ascribed and inevitable is in itself merely ideological and strategic, not factual.

A refuge for apartheid. In the early 1990s Mwene Kahare put himself in the debt of a dozen South African White, Afrikaans-speaking commercial farmers, to each of whom he issued a farm (a section of the people's communal land) of the general Zambian standard size of 2500 ha i.e. 25 km^2 (!). After surveying this land is registered as freehold land in the hands of these stranger entrepreneurs, who have already managed to establish apartheid-style rural labour relations in Mwene Kahare's area. However, the local peasants are prepared to turn themselves into underpaid farm hands, despite the obsolete and racialist labour conditions offered. Small-scale subsistence and commercial farming is therefore grinding to a halt and entire villages resettle near the farms because they constitute the only source of local cash income. These short-term economic opportunities have persuaded the average villagers to accept the alienation of their communal land; protests, and accusations to the effect that the chief has actually sold the land to the immigrant Boers, are only heard from educated locals with a senior-ranking urban career behind them and themselves engaging in commercial farming. They realise, more than their kinsmen in the villages, that Nkoya/Lozi ethnic conflict in Zambia Western's Province is increasingly going to be a conflict over arable land as a major economic resource, so that the introduction of a third party, the stranger farmers, in the long run can only be to the detriment of the local peasants.

A Paramount Chief's church. Another actor on the local scene since 1990 has been the Seventh-Day Adventist Church (SDAC), whose close association with the Lozi Paramount Chief made it an unwelcome but insistent newcomer in an area which in the 1920s-1950s was missionised by the evangelical South African General Mission (which led on the Evangelic Church of Zambia), as from the 1930s has seen a militant Watchtower movement settle down to become the emphatic religious identity of selected local villages, where the Roman Catholic Church also has made some inroads as from the 1940s, but where by and large cults of affliction and other historic forms of African religiosity have constituted the dominant religious expression also in the second half of the 20th century. Near Mwene Kahare's palace, the SDAC quickly finished a self-help clinic project initiated as long ago as the late 1970s. In return, the chief who had frequented the Evangelic Church of Zambia services prior to a spell of polygamy, had no option but to join the SDAC and to allow his orchestra to be silenced on Saturdays — before the drums were finally silenced throughout the week for the musician's lack of remuneration.

One group of actors which significantly have scarcely bothered to woo the chiefs are national and regional politicians. The end of the Kaunda/UNIP administration and the coming to power of Chiluba/MMD in 1991 further opened national opportunities for the

Nkoya; they obtained one fully-fledged Nkoya MP for one of the district's three wards, and one MP/junior minister who is half Nkoya half Mbunda) for another. The third ward was carried by a candidate representing the Luvale, Mbunda, Chokwe and Luchazi groups[15] which since the 1920s have immigrated into the district and which are now numerically dominant. With the rallying for votes, and for a lasting following on a regionalist and ethnic basis, the political new men of the MMD government as from 1991 made a point of visiting the chief's capitals from time to time, kneeling and clapping hands in ceremonial respect, and leaving some tribute. It was however clear to them that the key to voting support was no longer to be found at the chief's capitals but at the meetings of farmers' co-operatives and development committees both in the villages and at the Nkeyema agricultural scheme, and among the politically ambitious chief's relatives who, after successful careers in the urban formal sector, had returned to the district to be commercial farmers. The latter have dominated the executive meetings and the massive annual festival of the Kazanga Cultural Association, the ethnic association which bundles local ethnic resentment. At the highest national level a similar attitude towards the chiefs could be discerned, when in 1993 the Brigadier-General G. Miyanga, as Minister without Portfolio third in rank in the Zambian government, went on a fact-finding mission to Kaoma district in order to ascertain the extent of Lozi-Nkoya ethnic conflict. The trip was covered extensively on Zambian television,[16] in a way which was greatly partial to the Nkoya point of view. Chief's capitals were visited, but most time was spent with vocal, educated Nkoya familiar with court circles but with an open eye to the wider world, and prominent in the Kazanga Cultural Association.

The SDAC was neither the first nor the most conspicuous non-governmental organisation to encroach on the Nkoya chieftainship. For with their limited and dwindling power base, the failure of nostalgic initiatives to enlarge it, and while they are exploited, bullied or ignored by outside actors, the chiefs of western central Zambia at first welcomed the initiatives of the Kazanga Cultural Association as a possible solution to the predicament of having to adapt to current political and economic circumstances.

The Kazanga Cultural Association

The birth of the Kazanga Cultural Association

In postcolonial South Central Africa, ethnic associations have been rather less conspicuous than in the colonial period. The colonial state was suspicious of all forms of

---

[15] Closely related to one another by language, male circumcision, and identification with the Lunda heritage and with Mwatiyamvo; and as such much less different from today's Nkoya than the latter would care to admit; cf. my study of the vicissitudes of male circumcision among the Nkoya as an ethnic boundary marker, van Binsbergen 1993b.

[16] 'An olive branch for Kaoma district', 26 minutes production, Zambia Broadcasting Corporation, December 1993, videotape in the author's collection.

African self-organisation which might have political implications, and became all the more so during the struggle for independence in the 1950s and early 1960s. The postcolonial state, whose functioning was based on alliances between broad regionalist blocks, feared expressions of what was then called 'tribalism'; they might upset that delicate balance — although they were discouraged in the name not of existing ethnic relations, but of a pretended constitutional universalism which supposedly rendered all ethnic particularism anathema. In the first fifteen years of independence open expressions of ethnicity were therefore frowned upon, and if involving a small and powerless minority like the Nkoya, were effectively discouraged. A number of factors however made it possible that a thinly disguised ethnic association like the Kazanga Cultural Association was registered in 1980s:

- the awareness that small local ethnic movements could erode far more powerful ethnic blocks (especially that of the Lozi) opposing the ruling ethnic alliances at the state's centre;
- the rise to prominence of one Nkoya politician, Mr J. Kalaluka, which in itself reflected the previous point;
- the growing awareness among Zambian politicians and UNIP party ideologists that controlled expression of ethnic identity could have a integrating, rather than a divisive effect on the nation-state
- while the state recognition that was the central goal of ethnic minority expressions, was realised to win precious votes in a situation of political and economic decline, such as UNIP was facing in the 1980s.

For a long time the urban component of the village community was not formalised into an ethnic association. Only in 1982 the 'Kazanga Cultural Association' materialised as a formally registered society under the patronage of the Nkoya minister. This was an initiative of a handful of people from Kaoma district who, by their middle age, and against all odds, had made the grade from insecure circulatory migrant labourer to member of the capital's middle class. With the drop in copper prizes in 1975 Zambia entered into a crisis which has lasted until today. Therefore even the urban middle class could not ignore the economic developments which were meanwhile taking place in Kaoma district. Some returned to the district forever; other started a farm there but continued to live in town. Their enthusiasm for the Nkoya identity which became ever more articulated, and whose political and (through access to rural land and labour) economic potential they more and more appreciated, brought these urbanites in close contact with the district's political elite, according them new credit in the eyes of the villagers from which they had earlier taken a distance through their class position and urbanisation. From the 18th-century name of a forest, via that of a nineteenth century dynasty and an early 20th-century, colonial district, the name Nkoya had developed to designate an ethnic group found in several districts, and at the same time a language, a culture, and a cultural project intended to articulate this newly emerged group at the regional and national level.

Founded in the Zambian capital, Lusaka, in 1982, the Kazanga Cultural Association has provided an urban reception structure for prospective migrants, has contributed to Nkoya Bible translation and the publication of ethnic history texts, has championed existing and dormant local chieftainships, and within various political parties and publicity media has campaigned against the Lozi and for the Nkoya cause. The association's main achievement, however, has been the annual organisation (since 1988) of the Kazanga festival, in the course of which a large audience (including Zambian national dignitaries, the four Nkoya royal chiefs, people identifying as Nkoya, and outsiders), for two days is treated to an overview of Nkoya songs, dances and staged rituals. What we have here is a form of bricolage and of invention of tradition (Hobsbawm & Ranger 1983). The details of the contemporary Kazanga festival I have treated elsewhere. In the present context, it is important to look at the association behind the festival.

The Kazanga Cultural Association as a formal organisation

The Kazanga Cultural Association is a society registered under the Zambian Societies Act, and as such a non-governmental organisation of the type so much stressed in Africanist literature of the 1990s. Its formal nature however is largely illusory. The Kazanga association has no paying members and no membership list. Its minimal financial resources derive from voluntary individual contributions, mainly from the members of the executive themselves, who in this way gain popularity and influence. On the other hand, an executive position accords one a petty source of income via expense accounts. The Societies Act requires an Annual General Meeting which is held at the evening of the second day of the Kazanga festival. In the absence of a membership list and of fee paying, this is in practice a meeting not of members but merely of several dozens of interested persons. Executive elections mean that from these several dozens of interested persons groups of ten people are formed according to place of residence or of origin. Depending on which people happen to be present, such a group may comprise representatives from a few neighbouring villages, from an entire valley, from an official polling district as delineated by the Zambian state for the purpose of official elections, from a town at the Line of Rail (the urban areas of central Zambia), or even from the entire Line of Rail. With greater of lesser privacy these groups cast their votes for the available candidates, the votes are counted, the result announced via the festival's intercom system, after which the departing executive leaves under scorn and shame, while the new executive is formally installed and treats the voters to a 200 litres drum of traditional beer.

As basically a self-financing clique of successful urbanites and post-urbanites, the executive of the Kazanga Cultural Association has a strong class element, which I have already stressed elsewhere in my analysis of the Kazanga festival proper. Only Nkoya who are high-ranking in terms of education, formal sector career, church leadership, entrepreneurship, wealth, are eligible as candidates for the executive. Traditional status including royal birth or esoteric knowledge does not qualify. In principle all male Nkoya regardless of status have a right to vote for the executive, but in practice only a few score do vote who have the stamina to spend another night at the festival grounds after the two day's festival, and have cash to pay for transport home or have friends who offer to provide such transport. The class element in the Kazanga executive is further reflected in the shift, during the Kazanga Annual meeting of 1994, away from an executive dominated by respected and educated, but economically insecure urban dwellers, and towards an executive whose chairman and secretary are successful entrepreneurs, retired to the district after a brilliant career:

> *The composition of the Kazanga executive.* In 1988-91 national chairman was Mr M. Malapa, who after an urban career as a state registered nurse has retired to Lukulu as a peasant farmer trying to establish a rural barber shop. He was succeeded by Mr W. Kambita, a town-dwelling aged lay pastor with the Zambia Evangelical Church without a personal source of income; Mr Kambita's national secretary was Mr W. Shihenya, a town-dwelling former accountant without a permanent source of income. Both Mr Kambita's son and Mr Shihenya's wife are employed in junior positions with Zambia Educational Publishing House, formerly the Kenneth Kaunda Foundation, and a UNIP stronghold. The election of the 1994 national executive marked not only a move from town to rural district, but also to far higher levels of career achievement (the new national chairman Mr Mayowe being a former managing director of a parastatal, his national secretary Mr Lutangu a former district secretary) and wealth (Mr Mayowe operates a commercial farmer, a bar, and has a lucrative trade in fertiliser; Mr Lutangu owns a thriving grocery in Kaoma township; moreover, both draw substantial pensions, and as well as rent from a formal-sector urban house.)

The political agenda of the Kazanga Cultural Association

With all the attention for ethnic cultural production at the Kazanga festival, it is clear that the Kazanga executive does not for one moment lose sight of the fact that the festival is primarily an attempt to exchange the one resource which one locally has in abundance, competence in symbolic production, for political and economic power. The national dignitaries, and not the royal chiefs, let alone the audience, constitute the spatial focus of the Kazanga festival, and a large part of the programme is devoted to the dignitaries' welcome speeches and other formal addresses. Since the political arena is indeed the right place (and not only in Zambia) to exchange symbolic production for development projects, political allocation and patronage, the harvest of the series of Kazanga festivals since 1988 is by now eminently manifest in a marked increase of Nkoya participation at the national level, in representative bodies and in the media, and in a marked decrease of the stigmatisation to which they used to be subjected under Lozi domination until well after independence. Kazanga is an example of how an ethnic group can not only articulate itself through symbolic production, but may actually lift itself by its own hairs out of the bog.

In 1992 the state delegation to the Kazanga festival was led by the Cabinet Minister for Education, the Hon. Arthur Wina M.P., a Zambian politician of very long standing, son of a former Lozi Ngambela (traditional Prime Minister), and in the early years a member of President Chiluba's MMD cabinet. In his speech, Minister Wina explicitly joked that, with the recent shortage of water in the Zambezi flood plain (where the Lozi Paramount Chief's residences are located) there was little point in going to the Lozi annual Kuomboka ceremony marking the Paramount Chief's annual move to higher grounds with the rising of the Zambezi river; Kazanga was said to provide an adequate alternative. In coded language this was understood by the audience as a statement on the limits, if not decline, of Lozi power under MMD conditions (although Mr Wina, and for instance a former Lozi king's grandson Mbikusita-Lewanika, are clear examples of Lozi ethnic prominence in MMD circles, which are however dominated by the Bemba ethnic coalition). Minister Wina's statement was interpreted as a sign of full acceptance of Nkoya ethnic aspirations also after Mr Kaunda's political demise, and of the fact that the Kazanga leaders are taken seriously by the state.

The members of the Association's executive usually had a solid urban career and, for their generation (born in the early 1940s), a fair level of education. This makes them adept at operating bureaucracies and politicians. At the same time they tend to be the close relatives of the chiefs, usually spent their early childhood at chief's capitals, and have kept up contact with the courtly milieu to a sufficient extent to be accepted and understood there. This puts them in the unique position of being able to mediate between chiefs and state bureaucracies, or in general between the outside world of modern political and economic life, and the narrow horizon of the village society. Since village society contains, in addition to chiefs whose powers were evidently declining, large numbers of voters, as well as potential rural workers and clients of rural divisions of bureaucracies, politicians have an interest to honour the invitations to the annual Kazanga festival extended to them by the Kazanga executive; moreover, the respectful treatment and the colourful ceremony awaiting them there make them not regret their trip.

Why a formal organisation? Ethnicisation and structural bridging

Kazanga's political agenda however could only be conceived and executed within the wider framework of ethnic processes in Zambia, and throughout sub-Saharan Africa, today. The formula of ethnic self-presentation through an annual cultural festival built, with much bricolage, out of an historic ritual, has been generally adopted in Zambia today. The television audience is regularly reminded of a growing series (now nearly a dozen) of regional festivals similar to Kazanga. Since all these festivals are created and maintained by ethnic associations, this reveals a recent revival of such formal organisations. They are at the heart of current ethnicisation processes in Zambia (cf. van Binsbergen, in press).

Ethnicisation constructs ethnonyms so as to mark ethnic boundaries, and pre-existing culture so as to fall within those boundaries and to offer distinctive boundary markers. The cultivated sense of a shared history makes sense of experiences of powerlessness, deprivation and estrangement, and kindles hope of improvement through ethnic self-presentation. The ethnonym and the principle of ascription governing ethnic group membership by birth, then produce for the actors the image of a bounded, particularist set of solidary people. The vulnerable individual's access to national resources, and the formal organisations (in state and industry) controlling them, become the object of group action. In postcolonial Central Africa, ethnicisation increasingly includes cultural politics. A set of people is restructured so as to become an ethnic group by designing a cultural package which in its own right constitutes a major stake in the negotiations with the outside world. One dissociates from rival ethnic groups at the local and regional scene through a strategic emphasis on cultural and linguistic elements; and at the national level one competes for the state's political and economic prizes via the state's recognition of the ethnically constructed cultural package. New intra-group inequalities emerge. The mediation takes place via brokers who are more than their fellow-members of the ethnic group in a position to exploit the opportunities at the interface between ethnic group and the outside world. Asserting the 'traditional', 'authentic' (but in fact newly reconstructed) culture appears as an important task and as a source of power and income for the brokers. Ethnic associations, publications, and festivals, constitute general strategies in this process.

Ethnicity displays a remarkable dialectics between inescapability and constructedness, which largely explains its great societal potential. On the one hand, as a classification system ethnicity offers a logical structure, which is further ossified through ascription and which presents itself as unconditional, bounded, inescapable and timeless. This is what made early researchers of Central African ethnicity stress *primordial attachments*. On the other hand, the social praxis of ethnicity as ethnicisation means flexibility, choice, constructedness and recent change. Together, these entirely contradictory aspects constitute *a devise to disguise strategy as inevitability*. This dialectics renders ethnicity particularly suitable for mediating, in processes of social change, between social contexts with each have a fundamentally different structure. Because of this internal contradiction, ethnicity offers the option of strategically effective particularism in a context of universalism, and hence enables individuals, as members of an ethnic group, to cross otherwise non-negotiable boundaries and to create a foothold or niche in structural contexts that would otherwise remain inaccessible; this is how recent urban immigrants (cf. urban markets of labour and housing) and citizens (cf. bureaucracies) use ethnicity.

Ethnicisation amounts to a conceptual and organisational focusing or framing, so as to make a social contradiction or conflict capable of being processed within the available technologies of communication, bureaucratic organisation, and political representation. The emergence of ethnic associations is one example at the organisational level.[17] What the Kazanga Cultural Association basically does is to provide an organisational framework for bridging the state on the one hand, indigenous politics (and the rural society that it stands for) on the other.

At this point, where we aim at structural interpretation, our analysis has to proceed beyond the transactionalism that has so far guided it. We are pressed to admit that in the Kazanga Cultural Association as context of ethnicisation, two contradictory processes occur at the same time:

- the state on the one hand, the chiefs (and the rural society they stand for) on the other, are caused to be in constant interaction with each other (which makes for merging and blurring of boundaries in actual political and economic practice),
- yet at a level of the explicit conceptualisations, by the actors involved, this constant movement back and forth between what they construct as a traditional and as a modern domain, only reinforces their view that here two fundamentally different modes of socio-political organisation are involved.

The following table presents the outline of an actors' model which, from the point of view of the Nkoya elite, the Nkoya chiefs and most Nkoya commoners, would seem to sum up the structural differences between the postcolonial state and chiefs.

postcolonial state	chief
legal authority (the letter of the written word)	traditional authority
impersonal	personal
universalist	particularist
imported within living memory	considered as local
culturally alien	considered as culturally familiar, self-evident
defective legitimation	self-evident legitimation
lack of cosmological anchorage	cosmological anchorage

Table 1. A model contrasting postcolonial state and chiefs.

---

[17] However, ethnicity is not unique in this respect. Elsewhere (van Binsbergen 1993a) I have presented a similar argument with regard to African independent churches and professional associations of traditional healers in Botswana, both forms of formal organisations present an organisational form in line with the logic of the postcolonial state (via the latter's Societies Act), while internally supporting ideological positions totally at variance with the principles informing the state.

This model allows us to make the point that the Kazanga executive as brokers are, at least in their own perception, truly bridging two fundamentally different structures. Against the background of African ethnicity and ethnicisation, it is no surprise that they do so in an idiom of ethnicisation.

The important thing to realise is that such bridging consists in the negotiation of conceptual boundaries *through concrete interaction*, where objects and people are positioned at the conceptual boundaries between two systems, where they can serve as interfaces between the two. In the dialectics of social praxis, conceptually different domains are drawn, first, within such contradictory perceptions, motivations and exchanges as each single actor is capable of; and secondly, these contradictions are to be made convergent, predictable, and persistent over time by their being imbedded in the social organisation of such individual actors. In other words, structural bridging inevitably requires, beyond conceptualisation, effective social organisation. The modern formal organisation corresponds morphologically with the organisational logic of the state; at the same time, in the field of ideology and symbolism it can maintain as much continuity as is needed towards structural domains that are conceived according to a logic totally different from that of the state (like chieftainship). Therefore the mode of mobilisation which structurally bridges state and chiefs had to take the form of a formal voluntary association.

Let us now examine what in practice was realised of such bridging, by considering the actual interaction between the Kazanga Cultural Association and the chiefs of western central Zambia.

The chiefs and the Kazanga cultural association

Royal cultural revival in the Kazanga festival

Up to a point of disaffection, which was reached in 1995, chiefs have sought to use the Kazanga Cultural Association for their own self-presentation. But the complementary process has been much more manifest: the attempt, on the part of the Kazanga Cultural Association, to use, increasingly even to harness, chieftainship for its own combined purpose of ethnic articulation, access to the state, and personal ascendance in terms of political and economic power and influence on the part of the association's executive.

Kazanga's effective negotiation between the state, the chieftainship and the villagers insists on a new symbolic and ceremonial role for all four Nkoya kings together along lines which are all bricolage and thoroughly un-historical, but which do result in restoring the kings to a level of emotional and symbolic significance perhaps unprecedented in twentieth century Nkoya history. At the annual Kazanga festival, the chiefs have grasped the opportunity to appear with all regality which they could summon and which their paraphernalia could earn them. Mwene Kahare, who used to be a somewhat pathetic, stammering and alcoholic figure dressed in a faded suit with ragged shirt collar, finally, in his seventies, appeared at the 1992 Kazanga festival covered in leopard skins and with a headband adorned with regal *zimpande* shell ornaments — regalia he has most probably never worn since his installation in 1955 — formidably brandishing his royal axe in a solo dance that kept the audience breathless and moved them to tears. At the climax the king (for that is what he shows himself to be, in a performative revival of early 19th-century royal autonomy and splendour) kneels down and drinks directly from a hole in the ground where beer has been poured out for his royal ancestors — the patrons of at least his part of the Nkoya nation, implied to share in the deeply emotional cheers from the audience.

The successful emergence of the Kazanga Cultural Association initially promised to offer to the chiefs the opportunity for self-assertion that was well in line with their anti-Lozi sentiments. However, the competition between the two Nkoya chiefs from Kaoma turned out to be a very severe constraint in this respect. The first few Kazanga festivals were staged at the capital of Mwene Mutondo, and were thus interpreted as a sign of his seniority over Kahare and over other royal chiefs from outside Kaoma district. A truce was struck by the adoption of new, special festival grounds smack at the boundary between either chief's areas. But this led to further complications as the above case of Mr Daniel Muchayila demonstrates.

Gradually, Mutondo dominance over the Kazanga festival and over Nkoya ethnicisation in general has dwindled. The suspiciously untimely death of Muchayila's successor Mwene Chipimbi in 1992 prevented Mutondo control over that year's festival (a successor is seldom installed within a year), and anyway rendered the Mutondo *lukena* inappropriate as festival grounds in this time of mourning. Mwene Kahare's royal dance centres, of course, on a shrine situated at the hub of the festival grounds; but it is no longer the thatched shrine of the Mutondo dynasty, nor the Kahare dynasty's own wooden pole adorned with buffalo trophies, but a neutral shrub of the type found, as headman's shrine, in most Nkoya villages.

The traditionalist revival on the part of the Kazanga Cultural Association is not limited to Nkoya circles and western Zambia, as the following case reveals:

> *Kazanga, and Soli ethnic revival in central Zambia.* One of the most interesting developments around Kazanga occurred in Lusaka in 1995. The Kazanga band under the direction of Mr Tom Taulo, the composer and dance leader, also gives paid guest performances in beer gardens etc. in the Lusaka area. This has produced such popularity for the band that Kazanga Cultural Association was invited to play a major advisory role on the creation of the first Soli ethnic festival at Undaunda, 100 km. east of Lusaka. After extensive preparatory meetings in which the experiences of the Kazanga Cultural Association since 1982 were lavishly shared, both the

band and the executive of the association's Lusaka branch were major official guests at the actual festival in October, 1995. It was almost exactly a hundred years after Mwene Mutondo Wahila, in the context of a diplomatic exchanges, across a distance of 500 km paid a state visit to the Soli Queen Nkomeshya. It is still too early to draw conclusions from the 1995 co-operation, yet is suggests that we are witnessing the formation of one large ethnic coalition (a 'mega-ethnic group') encompassing the whole of Central Zambia. The name 'Kafue' has already been suggested as its name, not only because this is the major river of this region, but also because this has been the historic name of various colonial administrative centres, at various locations between Lusaka and Kaoma district.

The Kazanga association has also been instrumental in reviving royal titles which did not survive Lozi expansion around 1900: the Shakalongo title, once senior to both Kahare and Mutondo, had for many years been carried by a mere village headman, but has now been reinstalled as that of a royal chief; and the reinstatement of Mwene Pumpola in Lukulu district has been imminent for some years. The Kazanga annual festival offers these new chiefs the opportunity to articulate themselves publicly, even if this means that for the time being they have to make shift in a cosmopolitan three-piece suit instead of leopard skin and other historic paraphernalia. However, their formal recognition and remuneration depends on the Lozi Paramount, whose refusal we have already discussed above.

Interestingly, the traditionalist and Mwene-orientated stance of the Kazanga society enables its leaders to draw on this same reservoir of tribute-related labour for the construction and maintenance of its festival grounds, not only when these were still situated at the *lukena* of Mwene Mutondo but also when subsequently the festival was moved to a new site at equal distances from the capitals of Mutondo and Kahare — which involved the major task of clearing the new sit and erecting the branch palaces and the spectators' shelters.

After the enthusiasm of the first years of the Kazanga festival, it gradually became clear that the executive of the Kazanga Cultural Association sought to use chieftainship as a resource for ulterior aims, instead of furthering it as what the chiefs and their councillors had been led to believe during the colonial period: the hub of Nkoya ethnic identity. The dramaturgy of the festival was revised so as to make clear that not Mwene Mutondo, or the royal chiefs collectively, but the association's executive was hosting the festival; by 1993 the chiefs saw themselves reduced to the status of picturesque ornaments who had to put in a ceremonial presence, avowedly as exalted guests of honour but in fact as the most senior *performers* at the festival, who imprisoned in their royal shelter, next to that of the national and regional politicians, did not even have a chance to engage in conversation with the latter.

Interaction between chiefs and the Kazanga executive beyond the Kazanga festival

The interaction between the Kazanga Cultural Association and the chiefs was not limited to the Kazanga festival but gradually extended to traditional politics at the chief's capitals themselves. Against the background of the postcolonial state and Zambian civil society, an extremely complex pattern emerged whose outlines are presented in diagram 1. It is difficult to imagine a better demonstration of the boundary crossings which are absolutely standard between the so-called modern political domain and the so-called traditional political domain. Moreover, the diagram makes it clear that the mediation between these two domains presupposes a third domain: that of the civil society, which in the Kazanga case concentrates on the executive of the Kazanga Cultural Association.

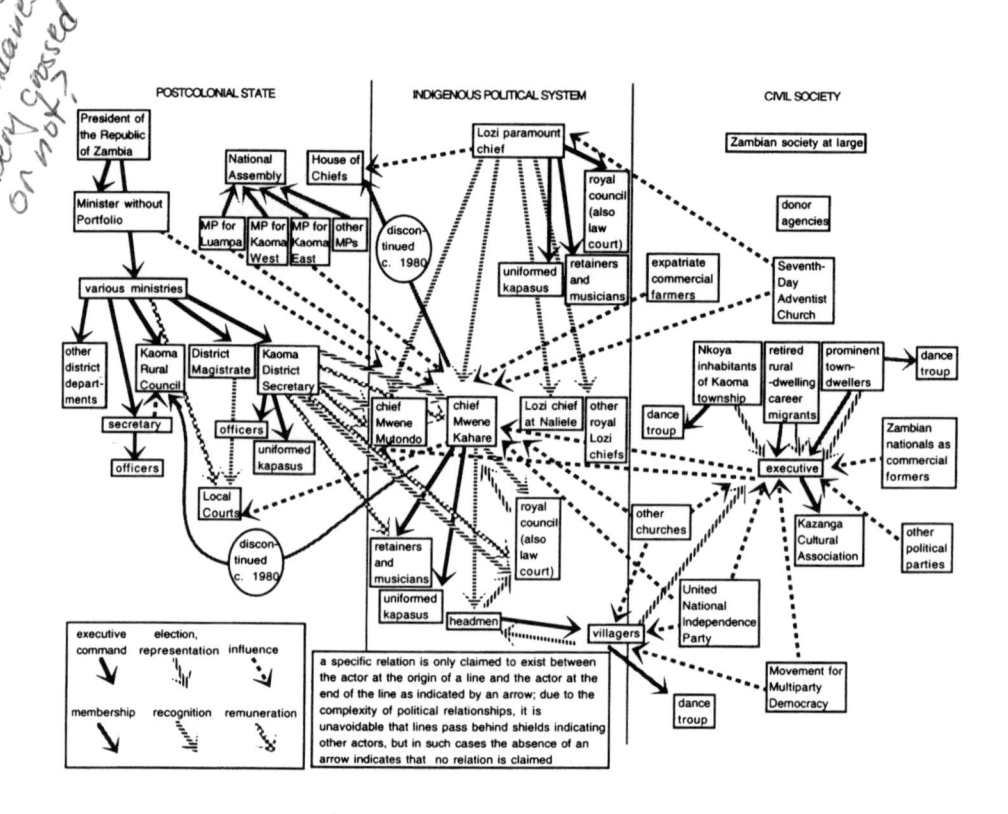

Diagram 1. Postcolonial state, indigenous political system and civil society: the background of political relations between Chief Kahare and the Kazanga Cultural Association executive.

- 124 -

A number of specific cases make clear that the Kazanga Cultural Association tried not only to further and revise, but actually to control chieftainship, and that this attempt was thwarted by the traditional guardians of that institution, the royal councils.

Mwene Mutondo Chipimbi's election, and its aftermath. A life-long town dweller an a middle-ranking officer with a Zambian parastatal, the later Mwene Mutondo Chipimbi was initially one of the founding members of the Kazanga Cultural Association in 1982. His accession to the throne in 1991 was the result of insistent rallying of the association's executive during the royal electoral process following the death of the aged Mwene Mutondo Muchayila in 1990. As we have seen, Mwene Chipimbi's untimely death (which others, along with the death of his wife around the same time, attributed to lack of resistance to malaria, as town dwellers) was interpreted as sign that the senior headmen greatly resented this intrusion from town dwelling careerists into rural traditional politics. His death was one of the reasons why the Kazanga festival had to be moved from the Mutondo capital, where the Kazanga executive during unavoidable personal and official visits in 1992-1993 literally feared for their lives. Initially, of course, the Mutondo courtiers refused to attend Kazanga at the new festival grounds, i.e. in a form which so effectively denied Mutondo hegemony. However, the Kazanga executive managed to bring a high-powered government delegation to the Kazanga festival of 1992, and made it clear to the Mutondo courtiers that their staying away would be interpreted by the new government as a anti-MMD demonstration and might therefore have unpleasant consequences. From a distant enemy, the state had become an ally; and from being introverted and divisive, ethnicity, at least in the form of ethnic mediation it has taken in Kazanga, has come to combine inward symbolic reconstruction with confident participation in the national space. But although a success from the point of view of the Nkoya ethnicisation project, its price was that the Kazanga executive had to openly deploy their state resources against the chief's council, thus revealing the contradictions between executive and chieftainship despite the former's further of chieftainship on less conflictive occasions.

The Kazanga executive at Kabulwebulwe's. Outside Kaoma district, at the Kabulwebulwe capital in Mumbwa district where most of the Kazanga executive are strangers, they did much better. They played a major part in the election of the new Chief Kabulwebulwe, in Mumbwa district in 1994, and were guests of honour both at the funeral of the previous incumbent and at the installation ceremony of his successor.

In the same year the throne of Mwene Kahare had to be filled after the aged Mwene Kahare Kabambi died in December 1993, after having ruled for 39 years. Here again, like at the court of Mutondo, the Kazanga Cultural Association's offensive intended to gain direct control over the chieftainship, but failed.

The Kazanga executive and the succession of Mwene Kahare, early 1994. During the final two months of the electoral process, the list of possible candidates had shortened to only four names (cf. diagram 2):

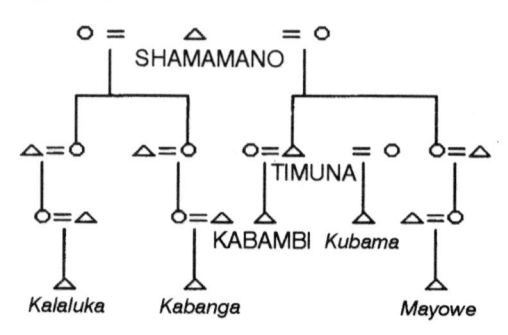

```
         ○ =   △    = ○
            SHAMAMANO
         ┌─────┼─────┐
    △=○   △=○   ○=△    = ○   ○=△
     │     │   │TIMUNA│        │
     ○=△   ○=△  △      △     △=○
      │     │  KABAMBI Kubama  │
      △     △                  △
   Kalaluka Kabanga          Mayowe
```

Diagram 2. Simplified genealogy illustrating the succession of Mwene Kahare Kabambi (1994 contenders for the chieftainship in italics; actual royal incumbents in capitals).

- Mr J. Kalaluka (a former MP, former Cabinet Minister and former Ambassador, awaiting trial for embezzlement which forced him to leave state service; commercial farmer; son of a Lozi father but, like the other three remaining candidates, raised at the Kahare court and locally identifying as Nkoya; founding patron of the Kazanga Cultural Association);
- Mr D. Kabanga (a retired state registered male nurse, former UNIP ward chairman in Lusaka, member of the Kazanga executive 1989-93, now a village farmer);
- Mr Kubama Kahare (peasant farmer from Namwala district; belongs on his mother's side to the Kambotwe/ Shipungu line from the Kawanga valley, Kaoma district, who are the original owners of the Kahare royal title);
- Mr S. Mayowe (a retired former manager of Lake Fisheries, a major parastatal; former member of the Kaoma rural council, commercial farmer, bar owner, general entrepreneur, Kaoma representative of the National Party (a Lozi-dominated opposition party), and member of the executive, Kazanga Cultural Association).

Campaigning involved conspicuous gift-giving to senior councillors and to royal women at the court, witchcraft accusations, etc. Mr Mayowe, accused of having caused, through sorcery, the death of Kabambi with whom he had repeated quarrelled over land issues, found that he lacked support, withdrew as a candidate and openly backed Kubama as the obvious and ideal traditional choice; Mayowe thus hoped that he would enhance his chances of succeeding Kubama, who was already in his mid-60s and reputed to be of ill health. Mr Kabanga was the least likely candidate of the four, for lack of wealth, ancestry and achievements. Mr Kalaluka, whose genealogical position was similar to that of Mr Kabanga, had already told his Lusaka elite friends that he was going to spend the rest of his life as a genuine chief, when the elders rejected him in favour of Mr Kubama. The latter lacked personal wealth, but his three sons were holding solid positions in government and industry, his fierce and upright character recalled that of his father Mwene Kahare Timuna, and considering his mother's ancestry he was indisputably the rightful owner of the title even in the eyes of those senior headmen who still resented the title's usurpation by Mwene Timuna's father Mwene Shamamano in the 1880s (!). When a few months later Mr Mayowe was elected national chairman of the Kazanga Cultural Association it was clear that the association, while playing a major role in the election of Chief Kubama, had given up hopes of controlling the chieftainship directly, but instead had opted for a division of labour between complementary sectors of modern and traditional politics, with close kin relations and trust between the leaders on both sides.

It is interesting to note how the contradictions between the royal courts and the Kazanga association, which became manifest in the course of the 1990s, also have complements in the religious and political affiliations of the people involved on either side. The MMD had a strong appeal among aspiring urbanites, the very category that makes up the Kazanga executive. By contrast, the chiefs' courts largely remained loyal to what over the years had emerged as their main ally in the struggle against the Lozi: UNIP and its leader Kaunda, who only as recently as in 1990 had prevented a move by the Lozi Paramount Chief to abolish the Nkoya chieftainships. Mr Mayowe meanwhile dabbled in opposition politics and in 194 was the district representative of the National Party, which carried the Mongu by-elections in early 1994; this lonely political stance in a UNIP-oriented rural environment helped to tilt the scales against him at the royal election. In the religious field Lozi/chief antagonism was temporarily suspended when Mwene Kahare welcomed the oppressive intervention on the part of the Seventh Day Adventist Church; however, most of the Kazanga executive have remained loyal to the Evangelic Church of Zambia, the first missionary presence in the region, since it had provided their formal education.

The breaking point in the relations between the chiefs and the Kazanga Cultural Association was reached in 1995:

The 1995 conflict between chiefs and the Kazanga executive. On the first day of the 1995 festival the chiefs refused to return to the shelter after lunch, under the pretext that the royal wives had not been accommodated with them in the royal shelter but had been seated, with other prominent commoners, on the seats provided along the rim of the arena, in July's mild winter sun. Both Myene were new incumbents, installed less than two years, and with only one Kazanga festival behind them; in the earliest Kazanga festivals, the Myene were old men without formal royal wives; on the occasion of the 1991 Kazanga, Mwene Mutondo Chipimbi had just acceded while his wife was already seriously ill. So this issue of protocol had not arisen before. For most of the remaining programme the 1995

proceedings took the form of a different historic Nkoya performance: the court case. The conflict destroyed the 1995 festival; visitors left in anger. Various contradictions reverberate in this conflict:
- gender, now beginning to be a modern political issue in this rural area, has always been an underlying current in local chieftainship: in the 18th and early 19th century, all Myene were women.
- the Kazanga festival as a celebration of viable royalty, of the kingdom (the way the festival was celebrated in the 19th century), rather as a mere nostalgic production of performative fragments (as the festival has turned out under the Kazanga Cultural Association).
- conflict between court officials and Kazanga officials; the court officials feel that their power over chieftainship is being usurped by the Kazanga executive, and seek to reclaim control by insistence on proper protocol.

These senior headmen may have spent many years in distant urban employment but in middle age can afford to have no other commitment than the preservation of *shihemuwa shetu*, 'our custom'. Far from being a dying concern, traditional politics (even if no longer remunerated) has remained a central career goals for many men from western Central Zambia.

The interaction between the Kazanga Cultural Association and the chiefs has made clear that ethnicisation does not necessarily lead to resilience of chieftainship. In the Nkoya case it has led to folklorisation: the reduction of chiefs to nostalgic ornaments of symbolic production in a festival context which is dominated by ethnic brokers orientated to the modern economy and the state.

In the early 1970s the Nkoya neo-traditional court culture was marked by a rigid, wholly introverted splendour. The maintenance of nostalgic historic forms of protocol and symbolic, particularly musical, production (which no longer correspond with any real power invested in the kingship under conditions of incorporation by the Barotse indigenous state and by the colonial and post-colonial central state) reflected the fact that *boundary maintenance* vis-à-vis the outside world was at its peak. All this strikingly contrasts with the laxity of court life at the *zinkena* today. The drums are no longer played. Court protocol which used to be extremely strict and enforced by physical sanctions (only a century ago still by capital punishment), is hardly observed today. Chiefs are no longer recognised nor remunerated, and expatriate commercial farmers with their racialist labour relations are literally taking over the land.

Under such circumstances, Nkoya ethnicisation could even lead to the virtual destruction of the chieftainships that featured so prominently as a sign of ethnic identity, ethnohistorical reconstruction, and the reinvention of tradition in the context of the Kazanga festival. The near future will learn if and how the current Nkoya royal chiefs, both of them new incumbents although in advanced middle age, will meet these challenges.

Conclusion

In Zambia's Kaoma district today, the two royal Nkoya chiefs (Mwene Kahare and Mwene Mutondo) are reluctant senior members of the Lozi indigenous administration headed by the Lozi Paramount Chief. Their financial situation is miserable and leads to the further decline of chieftainship and its courtly institutions. Nor can it justifiably be said that the chiefs exist on a plane outside the postcolonial state. Until recently they participated in many governing and representative bodies of the postcolonial state, and they have no formal source of income except from the state. The latter largely controls the reproduction (which is greatly defective, anyway) of chieftainship. Besides indirect influence over the lowest law courts with jurisdiction only in the field of family law and traditional political structure, the chiefs' main independent source of power is their continued control over rural land. However, this prerogative may be used, and is used, destructively. Issuing land to strangers hardly benefits the chief beyond covering part of his modest household expenses, but does lead to proletarianisation among the chiefs' local subjects and destroys the territorial basis for chieftainship.

Thus royal chief in western central Zambia constitute a limiting case for some of the general themes in African chieftainship today, as emerging from the present collective volume as a whole. They do not display the remarkable resilience of other African chiefs in adapting to social and political change. Their power base is small and diminishing. Whereas in the first decades of the postcolonial era they effectively expanded into formal administrative and representative bodies of the modern state, this process has now been reversed, largely as a result of regional ethnic conflict. These chiefs can certainly not afford to consider the bureaucratic logic of the African state merely as an accidental, foreign and imposed system. That they do not actually hold such views, and in the recent past have effectively blended with state institutions, is also partly attributable to their own formal sector employment (often as court clerks or low-ranking administrative officers at the district level) prior to accession. Meanwhile they are financially dependent upon the colonial state and upon recognition both by the state and by the indigenous administration under the Lozi Paramount Chief. Under these circumstances, chieftainship in western central Zambia does not emerge as an obvious focus for democratisation processes. Instead, it is subject to folklorisation, becoming a nostalgic element in an ethnicisation process which creates new inequalities (those between on the one hand proletarianising peasants, and on the other successful post-migrant pensioners and other agricultural and commercial entrepreneurs), while seeking to abolish one particular form of politico-ethnic domination.

Under the circumstances, the annihilation of the particular form chieftainship as found in western central Zambia is a serious possibility, which opens up further horizons of analysis. At an abstract level, the interaction between the Kazanga Cultural Association (and other formal organisations, e.g. the SDAC) and the chiefs may ultimately have to be interpreted, not as mere *bridging* (which presupposes the continued independent existence of social contexts - chiefs and state - to be bridged), but rather as the *replacement* of one historic mode of organisation (that of the indigenous political system centring on the *lukena*) by another, formal, global mode of organisation (that of the state-registered voluntary association). Both modes organise the villagers of western central Zambia, by trading exploitation by an elite (the chiefs, the executive) for old and new goals (the chiefs: social and cosmological order, judicial and military regulation of violence, regulation of long-distance trade; the executive: ethnic cultural self-expression, economic and political access to the wider world).

In less than a hundred years, the formal organisation has established itself on African soil as the principal format for social, political, economic and religious organisation, complementing and often replacing time honoured, historic local forms of organisation. I have often stressed[18] that from a sociological point of view, this is one of the most significant transformations of African life, and one of the greatest blind spots in African studies today. We have largely contented ourselves with demonstrating why (for informal undercurrents, corruption, continued allegiance to older forms of organisation, lack of appreciation of legal authority etc.) the formal organisation cannot work in Africa, rather than acknowledging that defective or latent functioning of formal organisations is not peculiar to Africa, and can only be understood once the formal organisation in itself has been accepted to set the framework.

References

AGREEMENT
1964 *The Barotseland Agreement 1964 presented to Parliament by the Secretary of State for Commonwealth Relations by Command of Her Majesty, May 1964*, London: Her Majesty's Stationery Office

APTER, David E.
1961 *The political kingdom in Uganda*, Princeton: Princeton University Press

APTHORPE, Raymond J. (ed.)
1959 *From tribal rule to modern government*, Thirteenth Conference Proceedings, Lusaka: Rhodes-Livingstone Institute

BAILEY, Fred G.
1969 *Stratagems and spoils*, Oxford: Blackwell

BARTH, Fredrik (ed.)
1966 *Models of social organization*, London: Royal Anthropological Institute of Great Britain and Ireland, Occasional Papers no. 23

---

[18] van Binsbergen 1985, 1993a, 1993c, 1997

BARTH, Fredrik (ed.)
1969   ed., *Ethnic groups and boundaries: The social organization of culture differences.* Boston: Little, Brown & Co

BEINART, William
1985   'Chieftaincy and the concept of articulation: South Africa ca. 1900-1950. Pp. 91-98. In: *Modes of Production: The challenge of Africa*, B. Jewsiewicki with J. Létourneau (eds.). Ste-Foy (Can.)

BENTSI-ENCHILL, Kwamena
1969   The colonial heritage of legal pluralism: The British schema. Pp. 1-30. In: *Zambia Law Journal*, 1, 2

BINSBERGEN, Wim M. J. van
1977   Law in the context of Nkoya society. Pp. 39-68. In: *Law and the family in Africa.* S. Roberts (ed). The Hague/Paris: Mouton

1985   Samenlevingen en culturen in Zwart Afrika: Honderd jaar na de wedloop: Struktuurveranderingen op kontinentale schaal. Pp. 30-43. In: *Tijdschrift voor Ontwikkelingssamenwerking (TvO)* (Antwerp), special issue on 'Africa hundred years after the Berlin Conference',10, 2

1987   Chiefs and the state in independent Zambia: Exploring the Zambian National Press'. Pp. 139-201. In: *Chieftaincy and the state in Africa.* Special issue of the *Journal of Legal Pluralism*, nos. 25 & 26 (guest-ed. E.A.B. van Rouveroy van Nieuwaal)

1992   *Tears of Rain: Ethnicity and history in central western Zambia*, London/Boston: Kegan Paul International

1993a   African Independent churches and the state in Botswana. Pp. 24-56. In: *Power and prayer: Essays on Religion and politics.* M. Bax & A. de Koster (eds.). CentREPOL-VU Studies 2, Amsterdam: VU University Press

1993b   *MUKANDA:* Towards a history of circumcision rites in western Zambia, 18th-20th century. Pp. 49-103. In: *L'invention religieuse en Afrique: Histoire et religion en Afrique noire.* J.P. Chrétien avec collaboration de C.H. Perrot, G. Prunier & D. Raison-Lourde (eds.). Paris: Agence de culture et de Coopération Technique/Karthala

1993c   Nederlands Afrika-onderzoek tot het jaar 2000: Hulpbronnen, personeel, organisatie, onderzoeksthema's. Pp. 81-104. In: *De maatschappelijke betekenis van Nederlands Afrika-onderzoek in deze tijd: Een symposium.* W.M.J. van Binsbergen, (ed.). Leiden: Netherlands Association of African Studies

1994a   Minority language, ethnicity and the state in two African situations: the Nkoya of Zambia and the Kalanga of Botswana. Pp. 142-188. In: *African languages, development and the state.* R. Fardon & G. Furniss (eds). London etc.: Routledge

1994b   The Kazanga festival: Ethnicity as cultural mediation and transformation in central western Zambia. Pp. 92-125. In: *African Studies*, 53, 2

1997   *Virtuality as a key concept in the study of globalisation: Aspects of the symbolic transformation of contemporary Africa.* The Hague: WOTRO, Working papers on Globalisation and the construction of communal identity, 3

In press Ethnicity and identity in Central Africa. In: *Encyclopaedia of Africa south of the Sahara.* J.M. Middleton (ed.). New York: Scribner's

BINSBERGEN, Wim M. J. van & Peter L. GESCHIERE
1985   Marxist theory and anthropological practice: The application of French Marxist anthropology in fieldwork. Pp. 235-289. In: *Old modes of production and capitalist encroachment: Anthropological explorations in Africa.* W.M.J. van Binsbergen & P.L. Geschiere (eds). London/Boston: Kegan Paul International

BOISSEVAIN, Jeremy F.
1968   The place of non-groups in the social sciences. PP. 542-556. In: *Man* (NS), 3

BROWN, Edward D.
1984   Drums of life: Royal music and social life in Western Zambia. Ph.D. thesis, University of Washington, School of Music; University Microfilms, Ann Arbor

BROWN, Richard
1973   Passages in the life of a white anthropologist: Max Gluckman. In: *Anthropology and the colonial encounter,* T. Asad (ed.). London: Ithaca Press

BUSTIN, Edouard
1975   *Lunda under Belgian rule: The politics of ethnicity.* Cambridge (Mass.)/London: Harvard University Press

CHANOCK, Martin
1985   *Law, custom and social order: The colonial experience in Malawi and Zambia.* Cambridge University Press

FALLERS, Lloyd A.
1955   The predicament of the modern African chief. Pp. 290-305. In: *American Anthropologist,* n.s., 57

FORTES, Meijer & Edward E. Evans-Pritchard
1969   *African political systems.* London: Oxford University Press, 13th impression (first impression 1940)

GRIFFITHS, John
1986   What is legal pluralism? Pp. 1-50. In: *Journal of Legal Pluralism* no. 24

HOBSBAWM, Eric & Terence O. RANGER (eds.)
1983   *The invention of tradition.* Cambridge: Cambridge University Press

MAIR, Lucy P.
1936   Chieftainship in modern Africa, Pp. 305-316. In: *Africa,* 9

PRINS, Gwynn
1980   *The hidden hippopotamus.* Cambridge: Cambridge University Press

RICHARDS, Audrey I.
1935   Tribal government in transition: The Babemba of Northern Rhodesia. In: *Journal of the Royal African Society*, 34, supplement

RICHARDS, Audrey I. (ed.)
1960   *East African chiefs*. London: Faber & Faber

ROUVEROY VAN NIEUWAAL, E. Adriaan B. van
1984   Volkshoofden en jonge staten in Afrika. *Le chef coutumier est-il mort? Inaugural lecture*. Leiden University
1987   (ed.) *Chieftaincy and the state in Africa*. In: Journal of Legal Pluralism and Unofficial Law, nos. 25 & 26
1992   The Togolese Chiefs: Caught between Scylla and Charybdis? Pp. 19-46. In: *Journal of Legal Pluralism and Unofficial Law*, no. 32
1994   Et toujours ce chef coutumier: Résistance au pouvoir étatique au Sud-Togo sous la tutelle française. Pp. 129-157. In: *Legitimation von Herrschaft und Recht*. W.J.G. Möhlig & T. von Trotha (eds.). Köln: Rüdiger Köppe Verlag
1995   State and Chiefs in Africa: Are Chiefs Mere Puppets?, Pp. 49-88. In: *Proceedings of the Conference on the Contribution of Traditional Authority to Development, Human Rights and Environmental Protection: Strategies for Africa, Accra-Kumasi, 2-6 September, 1994*. Nana. K. Arhin, D.I. Ray & E.A.B. van Rouveroy van Nieuwaal (eds.). Leiden: African Studies Centre

SCHAPERA, Isaac
1943   *Tribal legislation among the Tswana of the Bechuanaland Protectorate*. London: Lund, Humpries & Co
1963   *Government and politics in tribal societies: Josiah Mason lectures delivered at the University of Birmingham*. London: Watts, first published 1956

SPALDING, Fred O.
1970   The jurisdiction of the lower courts. Pp. 219-282. In: *Zambia Law Journal*, 2, 12

VANDERLINDEN, Jacques
1989   Return to legal pluralism: Twenty years later. Pp. 149-157. In: *Journal of Legal Pluralism*, no. 28

WEBER, Max
1969   *The theory of social and economic organization*, Glencoe: Free Press, 6th reprint of the 1964 paperback edition, [*Wirtschaft und Gesellschaft*, part I]

TRADITIONAL CHIEFS AND MODERN LAND TENURE LAW IN NIGER

Christian Lund and Gerti Hesseling

Introduction

Can land tenure legislation be modernised by integrating traditional chiefs into the legal framework and are tenure rules be clarified by referring to something as elusive as custom? Legislators and planners of rural development in Niger seem to have been thus persuaded when the new land tenure reform – the *Code rural* – was drawn up in the late 1980s and adopted in 1993 (Ordonnance no. 93-015 du 2 Mars 1993). The legislation has been considered path-breaking and innovative because it seeks to modernise tenure rules without breaking with tradition. It seeks to elevate customs to law.

When the government produces legislation that is a codification of customs, chiefs are central but their position is full of ambiguity. Chiefs are regarded at once as guardians of 'tradition' and as intermediaries between state and society; they are continually negotiating their social and politico-legal position vis-à-vis other politico-legal institutions, in particular the civil administration and the judiciary (van Rouveroy van Nieuwaal n.d.; Lund 1997). The competition over jurisdiction between chiefs and the government – generally the *sous-préfets* – is often characterised by self-contradictory efforts by both to claim legitimacy in dispute resolution, and hence in the interpretation of custom and law. On the one hand, both attempt to maintain a strict separation between their own realm and that of the other, in order to keep certain cultural entitlements to legitimacy out of the reach of other institutional actors. But at the same time each also tries to take possession of the codes, norms and procedures of the other institutions whenever that seems expedient. Chiefs refer to themselves and their jurisdictions as based on *'tradition'*. Their role as guardians of tradition is said to qualify them to decide how tradition is to be interpreted. However, chiefs are not able to monopolise references to tradition – these are often 'borrowed' by institutional actors whose mandate is grounded elsewhere. Thus, the government often takes the Quran as a normative referent for checking the validity of statements by litigants. Another way of establishing discursive boundaries and institutional domains is to claim that *legality* is the constituent force of the legitimate authority whereby politico-legal institutions may adjudicate in disputes and interpret the law. This is a strategy used typically by the governmental authorities – most commonly in direct confrontations with other politico-legal institutions, such as village and canton chiefs, to call them to order. Chiefs, for their part, rarely employ formal administrative rhetoric in confrontations with governmental authorities, but they do invoke administrative hierarchies and procedures vis-à-vis farmers to assert their position in the hierarchy and keep from being bypassed.

The two sets of discourses are thus used for different purposes. *Reference to tradition* is used for asserting *substantive* competence or jurisdiction – knowledge about land tenure, legal processes and 'right and wrong'. Legitimation through *reference to legality* is used in asserting *formal* competencies or jurisdictions, their hierarchical order and the formal legal process of litigation. Both politico-legal institutions use rhetoric from both types of discursive domain, but they use it in different confrontational situations.

Since the 1950s, relations between the Nigerien state and chieftaincy have been characterised by a pendulous movement. In some periods, the political elite's efforts to clip the wings of chiefs and reduce them to mere auxiliary staff of the administration gave rise to great animosity between the two institutions; in other periods, chiefs have been pivotal in the political and social organisation and mobilisation of the population. More recently the role and legitimacy of chiefs is being sanctioned 'from above' by the constitution and various forms of legislation. One significant piece of legislation is the *Code rural* (Bako-Arifari 1996; Lund 1995; Ngaido 1996).

Obviously a reform process under the conditions just described is not without its contradictions. We will examine some of them here and show how they translate into legislative challenges.

The Code rural

In most countries of the Sahel during the 1980s, attention was directed towards land tenure legislation. A whole range of observations had been made by governments, aid agencies and researchers concerning the stagnating rural development, the degradation of the physical environment and the deterioration of long-term productive capacities. Land tenure insecurity was judged to be a key factor in such trends; legal reforms were considered a good way to establish tenure security, and thereby incentives for improved natural resource management.[1] From its inception in the late 1980s, the project of establishing a tenure reform – a *Code rural* – in Niger was an ambitious one. A clarification of the modes of tenure and of transfer of natural resources – land in particular – was considered an important step towards reversing some of the unfavourable trends.[2] A special *Secrétariat permanent du Code rural* was established under the Ministry of Agriculture with the task of designing such a rural code. The people behind the reform efforts were keenly aware of the importance of the workability of the reform; they recognised the risk of drawing up something very elaborate and coherent but impossible to implement. It was therefore their ambition to avoid changes in the *actual* distribution of land while clarifying the conditions under which that land was held. The permanent secretary of the *Code rural* in 1989, Michel Keita, put it like this:

> Rather than provoking an upheaval, this reform should bring about a improvement of the existing situation. It is not a question of giving certain forms of land tenure priority over others. This implies that the reform is limited in the following ways:
> - There will be no 'state ownership' of lands;
> - Nor will there be 'de facto expropriation' on a national scale;
> - Nor will the land be 'redistributed'.
>
> But it is, nevertheless, our ambition to propose a law that will allow the coordination of all the rights of the different right-holders (Keita 1989: 14, our translation[3]).

In order to understand the different 'forms of land tenure', the authorities conducted a series of regional seminars, from which a somewhat sketchy idea of the complexity of the tenure situation emerged. One peculiar element was the overwhelming desire among the various respondents for private property.[4] It was decided that agricultural land could

---

[1] For a discussion of legal and institutional incentives for natural resource management, see Hesseling 1996

[2] This policy was significantly fuelled by analyses and funding from various donors, in particular France, the United States and the World Bank (Comité ad hoc chargé de l'élaboration du Code Rural 1986; Caverivière 1989; Rochegude 1987).

[3] 'Plus qu'un bouleversement, ce code doit réaliser un aménagement de l'ensemble des réalités existantes. Il n'est pas question de privilégier certains modes juridiques de maîtrise du sol plutôt que d'autres. Cela implique que la réforme est à la fois limitée:

- Il n'y aura pas 'd'étatisation' des terres, par exemple; – ni 'd'expropriation de fait' organisée à l'échelle nationale; – ni de 'redistribution de terres' mais également ambitieuse en ce sens qu'elle vise à proposer un texte qui permette de coordonner les droits des divers utilisateurs du sol' (Keita 1989: 14).

[4] Personal communication with Peter Bloch, Land Tenure Center, and Moussa Yacouba, *Sécretariat du Code Rural*. It is worth noting here that information was largely gathered from the village and canton elites (Arrondissement de Mirriah 1989:1), so it is not surprising that they should prefer private property to be the recognised principle of tenure.

become the private property of an individual, while pasturelands should be protected common property with priority access for the pastoral groups of the area.[5]

For the agricultural land, private property was to be the culmination of a series of steps towards official initial recognition. If customary rights could be asserted, a written *dossier rural* was to be created, and the rights would be transformed into private ownership after an unspecified lapse of time. The political ambitions were therefore to achieve a merger between tradition and modernity, rationalising the tenure system without breaking with tradition. Thus, the state would not *grant* modern property rights to customary land owners, it would simply *recognise* them. The ways in which customary rights were to be recognised were specified in Article 9 of the *Principes d'Orientation du Code Rural.*[6]

Driven by the desire to provoke as little disruption of social relations as possible and to base any change on local knowledge, rather loose and flexible concepts like 'time immemorial', 'collective memory' and 'customs of the area' were accorded decisive importance. The *autorité coutumière compétente* – i.e. the canton chief – was recognised as the institution through which people must pass to get private property rights formally established. Another decree from 1993 confirmed the central role of this authority in the event of disagreement about the 'collective memory' or about what is customary:

> Decree no. 93-28 of 30 March 1993 concerning traditional chieftaincy in Niger reaffirms that the traditional authorities decide on the use by families or individuals of cultivated land and other areas to which the communities under their authority have recognised customary rights (*Secrétariat permanent du Code rural* 1994: 4-3, our translation[7]).

---

[5] This last element creates problems of definition related especially to *'terroir d'attache'*, or 'land where specific pastoral groups have access priority', in the nomadic/pastoral zone.

[6] 'Customary property is the result of 1) acquisition of land through succession, confirmed since time immemorial by the collective memory; 2) permanent allocation of land by a competent customary authority; 3) any means of acquisition recognised by local customs. Customary property confers full and effective ownership on the proprietor.' ('La propriété coutumière résulte de: 1) l'acquisition de la propriété foncière rurale par succession depuis des temps immémoriaux et confirmée par la mémoire collective; 2) l'attribution à titre définitif de la terre à une personne par l'autorité coutumière compétente; 3) tout autre mode d'acquisition prévu par les coutumes des terroirs. La propriété coutumière confère à son titulaire la propriété pleine et effective de la terre.') (our translation)

[7] 'Le décret no. 93-28 du 30 mars 1993 portant de la chefferie traditionnelle du Niger réaffirme que les autorités coutumières règlent selon la coutume, l'utilisation par les familles ou les individus, des terres de culture et espaces ruraux sur lesquels la communauté coutumière dont elles ont la charge, possède des droits coutumières reconnus' (*Secrétariat Permanent du Code Rural* 1994: 4-3).

Canton chiefs – the link between custom and state law

The pivotal elements in the reform are customary rights and chiefs who are authorised to interpret them. While chieftaincy was established and developed well before colonisation, it was transformed by the French administration. The latter altered the territorial jurisdictions of chiefs, modified their numbers, changed their prerogatives and integrated them into the state as administrative auxiliaries. In contrast to many former French colonies, this organisation was maintained in Niger after independence (Guillemin 1983; Le Roy 1979:114; Raynal 1993; Robinson 1975; 1983; 1992).

A system of cantons and *groupements* was created by the French colonial administration between 1904 and 1924. Basic traditional entities were split up and reorganised, and persons who had proved their loyalty to or compliance with the French were appointed traditional leaders – canton chiefs.[8] Generally, the French administration was careful to seek out candidates who had some claim to being noblemen (Olivier de Sardan 1984: 221). However, candidates also included people like interpreters, domestic servants of the French, or African soldiers retired from the French army[9] (Gamory-Dubourdeau 1924; Abba 1990: 51; Salifou 1981; Fuglestad 1983: 84-89; Suret-Canale 1970: 64). Some chiefly claims to an ancient royal pedigree are hence somewhat of a fabrication, as illustrated by the anecdote about the chief's access to the throne in the Canton Gao.

> *Sometime in the 1950s, a French film crew had visited Niger to document traditional festivals, rites and ceremonies. The film crew's schedule did not coincide with the death of any canton chief and the subsequent crowning of his successor, so it was decided to stage one. The 'cinéastres' asked the canton chief of Gao if he would allow his son, Issaka Yahaya, to act out his future crowning in the documentary. The chief was dismayed, and refused to allow it. Finally, he did accept to let his Galadima [a Hausa term for a kind of minister of home affairs, Nicolas 1975] wear the crowning outfit and*

---

[8] The qualities the French desired of a chief were aptly illustrated in a letter from one Capitaine Brounin to his superiors in 1937: 'On a fait au chef de canton une bien triste réputation, la vérité m'oblige à dire qu'il présente à côté de défauts incontestables de sérieuses qualités qui sont: l'endurance, la volonté, la perspicacité et l'autorité, il suffit de le secouer un peu et de le surveiller, il a montré en plusieurs occasions qu'il était capable de décision; il se décharge aujourd'hui de la presque totalité de son travail sur son fils Yérima: personnage énergique, autoritaire, ambitieux et violent, son activité doit être contrôlée, peu aimé de tous il est craint et redouté; il possède au demeurant de réelles qualités de chef. Je pense pour l'avoir mainte fois constaté ailleurs que les meilleurs à nos yeux ne sont pas très bien vus de la population.' Zinder, 5 avril 1937. (From Archives Nationales de la République du Niger, Niamey. Rapport de tourné dans le canton de Dogo, Zinder, 3-27 mars, 1937. Filed under: Zinder, 1937).

[9] One of the best researched examples is the story of Aouta from Dosso. From being a depraved princeling with no authority or economic wealth struggling through as a rural merchant-cum-highwayman, he was enrolled as an *'agent politique auxilliaire'* and subsequently appointed Zarmakoye (leader of all canton chiefs) of Dosso by the French (Rothiot 1988).

promenade on a horse before the camera. The scenes were shot and the film crew left.

The chief had previously had some controversy with the Sultan of Zinder – the latter considered that the canton chief owed him 900 measures of millet. The chief did not accept this. It was by no means an unusual occurrence, but it was successfully exploited by the ambitious Galadima when the real death of the canton chief occurred. While Issaka Yahaya campaigned among the village chiefs in the Canton to become his father's successor, the Galadima went to the Sultan. There he struck a bargain: he would pledge loyalty with the Sultan and deliver the 900 measures of millet if the Sultan would support his candidature. While the Galadima was not of the noblest blood, the earlier documentary proved to the government authorities that he was indeed the dauphin and rightful heir to the title. Subsequently, he was inscribed in the register as the state-recognised traditional chief with corresponding prerogatives, notably to collect taxes, supervise land transactions and resolve local disputes.

The followers of the previous chief soon found their pastures and fallowed fields under the control of this new and energetic chief who was eager to make money by granting-cum-selling access to alleged unoccupied land. Thenceforth, spite and vendetta characterised relations between Issaka Yahaya and the new canton chief. (Lund 1995: 91)

Canton chiefs became the link between the emerging modern state and the population. The colonial administrator depended on the canton chiefs for maintaining law and order and for tax collection, and this social position gave the chiefs several advantages. The French colonial officer was supposed to dispense justice according to legal decisions and local customs. For this, he depended entirely upon the partly-invented chiefs, and this left considerable scope for the imaginative and opportunistic invention of customs.[10] This legal set-up not only had consequences for the primary rules about who is entitled to what. It also put the power of secondary rule-making – the power to make rules about *how to decide* who is entitled to what – in the hands of chiefs.

How did this affect the development of various customs relating to land tenure? Customary land rights have always been somewhat ambiguous. If we take the customs prevailing in South Central and Southeastern Niger, where the Hausa culture is dominant,

---

[10] Arbitrary advice was frequent, and this encouraged the colonial administration to record local customs 'once and for all' in order to establish an unambiguous base for the rule of law. The Nigerien Rural Code is therefore by no means the first attempt in Francophone West Africa to merge tradition with modern law (Blanc-Jouvan 1971). According to Le Roy (1991b) this type of recording has been undertaken since 1905. Evidently, none of these efforts has solved the problems 'once and for all'.

the ambiguity between the rights of the descendants of the first occupant and the actual tiller of the soil allows for various interpretations.

Tenure systems are closely connected with production. When land was in abundance, shifting cultivation on the communal fields of the extended household was the most common mode of production, and fallow of long duration followed some years of cultivation. In practice, if an individual brought uncultivated land in the bush under cultivation, he would do this as a member of a lineage, performing its particular cults; the land would thereby enter the patrimony of his clan and lineage. The person (and household) cultivating the land retained the right to do so until they ceased cultivation and no trace of cultivation remained. Their rights entitled them to use it, but not to sell it, and their rights were extinctive, i.e. if they ceased to cultivate it they would eventually lose their rights to the land (Raulin 1965: 134; Latour-Dejean 1973: 6). This interpretation of tenurial rights accords primacy to *work* as the feature that defines rights. The one who tills the soil has an inalienable right to continue doing so, and to enjoy the fruits of that labour. The right to control the land was thus limited to the time the farmers themselves farmed it, and it did not include control of it after transfer to another.

Competing notions of property rights also prevailed, however. Migration, settlement and the increased commercialisation in the zone seem to have favoured notions of non-extinctive rights. The evolution of certain rights of inheritance, combined with the growth of a more hierarchical social structure, influenced the concept of land tenure and undermined the older principles.

Thus, even if land was abandoned, the person who first cleared the land (and his descendants) retained a preeminent right to it. This hereditary right of the first occupant was not affected by the actual land use. The land could be cultivated or could lie fallow for many years, but the first occupant and his descendants still retained a preeminent right to it (Latour-Dejean 1973: 6). The right to control thus seemed inalienable. The transfer of land to households outside the first occupant's lineage established a sort of landlord-tenant relationship, so that the founding lineage of a village constituted a class of landowners. Important members of this group became the nobles. In this line of reasoning, the notion of extinctive rights pertained to the actual household and its access and cultivation of the land. So, contrary to the norms in the previously described system, the *access right,* rather than the right of control, was extinctive.

On top of this ambiguous normative repertoire came state regulation and a recognition of the tenure system through the tax system. The colonial administration institutionalised the payment of taxes to both the state and chiefs. As tax collectors, chiefs were given a percentage of state taxes, and this incentive to zealous collection has been maintained to this day. At the same time, however, a new fiscal tradition was also invented. While gifts had, of course, been offered to chiefs before, it was during the period of colonisation that *tithes* to chiefs were sanctioned as an obligation. However, as Olivier de Sardan has observed, 'The tithe is neither a traditional concept, nor a legal one; nor is it a religious obligation, a political institution or a land tax; it is a bone of contention' (1989: 224, our translation[11]). Thus, the tithe has no clear normative reference but is an ambiguous and negotiable sociopolitical transaction. Nonetheless, tithe payments were also linked to the tenurial status and rights of the chieftaincy.

The position of the colonial administration was also ambiguous. In the first place, it asserted the state's ultimate right to land, and any specific land rights were granted in principle by the state. The administration recognised farmers' use-rights and local tenure customs only as long as these were considered use-rights only.

The colonial criterion for retaining the use-right was that the land was being 'put to use' (*mise en valeur*). On the one hand, this concept favoured some of the local interpretations of custom, whereby those who work on the land hold the use-right for as long as they continue to work. On the other hand, the state depended heavily on chieftaincy for the administration of the colony and did not seriously challenge the authority of the chiefs vis-à-vis the farmers. It therefore also supported the notion of an inalienable right *vested in the chiefs* to control land allocation, and it regarded the tithe as the commoner's payment to the chief for being allowed to cultivate the land. The tenancy relationship that existed before colonisation between the first occupant and the person cultivating the land, thereby had a generalised version of a tenancy contract superimposed upon it in many cases. Vast tracts of land were declared *terres de chefferie,* or 'chiefs' land', during the creation of the chieftaincy by the colonial rulers.

This ambiguity persisted after independence. The successive governments needed popular legitimacy, and it was especially important for the government and the central administration – composed of the educated, political, urban elite with ambitions of modernisation – to limit the political, social and economic power of chiefs.

Both the Diori government (1960-74) and the Kountché government (1974-1987) took steps to curtail the powers of the chieftaincy and landowners vis-à-vis the use-right holders (Ngaido 1993: 3; Charlick 1991). The payment of tithes was therefore prohibited in 1960, and a series of other laws were enacted during the 1960s.[12]

---

[11] 'La dîme n'est d'abord ni un concept traditionnel, ni une notion juridique, ni une obligation religieuse, ni une institution politique, ni une redevance foncière: c'est un enjeu' (Olivier de Sardan 1989: 224).

[12] The most significant of these laws were 1) the Act of 25 May 1960 (Loi no. 60-28), which set the conditions for developing and managing state-funded irrigation projects; 2) the Act of 25 May 1960 (Loi no. 60-29), which prohibited the payment of tithes; 3) the Acts of 26 and 27 May 1961 (Loi nos. 61-5 and 61-6), which fixed the northern limit for crop cultivation and declared the land north of that line to be reserved for pastoralism. This limit was meant to separate the different regions of Niger by vocation; 4) the Act of 19 July 1961 (Loi no. 61-30), which laid down the procedures for confirming or expropriating customary tenure rights; 5) the Act of 12 March 1962

Generally, the formal abolition of the tithe provoked a large number of conflicts between use-right holders and owners of the land, with the latter defying the ban and insisting that tithes be paid or some other symbolic payment be made in recognition of their continued ownership. Basically, the acts and decrees had little fundamental impact on the powers of chiefs; the laws were simply not obeyed. Nor did people claim formal title to their land, even though that was the intention of the 1961 law (Loi 61-30). The non-enforcement of all these laws and decrees can be seen as a consequence of the state's, and in particular the local administration's, dependence on the chiefs and the authority they wielded over the general population. In spite of rhetoric and ambitious intentions to clip the chiefs' wings, little was effectively done to weaken their position. Rather, a profusion of ambiguous enactments, decrees and other authorised interpretations in the form of political speeches were propagated (see Ngaido 1996 for details).

Like his predecessor, President Kountché sought popular legitimacy for his regime partly by attempting to limit chiefly powers and gain the support of the farmers. Right after his 1974 takeover, Kountché declared on national radio that all land, no matter how it had been acquired and no matter what tenure rules it was held under, should henceforth be the private property of the person cultivating it (Rochegude 1987).

The fundamental ambiguity of tenure matters was compounded once again, however, by another decision to give local governmental and traditional institutions the mandate to mediate and resolve tenure conflicts. In a 1975 ordinance (Ordonnance no. 75-7), the *préfet*, the *sous-préfet*, the canton chief and the village chief were endowed with the power to conciliate in tenure conflicts (Ngaido 1993a: 9). This opportunity to reassert their privileges and prerogatives was not neglected by the chiefs. This again led to conflicts between use-right holders and the nobility and landowners, and the government resorted to issuing decrees and circulars which again aimed at curtailing chiefly power.[13] The most significant of these first limited, and then in 1977 forbade, the participation of local government and the chiefs in land conflict resolution. Despite this new decree, neither the conflicts nor their sources disappeared. Consequently, no

---

chiefs; and 6) the Decree of 29 May 1962 (Décret no. 62-128/PRN/SEP), which determined the composition and operation of the committees charged with assessing the number of plots controlled by traditional chiefs and the farmers cultivating those plots. These committees were composed of government officials, deputies and chiefs.

[13] The most important measures to be introduced were: 1) The 16 December 1977 Circular (no. 8/MI/SG) formally prohibited local authorities, administrative as well as customary, from participating in any procedure for resolving litigations over plots. 2) The 24 April 1980 Circular (no. 12/MI/SG/CIRC) quoted the president's speech to the nation which had stipulated that the local administrative and traditional authorities should not be involved in any cases of conflict resolution. 3) The annual circular (no. 004/MJ/GS) forbade any resolution of land litigation from 1 April to 31 October each year. In addition, in the event of litigation, a plot was to remain under the control of the farmer who had cultivated it the previous year. 4) A 1983 act required that everyone be registered in their village of residence. This meant that the farmers were registered in the villages where they had their lands. In cases where the village they lived in and the village where they had their land were different, many problems arose, such as conflicts between cantons and between villages.

institution had legal jurisdiction in land tenure questions; no conflict had a predictable course; and none of the institutions operating in the rural areas had formal powers to give a final, let alone written, decision in land conflicts. The result was an absolute intransparency of rules and jurisprudence. Everything was in limbo.

With the *Code rural,* the pendulum has now swung back once more, and chiefs have now again become pivotal in the defining of tenure rules meant to embody the customs the new law is based on.

Contradictions and legislative challenges

Basing the tenure reform on local custom is appealing because of its seeming simplicity. However, it does raise a series of questions: How will chiefs determine local customary law? Will it be possible to maintain the flexible, dynamic character of local tenure arrangements in Niger, which, both historically and in the present-day, ensure that several groups of users can exercise claims on natural resources in a given territory, either simultaneously or in sequence. Will the reforms alter the social structures of society? While full implementation of the rural code is still a long way off, the history and the recent development of Niger enable us to discuss some of these points.

Customary legal procedure and the new rural code

The *Code rural* operates on the concepts of 'time immemorial' and 'collective memory'. Property rights are thereby recognised if the land has been in the claimant's possession since 'time immemorial'. How will the 'collective memory' and 'time immemorial' be established; whose memory epitomises the collective memory and how far back can we go? In a society where history is almost exclusively oral, historical facts and events undergo often unnoticeable changes over time. Like any other country in West Africa, Niger has a long history of migration and settlement, and there have probably been several 'first occupants' of many places. Hence, a situation often prevails where several 'truths' are possible, and this makes legal procedure a crucial moment.

Whenever a chief is approached to settle a conflict over land, unsettled debts, divorces or whatever, gifts change hands. Not only do plaintiffs and their adversaries present gifts at their audiences and convocations; after closure of the case the 'winners' offer gifts to display their gratitude, while the 'losers' give them as a token of appreciation that the judgment was moderate.

In practical terms, plaintiffs and defendants are summoned by the canton chief to take an oath on the Quran in support of their claims. Religion is an important normative referent, and swearing on the Quran is almost universally accepted to be a gesture of truth. The use of the Quran to check the veracity of statements in legal procedures is very common. Lying while under oath subjects the perjurer to unpleasant supernatural sanctions such as leprosy and impoverishment. This doctrine, warning of the grim consequences of violating what has been made sacred by using the Quran, is widely believed to be true in Niger. As a result of the doctrine's pervasive power, the Quran is widely invoked in disputes, by chiefs and administrative authorities alike, especially the *sous-préfets*. To decline to subject oneself to 'Quranic trial' is effectively admitting one is in the wrong. It has a further effect as well. Tactics of manipulation are recounted as anecdotes and stories, such as 'Some people have their old folks swear since they are going to die soon anyway' or 'The Quran was not hand-written, but from a printing house, so it had no power.' Hence, the result of employing the Quran is ambiguous: the individual fears it, but suspects that others fear it less. Since an oath on the Quran has to be ordered by the canton chief, he is in a position to control the situation to a large extent.

Furthermore, hearings are often riddled with 'traps'. For example, if a chief asks someone to state who first authorised their (or their ancestors') settlement, this person is trapped. If they answer 'the chief', then they recognise that the chief has the authority over the land and that they themselves do not own and control it. If they answer 'no one, we were the first', then they find themselves in deeper trouble, since they thereby admit having defied the politico-legal authority of the chiefs by just squatting on the land. The recall of 'collective memory' and the time period 'since time immemorial' are thus highly manipulable concepts, and the chiefs benefit greatly from the bribes that are forthcoming.

Rural property and the customary notion of 'time'

In both the French and the Anglo-Saxon legal traditions, proprietors must make their ownership known if another person is found to be using (cultivating) their property. Failure to do so generally leads to the loss of the property after a certain period, 20, 30 or perhaps 50 years. The person using the property in ignorance of another 'owner's' existence will thenceforth be considered the owner (Ouedraogo et al. 1996: annexe, p. 6; Rose 1994: 11 ff.). Since the *Code rural* contains no time limit to render claims outdated, the door is opened to indefinite claims, which will be dealt with in the highly manipulable procedure of providing proof.

As we have noted above, two different and often conflicting customs bear upon the question of which right will be transformed into the right of private property: Is it the inalienable right of the first occupant – interpreted in many cases as the chief – to control the distribution of the land, or is it the inexpropriable use-right of the present tenants? Since the reform holds out a future recognition of 'owners', those who can bolster their claims with references to 'traditional ownership' seem to be ahead of those who must count on 'traditional use-rights'. This seems even more likely if we consider the influence chiefs have on the interpretation of customs. This results in two very different outcomes for farmlands and pasturelands.

In cases of conflict between farmers over the ownership of a field, the 'inexpropriable, time-honoured' right of the actual user gives way to the 'inalienable' right of the first occupant, no matter how much time has passed. Good political connections and sound finances enabling bribery may then still make it possible to successfully take up the case again with the canton chief.

The importance of custom in the reforms gives chiefs a particularly favourable position when it comes to uncultivated lands. Such areas may be considered to be for pastoral use, but since no resource user is exploiting them in the conventional way (that is, cultivating them), they may also be considered chiefs' lands, even though that concept has been officially abolished.

Thus, in contrast with disputes between farmers over a cultivated field, the time elapsed need not always be so long to establish ownership in disputes over pastures. Whilst claims to a pastoral area for cultivation are generally backed by precedents, often the precedent only dates back to the previous year. It is therefore very rare for farmers to be evicted from what has been a pasture since 'time immemorial'. If cultivation has already taken place, the farmer can usually stay on. Many pastures are under pressure. The extension of cultivated fields into the pastoral areas is the predominant trend, even to the point that it is seen as a minor victory for pastoralists if they manage to maintain the status quo. Although some degree of interest in protecting the pastures can be detected among canton chiefs and civil servants, it seems to give way as soon as the confrontation becomes intense. Numbers may also be important in some ways: the farmers constitute a larger tax base for the canton chief, but a large group may also appear threatening. We illustrate how some of the ambiguities of the status of these lands has been exploited by chiefs:

Assistant sous-préfet confronts canton chief – but a compromise is reached

When Manzo's father settled in the village of Dinney in the 1960s he got some plots of land with the help of the village chief. With the division of property upon the death of Manzo's father, the plots had become too small to satisfy Manzo's needs. In 1994 Manzo and his cousin and neighbour, Ajagoula, asked the canton chief of Gao for land. The chief made sure that the requested land was not in the vicinity of a well or a cattle corridor, and he assigned some additional land in the pastures to Manzo and his cousin for money, but we do not know how much. The field was demarcated by one of the chief's courtiers.
A group of cattle owners who used the area for pasture went to see Salissou,

since he was considered a man of wit and courage and was suspected of harbouring a grudge against Manzo, whose origins were lost in the past but a genuine grudge nonetheless. At first, Salissou went to the canton chief to ask him to withdraw Manzo's licence to cultivate in the pasture. The chief refused, claiming a right to sell his canton if it pleased him. Expecting this type of answer, Salissou, unabashed, went to the sous-préfet in Mirriah town and obtained a summons for Manzo, Ajagoula and the canton chief on the disputed land, and a new round of negotiation ensued.

On the day of the settlement, the assistant sous-préfet argued that the chef de canton was in no position to sell land in the common pastures and that Manzo would have to abandon his new field. The chief, on the other hand, maintained that he was entitled to do so, and that it was unacceptable if the assistant sous-préfet insisted, since his credibility as a chief was at stake. The assistant sous-préfet did, nevertheless, insist and asked the neighbours of Manzo and Ajagoula to show the boundary between the pasture and the fields. This was done, and from here the sources differ somewhat: Salissou claimed that the assistant sous-préfet asked both Manzo and Ajagoula to vacate their new fields, while Manzo claimed that only Ajagoula was asked to do so. However, regarding the result their stories concurred: Ajagoula abandoned his field first, but when he saw that Manzo did not, he also recommenced cultivation, and both continued to cultivate their fields when the assistant sous-préfet went back to his office in town.

The result of the confrontation between Manzo and the pastoralists thus turned into a dispute over authority between the assistant sous-préfet and the canton chief. The dispute seemed to be impossible to settle without one of them going back on their word, but a subtle kind of compromise was actually reached. The assistant sous-préfet managed to retain his formal authority by demonstrating that he could overrule the canton chief and decide on the protection of the pastures (which was the objective of his mission). The canton chief succeeded in retaining effective authority, however, since his decision to grant Manzo and Ajagoula land also carried. The decision was formally reversed, but it was effectively maintained – though not as status quo. The fact that Manzo and Ajagoula got away with it, so to speak, was a message to their farming neighbours and the real root of anxiety among the pastoralists. The confrontation would buttress the image of the canton chief among his subjects as someone who stands up for them and was not shoved around by the administration. (Lund 1995: 141).

This case may give the impression that the canton chief is generally amenable to cultivation of pastureland. Indeed he is, unless the pastoral interests are important – that is, if he would benefit financially from defending them. This does not mean that pastureland in the agricultural zone is doomed, but that enterprising, experienced and committed political protection and leadership on behalf of pastoral interests are probably necessary prerequisites. And such is generally in short supply.

When the notion of pastoral lands and the rights of specific groups to these lands need to be established in practice, a number of unresolved questions are set to pose challenges to the legal system: How will these groups be defined? Can pastoral producers cultivate fields in pastures and, if so, how can cultivation by others be prevented (morally and practically)? How will priority access be understood; does it imply the right to exclude others (and if so whom)? etc. If these questions are left for the canton chiefs to decide, traditional pastoral groups are bound to lose out.

The problem of codification

A fundamental contradiction in the *Code rural* endeavour is the ambition to codify tenure rules while not disturbing the prevailing situation. The planners assumed that if they just codified the situation as it was, nothing would change dramatically. However, it is the codification itself which constitutes the greatest change. And this is so at several levels simultaneously.

The announcement of the tenure reform amounted to an invitation to have customary rights in land recognised now in order to secure irrevocable private property rights later. 'Get your customary rights to your land recognised before your neighbour does' seems to be the maxim distilled from the *Code rural* by the general population. Thus, while several different customary norms prevail and could potentially be invoked in support of property claims, the *Code rural* has now injected an idea of deadline into society.

Studies by Ngaido (1996) and Lund (1993; 1995) show that as a consequence of the announcement of the reform, the number of disputes brought before the canton chiefs and the administrative and judicial authorities has increased substantially. The *Code rural* did not *cause* such disputes, but it has unleashed them. In addition, political conditions in the late 1980s and early 1990s, with the downfall of the military regime and emerging political democracy, gave rise to a general contestation of the authority of politico-legal institutions, including that of chieftaincy. People have more readily rejected legal settlements and appealed. Thus, while the *Code rural* has triggered a large number of disputes, the nature of dispute settlement also seems to have undergone some transformation.

Codification also means change at a different level. Recent dispute settlements by chiefs seem to point in a certain direction: that the person granted property rights to the soil becomes owner and controller of all the natural resources attached to it, without seasonal interruption. This can result in a marginalisation of the secondary use-rights that historically have characterised the production system – fruit collection, dry-season grazing and other such uses of cultivated fields. Codification thus also tends to imply simplification. While the cohabitation of different user groups has historically been a source of both conflict and cooperation, codification will mean a once-and-for-all recognition of one group's rights at the expense of the others, with the permanent eviction of the latter as a consequence. This is likely to usher in bitter conflicts along ethnic lines on a massive scale.

At yet a different level, the reform has boosted the social position of chiefs. Settling the increasing numbers of disputes has yielded many chiefs a windfall income, and the rush on the pastures seems to be a virtual 'money-machine' in some parts. Conversely, tenure security seems to have declined markedly for those who have neither capital nor sociopolitical connections to protect them from others' claims to their land.

Finally, at a more general level, the reform – the codification – signifies a change in the relations between society and the state, in the form of both government authorities and the chieftaincy. Transactions that previously took place under informal, private conditions, with the threat of intervention from the chief as a potential disciplinary sanction, now appear to provoke direct formal intervention from a politico-legal institution, namely the chiefs. Historically, unequivocal exactitude was neither required nor desired, since land resources were more plentiful and transactions could hold multiple meanings. When land was transferred from A to B, it could be a loan, a gift or merely A showing B a good spot. Such transactions, which historically required less formal intervention from the authorities, are now frequently the object of legal proceedings by canton chiefs, *sous-préfets* and magistrates, and the present need for exactitude is projected into past transactions that were by nature opaque.

State regulation of tenure disputes has not only been accompanied by extension of the activities of legal or administrative authorities, but also by increased competition between the different politico-legal institutions. This has developed into quite a paradox. Because settlements are more readily rejected, the litigants take their cases from one institution to the other, exploiting this institutional competition. On the other hand, it would appear that some kind of socio-legal umpire is desired (otherwise people could have just ignored the settlements), and that rather than rejecting the state, rural citizens invoke state power in existing institutions. Thus, state control or arbitration is asked for by the citizens, not merely inflicted upon them. Consequently, the reform has thus far produced more regulation of society by politico-legal institutions, at a time when the legitimacy of these institutions is declining.

Legislators face a continual dilemma: To what extent should laws reflect reality, and to what extent should they change it? The Nigerien experience shows that even if you only want to reflect reality, the reflection itself changes it.

Conclusion

Many efforts at institutional reform in Africa have been hampered by the neglect of the existing politico-legal infrastructure. The Nigerien *Code rural* process stands out as an ambitious attempt to put that infrastructure to constructive use. There are a number of weaknesses in the reform, however.

The overall aim of enhancing tenure security has been turned into a transformation of certain customary rights to private property. This reflects a simplistic notion of customary tenure, and it proposes a linear transformation of tenure regimes which is patently inadequate. Secondary right-holders such as pastoralists and women also merit a degree of security of access and exploitation of specific resources. Therefore much more creativity is required to accommodate the nuances and the flexibility of local land, use practices into a codified form of customs. Different degrees of restrictions on the rights of primary right-holders to exclude others should be conceptualised. That would facilitate local negotiations that could do justice to the specificity of the varied localities in Nigerien society.

The idea of modernising rules on the basis of what is known to the population, thereby relying on institutions more decentralised than any purely civil servant-based administration could ever be, is certainly worth pursuing. Nevertheless, the developments in Niger also show it is naïve to trust in the ability of custom and chiefs to steer by themselves towards good governance, rule of law and social justice. A major challenge is therefore how to subject the chiefs and customs to public or democratic control without undercutting their authority. The chiefs have been regarded as instruments for implementing the *Code rural,* and their role and capacities as quite static. However, experience shows that chiefs readily project their authority into the rather different roles of 'administrators' of land rights and 'judges' in disputes. Chiefs are not mere receptacles of authority which can be opened and shut according to the needs of the legislators. Quite the contrary, chiefs are capable political actors in pursuit of interests. This may or may not favour the implementation of the *Code rural.* Consequently, if the chiefs are to have a central role in the reform, a serious effort to secure their commitment to the policy objectives seems absolutely essential. This, in turn, implies political negotiations to establish their role and to train them to perform it well. One key aspect of their role that needs clarification is to what extent the chiefs should be mere mediators (as the text of the law prescribes) or should have the authority to decide on disputes (as is often the practice). A pragmatic first step would be to modernise recording procedures. If the outcome of the litigation process at the level of the chiefs were to be put in writing, it would matter less whether it was a 'settled' or 'mediated' outcome that is being pursued further in the legal system, and in theory it could increase transparency and facilitate the chiefs' accountability.

The odds are, however, that written records would still have a limited effect as long as the average rural Nigerien is illiterate and ill-organised in unions or interest groups, thus remaining unequipped to confront and control authority.

The implementation of a legal reform, and especially a land tenure reform, in a society so immediately dependent on its natural resources is bound to have repercussions on social and political institutions. Even when labelled traditional, these are contemporary and modern, and they are constantly being renegotiated through the political process. If reformers disregard this, they run the risk of becoming policymakers in the virtual reality of their imaginations, thereby missing the point entirely.

References

ABBA, Souleymane
1990   La chefferie traditionnelle en question. Pp. 51-60. In: *Politique Africaine,* no. 38

BAKO-ARIFARI, Nassirou
1996   *De la résurgence et de la réjustification de la chefferie en contexte de démocratisation au Benin et au Niger.* Universität Hohenheim, Stuttgart, (mimeo) 35 p.

BLANC-JOUVAN, Xavier
1971
[1964] Problems of harmonization of traditional and modern concepts in the land law of French-speaking Africa and Madagascar. Pp. 215-238. In: *Integration of Customary and Modern Legal Systems in Africa.* A.N. Allott (ed.). Ile-Ife/New York: University of Ife

CAVERIVIÈRE, Monique
1989   *Code Rural – problématique et premières propositions d'orientation.* Mimeo, Niamey

CHARLICK, Robert B.
1974   *Power and Participation in the Modernization of Rural Hausa Communities.* PhD, University of California: Los Angeles

1991   *Niger – Personal Rule and Survival in the Sahel.* Westview Press: Boulder

FUGLESTAD, Finn
1983   *A History of Niger – 1850-1960.* Cambridge: Cambridge University Press

GAMORY-DUBOURDEAU, Capitaine
1924   Etude sur la création de cantons de sédentarisation dans le cercle de Zinder et particulièrement dans la subdivision centrale. Pp. 239-258. In: *Bulletin du Comité d'Études Historiques et Scientifiques de l'Afrique Occidentale Française*

GUILLEMIN, Jacques
1983 Chefferie traditionnelle et administration publique au Niger. Pp. 115-124. In: *Mois en Afrique,* nos. 213-214

HESSELING, Gerti
1996 Legal and institutional incentives for local environmental management. Pp. 98-134. In: *Improved Natural Resource Management – the Role of Formal Organisations and Informal Networks and Institutions.* H.S. Marcussen (ed.) International Development Studies, Roskilde University. *Occasional Paper* no. 17.

KEITA, Michel
1989 Code rural. Pp. 8, 14, 14. In: *Sahel Dimanche* 28/7-18/8-25/8.

LATOUR-DEJEAN, Éliane de
1973 *La transformation du régime foncier – appropriation des terres et formation de la classe dirigeante en pays Mawri (Niger).* Institut Africain de Développement Économique et de Planification: Dakar. 41 p.

LE ROY, Etienne
1979 Les chefferies traditionnelles et le problème de leur intégration. Pp. 105-132. In: *Les institutions constitutionnelles des Etats d'Afrique francophone et de la République Malgache.* G. Conac (ed.). Paris: Economica

1991a L'Etat, la réforme et le monopole foncier. Pp. 159-190. In: *L'appropriation de la terre en Afrique noire.* E. le Bris, E. le Roy & P. Mathieu (eds.). Karthala: Paris

1991b Les usages politiques du droit. Pp. 109-122. In: *Les Afriques politiques.* C. Coulon, & D.-C. Martin (eds.). Paris: Editions la Découverte

LUND, Christian
1993 Waiting for the Rural Code. *Drylands Network Working Paper* no. 44. 24 p.

1995 *Law, Power and Politics in Niger – Land Struggles and the Rural Code.* PhD Dissertation: Roskilde University

1997 Approaching twilight institutions – analytical dimensions of politico-legal institutions and disputes. In: *Forum for Development Studies,* no 2

NGAIDO, Tidiane
1993a *Land Use Conflicts in the Rural Areas of Niger – the Case of Kollo Arrondissement.* Land Tenure Center cooperative agreement with USAID-Niger, Discussion Paper no. 1. 30 p.

1993b *La mise en place du code rural – Perceptions et attentes du monde rural nigérien.* Land Tenure Center convention de coopération avec USAID-Niger, Document de Travail no. 7. Niamey. 39 p.

1996 *Redefining the Boundaries of Control: Post-Colonial Tenure Policies and Dynamics of Social and Tenure Change in Western Niger.* PhD Dissertation: University of Wisconsin, Madison

NICOLAS, Guy
1975   *Dynamique sociale et appréhension du monde au sien d'une société Hausa.* Paris: Muséum National d'Histoire Naturelle, Travaux et Mémoires de l'Institut d'Ethnologie. Vol. LXXVIII

OLIVIER de SARDAN, Jean-Pierre
1984   *Les sociétés Songhay-Zarma (Niger-Mali).* Karthala: Paris

OUEDRAOGO, H; FAURE, A.; CHRISTOPHERSEN, K.; LUND, C. & MATHIEU, P.
1996   *Evaluation des mechanismes de mise en œuvre du code rural à travers l'expérience des commissions foncières de Maïne Soroa et Mirriah.* USAID/DANIDA, Niamey

RAULIN, Henri
1965   Travail et régimes fonciers au Niger. Pp. 119-139. In: *Cahiers de l'Institut des Sciences Économiques Appliquées.* sér. V, no. 9

RAYNAL, Jean-Jacques
1993   *Les institutions politiques au Niger.* Saint-Maur: Sépia

ROBINSON, Pearl Theodora
1975   *African Traditional Rulers and the Modern State – the Linkage Role of Chiefs in the Republic of Niger.* PhD Dissertation: Columbia University

1983   Traditional clientage and political change in a Hausa community. Pp. 105-128. In: *Transformation and Resiliency in Africa.* P.S. Robinson & E.P. Skinner (eds.). Washington D.C.: Howard University Press

1992   Grassroots legitimation of military governance in Burkina Faso and Niger – The core contradictions. Pp. 143-165. In: *Governance and Politics in Africa.* G. Hyden, & M. Bratton (eds.). Boulder: Westview Press

ROCHEGUDE, Alain
1987   *Les aspects juridiques du code rural.* Projet code rural, République du Niger, Niamey. 28 p.

ROSE, Carol
1994   *Property and Persuasion – Essays on the History, Theory and Rhetoric of Ownership.* Boulder: Westview Press

ROTHIOT, Jean-Paul
1988   *L'ascension d'un chef africain au début de la colonisation – Aouta, le conquérant (Dosso – Niger).* Paris: L'Harmattan.

ROUVEROY van NIEUWAAL, E. Adriaan B. van
n.d.   *L'Etat moderne et sa contrepartie, le chef (néo)traditionnel au Togo: un mariage de raison?* Karthala: Paris. (forthcoming)

SALIFOU, André
1981   La chefferie du Niger "revue et corrigée" par le colonisateur. Pp. 30-34. In: *Afrique Histoire,* no. 1

SURET-CANALE, Jean
1970   *French Colonialism in Tropical Africa 1900-45.* London: Hurst & Company
[1964]

Nigerien Législation
-   *Loi portant régime de l'eau* (Ordonnance no. 93-014 du 2 mars 1993) 21 p.
-   *Principes d'orientation du Code Rural* (Ordonnance no. 93-015 du 2 mars 1993) 28p. *Official Nigerien Documents*

ARRONDISSEMENT DE MIRRIAH (Département de Zinder/République du Niger)
1989   *Réponses aux questionnaires relatifs à l'élaboration du Code Rural* . 6 p.

SECRÉTARIAT PERMANENT DU CODE RURAL (Ministère de l'Agriculture et de l'Elevage/ République du Niger)
1994   *Problématique foncière et code rural.* Session de formation des membres des Commissions Foncières des arrondissements Maïne Soroa et Mirriah. 13 p.

"ONE CHIEF, ONE VOTE": THE REVIVAL OF TRADITIONAL AUTHORITIES IN POST-APARTHEID SOUTH AFRICA[1]

Ineke van Kessel and Barbara Oomen

Introduction

About 40 percent of the people of South Africa and 17 percent of its territory are ruled by traditional authorities. These 17 million subjects of chiefly rule are governed by about 800 traditional leaders.[2] Like almost everything else regarding chieftaincy, these figures are disputed. Depending on one's definition of "traditional leader", their numbers could multiply to perhaps 10.000.

Rather than being phased out as relics of pre-modern times, chiefs are re-asserting themselves in post-apartheid South Africa. Nor are they satisfied with a ceremonial role as guardians of African custom. They demanded and obtained constitutional guarantees for their position and their representation in the local, provincial and national administration. In view of South Africa's history, this is a surprising outcome of a long liberation struggle.

The first part of this article is a brief survey of the changing perspectives on chieftaincy within the African National Congress and its allied movements. Secondly, we describe the position of traditional authorities during the present transition period (1994-1999),

---

[1] An earlier version of this article has been published in *African Affairs*, 1997, no. 96: 561-585

[2] Figures provided by the Department of Constitutional Development in Nov. 1995

and the main themes of discussion in the constitutional negotiations.[3] Is the revival of traditional authorities likely to be a lasting phenomenon or just a passing phase? The last part presents a case study in the Northern Province (formerly the Northern Transvaal), a province with a high proportion of chiefs since it incorporates three former bantustans. One constant theme over time is that of shifting alliances: chiefs often align themselves - whether wholeheartedly or for tactical reasons - with the powers that seem to offer the best chances of safeguarding their positions. This strategy is of course not the exclusive preserve of traditional leaders. But being traditional leaders, chiefs have a resource which is not so readily available to commoners: tradition.

What is a tradition? Webster's dictionary gives the following definition: "A cultural continuity transmitted in the form of social attitudes, beliefs, principles and conventions of behaviour etc. deriving from past experience and helping to shape the present" (New Webster's Dictionary 1992: 1046). In the context of this article, "helping to shape the present" is the crucial element.

In post-apartheid South Africa, numerous chiefs have become adept in combining the resource of tradition with appeals to western models and the discourse of liberation politics. Thus, chiefs project themselves as guardians of African custom, but simultaneously as pioneers of rural development.[4] They campaign for the establishment of a House of Traditional Leaders based on the model of the British House of Lords and demand simultaneously that their representation in this House ought to be based on the democratic principles advocated by liberation movements. The principle of "One Man, One Vote", after having gone through the non-sexist phase of "One Person, One Vote" is being transformed by some traditional leaders into the "time-tested" principle of "One Chief, one Vote".

Chiefs and liberation politics

Among the founding members of the African National Congress[5] were a considerable number of chiefs. Upon the formation of the ANC in 1912, an Upper House was created to accommodate traditional leaders who joined the organisation. In its early days, the ANC represented the concerns of a small professional middle class which maintained close links with the African aristocracy, the rural chieftaincy. South Africa's industrial

---

[3] In this article we focus on the political dimensions and the changing perspectives of political elites with regard to chieftaincy. For a discussion of the role of traditional leaders in local government and the prospects for 'mixed government' in various parts of South Africa, see: Bank and Southall, 1996

[4] See for a general discussion of chieftaincy in Africa and the capacity of traditional leaders to adapt to changing conditions: van Rouveroy van Nieuwaal, 1987

[5] At the time of its formation in 1912, the organisation was known as the South African Native National Congress.

revolution in the 1940s and 1950s transformed the ANC into a mass movement with a following mainly located in the main industrial centres. From the second half of the 1940s, the ANC went through a radicalisation process which was inspired both by its growing working class base and by the coming to power of the National Party in the 1948 elections. During the 1950s, the National Party government engaged in a profound restructuring of rural society, which would fundamentally alter the relationship between the ANC and the rural aristocracy. The African reserves in the countryside played a crucial role in the governments' efforts to establish tighter control over African labour. Labour bureaux regulated the supply of labour to the mines, commercial agriculture and industry. Labour mobility was further controlled by a tightening of the pass laws. In the rural village, the administration of the pass book and the running of the labour bureaux, where permits had to be annually renewed, were the responsibility of the chief. Local government in rural areas was reshaped by the 1951 Black Authorities Act[6], which aimed at self rule and ultimately "independence" for the Bantustans. Powerrested with a hierarchy of compliant chiefs, who were made utterly dependent on the patronage of the Department of Native Affairs. Chiefs were no longer accountable to their subjects, but to the Department. Their powers were increased while their legitimacy was being eroded. Adding to their unpopularity was their role in the implementation of the policies of agricultural betterment, which involved cattle culling and land demarcation.

Not all chiefs were willingly incorporated in this new dispensation. During the 1950s and early 1960s, South Africa experienced a series of rural revolts, ranging from Zoutpansberg in the far north to Mpondo-land and Tembu-land in the Eastern Cape. Paramount Chief Sabata Dalindyebo headed the revolt in Tembu-land. He was sidelined and later deposed by his rival Kaiser Matanzima, who as the more compliant chief profited from government patronage to become prime minister and subsequently president of the Transkei. (Lodge 1983, ch. 11). Later Dalindyebo went into exile where he linked up with the ANC. He died in exile, but his reburial in the Transkei in 1989 turned into a massive demonstration of support for the ANC in the countryside. In the Northern Transvaal, the acting Paramount Chief of Sekhukhuneland, Morwamoche Sekhukhune, and a majority of his people actively opposed the Bantu Authorities system. The Paramount Chief was deposed and sent into internal exile (Delius 1989, 1990).

The imposition of Bantu Authorities not only changed the relationship between the chief and his subjects. It also upset the balance within the tribal hierarchy. In Sekhukhuneland, and in numerous other regions, the Native Affairs Department undermined the opposition by breaking the power of the paramountcy. Subordinate headmen were offered recognition as chiefs if they accepted the establishment of Tribal Authorities. This scheme resulted in a proliferation of chieftaincies. Initially, Sekhukhuneland counted nine chieftaincies, but by the mid 1970s more than 50 chiefs had been officially

---

[6]   Act 68 of 1951

recognised (Bothma 1976: 179). The paramountcy had been abolished. The doubtful origins of many chiefs served to further weaken their legitimacy, as many "chiefs" were considered to be only "headmen" who had usurped chiefly powers. On the other hand, this history of resistance on the part of a number of chiefs could be drawn upon to demonstrate the role played by traditional leaders in the fight against white domination. When, in the late 1980s, chiefs were seeking to secure their future in a post apartheid state by linking up with the ANC, they constructed a sense of historical continuity by focusing on these examples of resistance rather than on the mainstream pattern of chiefly compliance.

Until about 1950, the ANC's organisational strategy aimed at establishing rural branches through chiefs. This approach limited its capacity to mobilise a mass constituency, as popular grievances were accumulating against chiefs. In the eyes of many, the office had been corrupted by the control exercised by the Native Affairs Department. The ANC's rural strategy had reached the end of its potential by the early 1950s. With the introduction of Bantu Authorities in the 1950s, which made chiefs into civil servants accountable to banstustan governments, state recognition had become more vital for the chieftaincy than popular support. Chiefs had become civil servants, to be hired and fired and paid — and if necessary, created — by the government. If they were lucky enough to be designated a member of a homeland parliament they would also receive a car and some other perks. The Black Authorities Act had further upset the customary system of checks and balances. Chiefs came to be seen more as coercive agents of the bantustan regimes.

However, chiefs continued to play a role in the ANC, as demonstrated by chief Albert Luthuli, who was elected ANC president in 1952. Luthuli was a — relatively minor — Zulu chief, whose memory can nowadays be exploited for a double purpose: to stress the historical continuity of the role of chiefs in liberation politics, but also to establish the credentials of the ANC as a movement with a firm base among the Zulu people, an important asset for the ANC when contesting the monopolisation of Zulu tradition by Inkatha. Originally a cultural movement of the Zulu people, Inkatha subsequently was transformed into a nation-wide political party, the Inkatha Freedom Party (IFP).
But by the early 1960s, chiefs were no longer perceived as potential allies in the liberation struggle. The ANC had been banned in 1960 and concentrated on rebuilding the movement in exile and enlisting international support for the anti-apartheid struggle. During the 1960s, the ANC remained hopeful about the revolutionary potential of the bantustans, even though the rural revolts had been crushed by severe repression. A strategic review, undertaken after the Soweto rising of 1976, shifted the thrust of ANC strategic thinking towards the urban areas. The road to power, it was now believed, was not through rural rebellion, but through urban guerrilla in combination with indefinite strikes and mass risings.

The ANC had no clear cut policy on chiefs. Although the institution as such was never officially denounced by the liberation movement, many leading figures in the ANC assumed that chieftaincy would either die of its own accord or otherwise would be abolished. Govan Mbeki, writing on the peasant revolts of the 1950s, questioned the role of chiefs in the industrial age. "If the Africans have had chiefs, it was because all human societies have had them at one stage or another. But when a people have developed to a stage which discards chieftainship, when their social development contradicts the need for such an institution, then to force it on them is not liberation but enslavement." (Mbeki 1984: 47) Writing a quarter of century later, another leading ANC intellectual was more straightforward: "Backward tribal and other relationships, such as the role of the chiefs in such situations, will by replaced by democratic institutions founded on the organs of people's power." (Mzala 1988: 224)

Chiefs in the 1980s: enemies of the liberation struggle

These pronouncements of ANC leaders in prison or exile were in line with the prevailing opinions among leaders of the internally-based anti-apartheid opposition. During the 1980s, a multitude of organisations found common ground under the umbrella of the United Democratic Front (UDF), which functioned more or less as the internal ally of the banned liberation movement. Chiefs were on the margins of the UDF's concerns. As with the ANC in the preceding decades, most UDF campaigns were geared towards urban areas. Its rural affiliates consisted mainly of youth organisations, led by students at secondary and tertiary schools. Attempts to recruit migrant workers were not pursued with much vigour. Generational cleavages in the liberation movement, a well-known feature of urban resistance, became even more pronounced in the rural setting, where power was wielded by chiefs, teachers and elders. Grievances against the authoritarian rule and frequent misappropriation by the chief were by no means limited to youth, but the youth movement — with few exceptions — did not succeed in building a broad alliance around their campaigns against chieftaincy. Radicalised youth movements often acted in isolation.

The abolition of the pass laws in 1986 meant that migrants no longer had to present themselves at the chief's office in their home village. Chiefs lost their income from registration fees and their control over the movements of their subjects. Recalcitrant villagers could no more be punished by withholding labour permits and travel documents. It also meant that the chief no longer had the opportunity to collect arrears from their migrant subjects. Faced with diminishing control, chiefs frequently reacted by imposing new taxes to make up for the lost revenue. One way of increasing their income was to seize control over the boreholes which were provided in drought relief programmes. People were then made to pay for the water.

There is an interesting parallel between the changing position of the Black Local Authorities in the administration of the townships and the changing position of the chieftaincy during the 1980s. Both experienced an important loss of revenue: in the case of the townships, privatisation caused the loss of revenue from the monopoly on liquor sales and sorghum beer. The resulting increase of financial burdens on the inhabitants was an important ingredient in the build-up of both the urban and the rural crisis. The dilemmas of the new black township authorities, whose position has been characterised as one of "responsibility without power", have been the subject of several studies.[7] By contrast, the changing role of the chieftaincy during the 1980s and the effects on the popular legitimacy of the tribal hierarchies have scarcely been explored. As the chiefs lost many of their previous responsibilities and proved largely incapable of delivering services to their communities, the burdens imposed by them were felt as increasingly onerous. Grievances centred around tribal levies and tributes, and authoritarian rule.

Tribal levies can be raised for special purposes after the chief's council has gained the approval from the formal gathering of adult men. In practice, these meetings were often called during weekdays, thus excluding the migrants from the consultation process. Upon their return to the village, migrants were presented with the bill which the chief and the elder men had decided upon. The special purposes generally include the building of a school, clinic or post office; paying for legal advice in cases involving the chief or the tribe; contributing to his marriage goods, or to the costs of his funeral; procuring the services of rain-makers. Frequently, the taxes were of more benefit to the chief's private affairs than to the community. Tributes were raised to buy a car for the chief, or to pay his repair bill; to build him a brick house, preferably with two stories and modern amenities. The more extreme stories of arbitrary chiefly taxes included levies to pay for his traffic fines and for the nappies of his children.

This system of "taxation without representation" was at the root of many grievances against the chieftaincy. The migrants' organisation NOTPECO (Northern Transvaal People's Congress), a UDF affiliate in the Northern Transvaal, mobilised its following mainly on this issue, by impressing on the migrants that they were entitled to be part of the decision-making process.

Apart from taxation, free labour was also perceived as a form of exploitation. Free labour is exacted mainly from women and school-children. It involves mostly maintenance work on the chiefs' homestead and work on the tribal land held by the chief. Youth activists frequently mentioned tribal custom as a "source of oppression". There are numerous examples of villages where youth activists in the 1980s demanded transparency of the tribal finances, sometimes seizing control over the school fund. In several cases, chiefs were chased away from their village and in few villages the chief was actually killed.

---

[7] e.g. Seekings 1990

Faced with these challenges to their authority from different quarters, many chiefs reacted by forming armed vigilantes to combat rebellious youth. Weapons were provided by the bantustan government. The tribal authorities were one of the key pillars of the "pacification" strategy of the South African army in the Northern Transvaal. From the point of view of UDF activists, chiefs were part and parcel of the repressive status quo. Village meetings could only be held with permission from the chief. Chiefs generally opposed attempts to establish a civic association, which they rightly perceived as an alternative power structure. Civics had multiplied in the African townships during the first half of the 1980s, organising residents around bread-and-butter issues such as rents, electricity and the costs of bus transport. By virtue of the affiliation of the civics to the UDF, these campaigns around local issues became linked to the nation-wide liberation movement. In the second half of the decade, civics made their way to the rural villages, but they were far less effective in the rural context.

The UDF stood for a unitary South Africa, without ethnically-based bantustans. Since the tribal hierarchies had become part and parcel of bantustan administrations, it followed that both homeland governments and chiefs had to be abolished. The National Working Committee of the UDF resolved in 1986 that "tribal structures should be replaced with democratic organisations".[8] Other UDF publications suggested that short-term alliances with chiefs could be expedient in places where the chief still enjoyed popular support, but the objective in the long run was generally summed up as "Chiefs must go and the people must run the villages" (*SASPU National*, 7,4, 1986).

Changing perspectives on chieftaincy: 1987-1996

Against this background, it is not surprising that the emergence of an ANC-aligned organisation of chiefs came as a shock to many UDF and ANC adherents. The formation of the Congress of Traditional Leaders (CONTRALESA) met with an ambivalent response: could "progressive chiefs" be organized to further the liberation struggle?
CONTRALESA had its origins in the battle against independence in KwaNdebele and the resistance in the district of Moutse against incorporation into KwaNdebele. (Transvaal Rural Action Committee 1988; Ritchken 1989). KwaNdebele, the most recently established bantustan, was scheduled for "independence" in 1986. Moutse residents feared that the planned excision of their district from Lebowa and the incorporation into KwaNdebele would entail the loss of their South African citizenship. One of the prime movers of the anti-independence camp was Prince Klaas Makhosana Mahlangu of the Ndzundza royal family in KwaNdebele. The KwaNdebele government expelled him, along with several other senior tribal leaders, from the banstustan Legislative Assembly for his opposition to independence. Klaas Mahlangu and other opponents of independence, many of whom had to flee KwaNdebele in fear of their life,

---

[8]   UDF report of the National Working Committee conference, 24 and 25 May 1986

flocked to Johannesburg looking for help. Now a new problem posed itself to a UDF leadership which by this time was working in semi-clandestinity under the State of Emergency. What to do with chiefs who supported a progressive cause, i.e. the anti-independence struggle in the bantustans? Would organising chiefs serve the purpose of broadening out and further isolating the enemy?

The idea was discussed with Samson Ndou, vice-president of the UDF region Southern Transvaal, with Peter Mokaba, president of the South African Youth Congress (SAYCO -the largest UDF affiliate) and several others, including trade unionist Desmond Mahasha, who dipped into the coffers of the General and Allied Workers Union to provide funds to get the new organisation started. To his luck, this initiative was later sanctioned by the ANC who "bailed him out" when he risked losing his job because of misuse of union funds.[9] Ndou, Mokaba and Mahasha all come from the Northern Transvaal.

CONTRALESA was launched in September 1987 in Johannesburg, claiming a membership of 38 chiefs and sub-chiefs from KwaNdebele and Moutse. According to its Constitution, CONTRALESA aims to unite all traditional leaders in the country, to fight for the eradication of the bantustan system, to "school the traditional leaders about the aims of the South African liberation struggle and their role in it", to win back "the land of our forefathers and share it among those who work it in order to banish famine and land hunger" and to fight for a unitary, non-racial and democratic South Africa (*Race Relations Survey* 1987-88: 922). CONTRALESA emerged on the political scene couched in the discourse of liberation politics.

The involvement of SAYCO in the launch of CONTRALESA gave rise to the suspicion that this organisation was being formed with the ultimate goal of abolishing the institution of chieftaincy. That suspicion was not unfounded. Some of the activists involved in the formation of CONTRALESA were indeed motivated by the belief that there was no place for chiefs in the classless society they were striving for. In the meantime however, harnessing chiefs to the progressive cause would prevent them from subverting the struggle. Heeding the lessons from Angola and Mozambique, where "the destabilising factors such as Unita and Renamo found fertile ground in the disillusionment of rural people", it was imperative to "organise and unite all traditional leaders of our country and to refrain from alligning (sic) ourselves with any particular oppressive system today or in the future "(*CONTRALESA Newsletter*, 1,1, [1990]).

While the formation of CONTRALESA as a partner in the liberation movement was shocking news to many activists inside South Africa, the ANC was quick to give its blessing. In February 1988, a CONTRALESA deputation visited Lusaka to meet an ANC delegation headed by secretary-general Alfred Nzo. ANC, UDF and SAYCO all

---

[9] van Kessel interview with Desmond Mahasha, Mohlaletse, 23 September 1990

hailed the "heroic role" which chiefs had played in the past against the forces of colonialism, pointed at the significant role of the chiefs in the early years of the ANC and welcomed the "chiefs coming back to the people" (Zuma 1990).

It was, in part, the experience of exile which had prepared the ANC for a fresh look at the future position of chiefs. The spectre to be avoided was Mozambique, where RENAMO had found fertile recruiting ground among a rural aristocracy which was thoroughly alienated by the rule of marxist-inspired youngsters from town, representing the ruling FRELIMO government.

But it was perhaps the intractable Buthelezi and his Inkatha movement which carried most force of persuasion. From the mid-1980s, a low intensity civil war raged between Inkatha and the UDF in Natal, pitting traditionalists and rural villagers against militant youth intoxicated with the belief in impending revolution. In 1990, when Inkatha transformed itself into a nation-wide political party, the Inkatha Freedom Party, violent conflict spread to the townships of the Witwatersrand. Buthelezi and Inkatha benefited from the active support of the South African security forces in this battle against their common enemy. But unlike other bantustan rulers, he also had a distinct powerbase of his own. Therefore, Buthelezi could not so easily be dismissed as a puppet of the apartheid regime. The Inkatha leader offers a prime example of a successful straddling technique: while skilfully manipulating the appeal of tradition and Zulu identity in his home base, he also proved an expert player in the politics of the wider world. In order to contest Inkatha's claim to the sole guardianship of Zulu tradition, the ANC in 1992 made a conscious decision to enter the political arena in Natal on Inkatha's terms (Jung 1996). The discourse of "development" and non-racialism was unlikely to woo Zulu traditionalists. In the battle for the Zulu nation, the ANC attempted to "out-Zulu" its rival when paying respect to Zulu traditions which included of course royalty and chieftaincy. Control over the guardianship of Zulu tradition (presented as the soul of the Zulu nation) is a central theme in the conflict between ANC and Inkatha in KwaZulu-Natal, but also in the tug of war between King Goodwill Zwelethini and Chief Mangosuthu Buthelezi.

Constitutional guarantees for the Zulu kingdom were made into an almost insurmountable stumbling block in the run-up to the 1994 elections. But subsequently the king has broken ranks with Buthelezi. Liberated from Buthelezi's control over the purse strings - the king is now being maintained by the central government - Zwelithini became a fervent advocate of the non-partisan nature of the office of traditional leader (Ewing 1995). Meanwhile, Buthelezi had himself appointed as chairman of the House of Traditional Leaders in KwaZulu-Natal. The king's royal council is of the opinion that the king himself should preside over the House. The dispute has been brought before the South African Constitutional Court.

KwaZulu-Natal obviously is a special case. But towards the end of the 1980s, it seemed that a similar rural reaction as in Natal was not beyond the imagination in the case of other bantustan elites who in tandem with the South African security forces were largely succeeding in suppressing the youth revolts in the homelands. In addition, the ANC was in need of a broader support base. Militant youth had alienated not only the tribal hierarchies, but also large sections of the adult population in the villages. With a military victory of the liberation forces becoming ever more unlikely, ANC strategists began to focus on a negotiated settlement. A negotiated transfer of power would have to be effected through elections. With the perspective of an electoral contest, the ANC modified its views on chieftaincy. With the promise of delivering their "block vote", chiefs assumed a new role: traditional leaders could no longer merely be considered as relics of a feudal past, but now had become strategic allies in the conquest of state power. As chief Mhlabunzima Maphumulo, a Zulu chief who was prominent in CONTRALESA, stated in 1990: "Once a chief has identified himself with us, then we know that the whole tribe or the majority of the people in that area are now with the progressive forces." (Payze 1992)[10]

After the unbanning of the ANC in 1990, CONTRALESA's membership increased dramatically. Its main powerbase was in the bantustans of the Northern Transvaal. Many chiefs began to perceive CONTRALESA as the best forum to safeguard their interests under a future ANC-led government. From the ANC's point of view, wooing chiefs made political sense. One of the ANC's major concerns in 1990-91 was to prevent the emergence of a National Party-led alliance, in which bantustan leaders and officials, and chiefs would provide the rural support base. In the 1994 elections, the Northern Transvaal proved to be the most solid ANC bastion of all nine provinces. But in 1990-91, this was by no means a foregone conclusion.

In 1990, CONTRALESA was regarded as an important rural partner in the ANC's strategy to "isolate De Klerk" by drawing all kinds of disparate forces into a broad alliance under ANC guidance. Chiefs were seen as constituting part of the middle ground between the ANC and the National Party government, hanging in the balance from where they could swing either way. The ANC leadership experienced great difficulty when trying to convince rural youth of the wisdom of this policy. The antagonism was not limited to youth only. The prospect of the ANC being swamped with yesterdays enemies elicited much criticism, also from old guard ANC activists, intellectuals and ordinary rank and file members. One bastion of opposition was the civic movement, now nation-wide organized under the umbrella of the South African National Civic Organisation (SANCO). Antagonism between civics and chiefs was particularly pronounced in the Eastern Cape. The issue equally served to accentuate the centre-periphery dichotomy: the strategy to win over chiefs and bantustan leaders was devised in the ANC head office in Johannesburg, where Nelson Mandela was known to

---

[10] Maphumulo was assassinated in 1991

be a particularly keen advocate of this rapprochement. The picture of ANC leaders wining and dining with bantustan leaders and paying homage to chiefs was thoroughly upsetting for rural activists.

The issues at stake: how do chiefs fit in a non-sexist, non-racial democracy?

Like other stakeholders, chiefs negotiated their entry in the New South Africa in the series of constitutional negotiations which began late 1991. Even if it rarely became front page news, the issue of traditional leadership posed certain fundamental questions which still prove difficult to tackle. During this transition process, various models of democracy were hotly debated (Konrad Adenauer Stiftung 1994). It was pointed out that the institution of chieftainship is not in accord with the precepts of democracy in its late 20th century version. Chiefs are not elected, but hereditary. Secondly, chiefs are mostly men, which goes against the principles of non-sexism. Thirdly, only Africans can become chiefs, which goes against the grain of having a non-racial society. Fourthly, chieftaincy serves to accentuate the forces of ethnicity, which had become thoroughly discredited in the apartheid years when it was used as the organising principle in the divide and rule strategy of ethnic homelands (Bekker 1994). In the popular mind, chieftaincy was equated with tribalism which could divide the African majority and derail the process of democratisation and nation building. If chiefs remained dependent on government patronage as in colonial times and apartheid years, they could be easily manipulated by the government of the day. How to determine which chiefs were "authentic" traditional leaders rather than creations of apartheid ethnographers and bantustan regimes? How far would their jurisdiction hold? Would it cover the migrants living in town? Would individuals be free to choose whether they wanted customary law to be applicable? What was the potential of chiefs as agents of rural development? Should they continue to control communal lands? Who should pay the chiefs? The national government, the province, or his subjects?

Writing in 1992, the ANC's constitutional expert Albie Sachs gave a highly optimistic assessment of the developmental potential of chiefs. "Traditional leaders are entitled to a dignified and respected role which enables them to take their place in and make their contribution towards building a new democratic South Africa. Their position in the new constitutional order should be such as to permit them to recapture the prestige which was undermined by colonialism, segregation and apartheid". The objective, Sachs believed, was not so much to democratise traditional institutions as to constitutionalise them (Sachs 1992:77-78). This is a far cry from Mbeki, Mzala and the classless society envisaged by activists in the 1980s. How were traditional authorities "constitutionalised"?

The "constitutionalisation" of traditional leaders

Both the interim constitution and the final constitution provide for the recognition of traditional leaders. A clause in the interim constitution specified that all traditional leaders who were functioning in this capacity at the time when the negotiations were concluded will be recognised as such for the duration of this five year transition period. The recognition of traditional leadership and customary law was enshrined in the constitutional principles which guided the deliberations in the Constitutional Assembly. This recognition would among other entail the right to a salary paid by the government, to settle certain disputes according to customary law and to representation on various levels of government. Provision is made for the establishment of a House of Traditional Leaders in each province which has traditional leaders and the establishment of a Council of Traditional Leaders at national level, to be elected by the provincial Houses. Each House of Traditional Leaders is empowered to advise its provincial legislature on matters relating to customary law and other traditional issues, while the Council of Traditional leaders is empowered to advise the national government on the same matters. These bodies do not have the power to reject or amend legislation. They are only entitled to advice the legislators. At most they can delay the passing of a bill by 60 days (*Survey of Race Relations 1993-94*: 556-557).

Nevertheless, there are some notable differences between the firm guarantees defined in the interim constitution and the hesitant phrasing of the final version adopted by the Constitutional Assembly in October 1996. Whilst the interim constitution explicitly states that there *shall* be Provincial Houses and a National Council of Traditional Leaders, its successor is more hesitant: national legislation *may* establish these institutions, without any obligation to do so. One reason for the watering down of this clause might be the problems experienced thus far with the formation of these Houses. By October 1996, Houses of Traditional Leaders had been established in only four of the six provinces which have state-appointed traditional leaders: KwaZulu/Natal, Northwest, Mpumalanga and the Free State. The process in the Eastern Cape remained deadlocked by the conflict between chiefs and civics, while in the Northern Province the issue hinged on the mode of representation of the chiefs. Gauteng, the Northern Cape and the Western Cape are not destined to have a House of Traditional Leaders as these provinces do not incorporate former bantustans. Since not all Provincial Houses have been constituted, it proved impossible to proceed towards the establishment of the National Council of Traditional Leaders. The Houses have to elect the members of the National Council. Legislation enabling the installation of a National Council was therefore withdrawn from parliament in October 1996.

One of the main functions of traditional leaders in terms of the constitution is the observance of customary law.[11] Customary law, apart from being a living reality in large

---

[11] S 211 Constitution of South Africa, as adopted on 10 December 1996

parts of rural South Africa, has also over the decades to a large extent been codified, most often by Afrikaner ethnologists in government service. It is this codified customary law, laid down in legislation such as the Black Authorities Act and the Native Administration Act, that because of its rigid and often outdated formulation is subject of fierce debate. At one point the rural women's movement threatened to boycott the 1994 elections if the ANC would abandon its non-sexist principles in order to placate chiefs. The Bill of Rights provides for equality before the law and to equal protection of the law. But in most systems of customary law, African women fall under the guardianship of their father or, after marriage, their husbands. They have no contractual capacity without the consent of their guardian and are not allowed to appear in court without the assistance of their guardian. They are excluded from the political process of the tribe and are sometimes precluded from obtaining land rights and from inheritance rights. [12] This minority status of African rural women was codified in the Native Administration Act of 1927.[13] How to reconcile customary law with the equality clause in the constitution? Against the argument that the low status of women under customary law was out of step with the basic tenets of contemporary human rights law, chiefs countered that "our culture cannot be outmoded" (Matlala 1993:2-4). The living customary law however has proved to be capable of adapting to change. These systems now face the major challenge of adapting to the equality clause in the constitution, which will prevail over customary law. According to a 1995 survey, the majority of South Africans favoured more female participation in traditional authorities, including the customary courts. These courts deal with minor crimes, family law and dispute settlement and thus relieve the state magistrature of a substantial workload (*Social Update* 1995).

The most thorny issue perhaps is the role of chiefs in local government. This was the central issue prompting the postponement of the local elections in KwaZulu-Natal: while the ANC believed that chiefs should play some part in local government, Inkatha maintained that chiefs *are* the local government.

The negotiators who produced the Local Government Transition Act (Act 209, 1993) were focused on urban areas, where formerly white towns and African townships had to merge into administratively viable units. The homelands lack an appropriate historical precedent of local government and their system of local administration was by no means uniform. The Act applies to rural areas as well, but pays scant attention to the specific characteristics of the former bantustan areas. The result was a momentous confusion at the time of the local elections in November 1995. There was no clarity about the functions of elected and traditional authorities, and therefore a great potential for conflict

---

[12] For a list of grievances, see the letter to the editor "Women not Kids" in *New Nation*, 29 Nov. 1996

[13] S11(3) (b) Native Administration Act: " A Black woman (excluding a black woman who permanently resides in the province of Natal) who is a partner in a customary union and who is living with her husband, shall be deemed to be a minor and her husband shall be deemed to be her guardian."

about the role of chiefs. (McIntosh and Vaughan 1994: 9) Unresolved for example was the responsibility for the allocation of land, previously one of the prerogatives of traditional leaders. Two modes of representation are possible under a proclamation issued by the government in August 1995. Chiefs can be appointed as ex officio members of the Transitional Local Council, or they can be represented on this council as an "interest group".

In the first case — ex officio members — all the recognised traditional leaders are entitled to a seat on the council. The extent of their powers is however unclear. In most provinces, the ex officio members have the same rights as the elected members, including the right to vote on issues before the council. In the Northern Province, the provincial government decided against this, because in numerous cases chiefs could have outvoted the elected members. It was never intended that chiefs would outnumber elected members, but in several parts of the ex-bantustans this happened to be the case.

But the proclamation also allows for another model: chiefs would then be represented as an "interest group", along with women, farm workers and farm owners. Each interest group would occupy not more than ten percent of the seats on the Transitional Representative Council. The total percentage of "representatives of interest groups" could not exceed 20 percent of the number of seats. The traditional leaders were up in arms against this model. They resented being put in the same category as rural women. (*Weekly Mail and Guardian,* 18-24 August 1995). And they objected to their minority position on an elected council. CONTRALESA chairman Patekile Holomisa protested that "this will put the position of the traditional leaders in the hands of the very people who are so hostile to us"(*The Star*, 23 August 1995), an assertion which casts some doubts on the claims of the chiefs that they enjoy wide popular legitimacy. He threatened to take the government to court. One other objection centred around the notion of representation as such. It was argued that one cannot expect one traditional leader to represent another.[14]

But chiefs were equally unhappy with the ex officio status, if this meant that they have less rights than the elected councillors. If the subjects of the chief are more powerful than the chief himself, a status problem poses itself. The definitive constitution leaves out all reference to the ex-officio membership of traditional leaders in local government bodies and confines itself to the non-committal statement that national legislation *may* provide for a role for traditional leadership as an institution at local level on matters affecting local communities.[15] While the position of traditional leaders who are ex-

---

[14] Interview by Oomen with officials of the Department of Constitutional Development, 17 November 1995

[15] S 212.1 of the constitution as adopted by the Constitutional Assembly, as adopted on 10 December 1996

officio members of local government is guaranteed until April 1999,[16] it seems likely that their official role will diminish after this date. Bridging legislation on local government, for instance, makes no mention of the chiefs.[17]

The reference to national legislation in this constitutional clause is noteworthy. While in the much contested balance of power between the provincial and central legislatures traditional leadership as well as local government fall under the exclusive legislative competence of the provinces, the power given to provinces such as KwaZulu-Natal in this respect was evidently perceived by the ANC-dominated government as sufficiently threatening to overrule it by constitution. At the time of writing, the issue of the representation of traditional leaders in local government in KwaZulu-Natal had not been resolved. Traditional leaders continue to form the primary form of rural local government. On an intermediate level, the province has seven elected regional councils, on which chiefs are represented.

Equally controversial is the control over the purse strings: who pays the chief? The Remuneration of Traditional Leaders Act, passed by the South African parliament in July 1995, makes payment a responsibility of the central government. The provinces, up till now responsible for footing the bill, may decide to add extra allowances, for example for attending sessions of the House of Traditional Leaders. The transfer of the control over salaries from the provinces to the central government is obviously meant to loosen Inkatha's grip on the Zulu chiefs. While Inkatha argued that chieftaincy matters fall under the competence of the provincial legislator, the central government stated that this, on the contrary, was one of those exceptional instances which called for uniform standards. The Inkatha-dominated provincial government of KwaZulu-Natal reacted furiously and passed legislation prohibiting traditional leaders (including the King!) to receive remuneration from the central government.[18] The case was put before the Constitutional Court, which ruled in July 1996 that this legislation was indeed within the competence of the province and that this prohibition was not inconsistent with the Constitution.[19] By the end of 1996, the legislation on remuneration had not yet been implemented, mainly because the Commission on the Remuneration of Representatives had not yet come up with recommendations on the payment of traditional leaders. It is expected that the Commission will recommend uniform payment scales for the same categories of traditional leaders all over the country. Presently enormous differences in

---

[16] S. 26 of the transitional arrangements in the definite constitution. Before 1999, the ex-officio membership can only be terminated by an Act of Parliament

[17] Draft Further Regulation of Local Government Bill, notice 1010 of 1996

[18] The payment of Salaries, Allowances and other Privileges to the Ingonyama Amendment Bill of 1995 and the KwaZulu/Natal Amakhosi and Iziphakanyiswa Amendment Bill of 1995. An interesting but yet undecided question is whether these remunerations should be considered salaries, thus putting traditional leaders on the same footing as civil servants.

[19] Case CCT 1/96 before the Constitutional Court, heard on 21 May 1996 and judgment delivered on 5 July 1996

salaries and benefits continue to exist between the provinces. In the Northern Province, a chief receives about 50.000 rand annually, while his colleague in the neighbouring North West Province has to be satisfied with on average 6.000 rand (Oomen 1996: 37).[20]

"Find the Chief"

As a corollary of new rules and new paymasters, it has to be established who will benefit from the Remuneration Act. Who are the "legitimate chiefs", as distinct from the creations of the apartheid state and the illegitimate usurpers of power? South Africa seems set for a new round in the familiar game of British colonial politics: "Find the Chief".

In the past, this issue was handled by the Department of Native Affairs. Since 1926, South African government ethnographers have collected evidence and compiled family trees of some 800 tribes. This work used to be the preserve of Afrikaner ethnographers, who up till now still dominate the scene in "native affairs". Their collections were mainly used in succession matters. But legitimacy and expediency do not always coincide: numerous "true" leaders have been disinherited while compliant marionettes were elevated to higher ranks. In nearly every discussion on chieftaincy, the issue keeps popping up: who are the chiefs? And who decides?

The answers vary. CONTRALESA has called for an independent commission of inquiry to sort out the issue "once and for all" (*Weekly Mail and Guardian* 23-29 June 1995). The Constitutional Assembly, when dealing with calls to establish the authenticity of chiefs, decided that this was the responsibility of the Department of Justice (*Constitutional Talk* 8 Sept. 1995). The Department of Constitutional Affairs also handles chieftaincy issues. Until new rules are adopted, the Native Administration Act (as adopted in 1927) continues to apply: the State President has the final say over who is appointed a traditional leader. Similarly, the president can define the duties, powers privileges and conditions of service of traditional leaders thus appointed and depose leaders when he deems this necessary (S.2 Black Administration Act).

What does all of this mean in real life in rural South Africa? For a glimpse of the practical implications of new laws and old institutions, we look in somewhat more detail at the situation in the Northern Province, formerly the Northern Transvaal.

---

[20] The rate of exchange of the Rand at the end of 1996 was 1 Rand: 0,22 US $

The Northern Province: old leaders and new masters

The Northern Transvaal is one of the most rural parts of South Africa. This was the heartland of conservative Afrikanerdom, dominated not by the National Party, but by the Conservative Party, the Afrikaner Weerstandsbeweging (Afrikaner Resistance Movement) and the latest addition to Afrikaner political parties, the Freedom Front. In the 1994 general elections, the ANC scored a massive victory. Among the nine provinces, the Northern Transvaal proved to be the most solid ANC bastion. In line with national politics, the ANC followed a conciliatory approach and included a representative of the Freedom Front in the provincial cabinet. But for Black South Africans, the Northern Province is a de facto one-party state: the ANC is the only game "in town". This means that conflicting interests are not represented by different parties, but have to be accommodated within the ANC. Phrased in the discourse of liberation politics: the "contested terrain" is now within the ANC. Civil servants, chiefs, youth, women, black business and other interest groups all seek ANC patronage. One major headache for the government of the Northern Province was the incorporation of three former bantustans: Venda, Ganzankulu (destined for the South African Tsonga/Shangaan; the majority of the Shangaan live on the other side of the border in Mozambique) and Lebowa (Northern BaSotho). The government inherited the costly legacy of Grand Apartheid. The bureaucracies of the former bantustans — reputed to be inefficient and corrupt — had to be absorbed in the new provincial administration. Traditional leaders, until recently maligned as the faithful servants of the apartheid government and the bantustan despots, had to be incorporated in provincial and local government and in the ANC's ambitious five-year development plan, the Reconstruction and Development Programme (RDP). Former enemies -chiefs, youth activists, civic associations- all became dependent on ANC patronage. This part explores how traditional leaders manoeuvre in this new game, forging new alliances in order to safeguard their position.[21]

Responsibility for policy vis-à-vis chiefs initially rested with the Commissioner for Traditional Authorities, a short-lived position which was abolished in 1996 as a result of an internal rearrangement of the provincial administration. The first and only Commissioner, Benny Boshielo, who also served as deputy secretary of the ANC in the Northern Province, was rather uncomfortable with his job. A young ANC activist who spent considerable time abroad studying in Amsterdam, he was not at all convinced that chiefs enjoy broad popular support. He basically believed that the institution is a waste of time and money. In his view, the ANC had rehabilitated the chiefs and given them a new role in post-apartheid South Africa. But in turn, the chiefs were most ungrateful. Some chiefs still did not allow civic associations in their village. Some had obstructed

---

[21] Most of the material for this section was gathered during a visit by Van Kessel to Pietersburg and Sekhukhuneland at the time of the local elections in November 1995 and by Oomen later that same month. Interviews were conducted i.a. with the Commissioner for Traditional Authorities in Pietersburg and with acting paramount chief K.K. Sekhukhune in Mohlaletse.

the local elections by contesting the delimitation of electoral districts in court. In several places, chiefs called for a boycott of the local elections. Some propped up their rule with armed vigilantes and refused to be disarmed. In some villages, chiefs managed to gain control over job creation under the RDP. Companies wanting to recruit labourers for RDP projects were told to report to the Chief's kraal. This provided the chief with a crucial network of patronage: jobs are the highest priority in any rural village. Boshielo tried to remove chiefly control over employment. With the election of new local councils in November 1995, an alternative network had been established to dispense jobs and contracts.

Interviewed in 1995, the Commissioner for Traditional Authorities sounded thoroughly frustrated with the lack of ANC policy on the issue of chieftaincy. "The ANC must make up its mind: do we want chiefs or not? If yes, then we must make them effective. If no, then we must do away with them."

His days were occupied with "endless bickering and protocol". The issue of the provincial House of Traditional Leaders was still unresolved (and remained unresolved at the time of writing). He handled numerous succession disputes and received scores of people who contested the legitimacy of "their" chief. His newly created position gave of course rise to another question: how legitimate was the youthful Commissioner for Traditional Authorities in the eyes of the chiefs? Chiefs obviously tried various avenues to further their interests: sometimes through the Commissioner, but they could also try to circumvent him in order to pull strings at national level in the ANC.

Boshielo controlled a substantial budget of R. 108 million, which was more than many other provincial departments. Chiefs were paid by the provincial government, rather to the chagrin of Boshielo who believes that chiefs ought to be maintained by their tribe. Why, he asked, should chiefs be maintained at the taxpayers' expense? Nevertheless, all 193 traditional leaders in the Northern Province receive a salary of R. 46.000 annually, plus R. 9.000 to run their tribal office and a *bakkie* (a van). After the administrative shake-up, traditional affairs became the responsibility of the provincial Department of Local Government.

The Commissioner was equally critical of the proposed House of Traditional Leaders, which he regarded as a waste of taxpayers' money. The chiefs most likely were expecting extra allowances for attending meetings, but Boshielo was determined to underplay the importance of this House and to limit expenditures. He was not unhappy with the delays in constituting the House of Traditional Leaders: up till the end of 1995, the savings were adequate for the construction of an extra 60 class rooms.

The dispute regarding the House of Traditional Leaders hinged on the mode of representation. The provincial government had allocated the 36 seats on the basis of equal representation of "cultural groups": one third each for the Venda, Shangaan and Sotho chiefs. But the Sotho chiefs campaigned for a system of proportional representation: "One Chief, One Vote". This would make them the dominant group in the House. Lebowa, the former bantustan for the Northern BaSotho, had 153 chiefs, while Venda had only 28 and Gazankulu 38. While the Commissioner waited for the chiefs to produce a compromise, the chiefs were waiting for the Commissioner to come up with a solution. The issue was potentially divisive, as passions could be mobilised along ethnic lines. Already the paramount chief of Sekhukhuneland, a part of former Lebowa, was expressing doubts whether the Shangaan chiefs ought to be represented at all. After all, "they came only yesterday, they are from Mozambique. They did not even have chiefs, and now they are claiming seats in the House of Traditional Leaders." He blamed the delay on the alleged dominance of Venda and Shangaan people in the provincial government.

Naturally, the Venda and Shangaan chiefs favoured the system of equal representation. Moreover, they questioned the legitimacy of this multitude of Sotho chiefs: surely, these could not be all "authentic" traditional leaders? As we have seen, many chieftaincies were indeed created with the introduction of the Bantustan authorities. In Venda, a clean-up of these newly created chiefs had already been carried out in 1990, when the previously quiescent homeland went through a period of turmoil. Therefore, the number of Venda chiefs was by 1995 substantially lower than that of the Sotho chiefs.

Commissioner Boshielo had instituted a Commission of Inquiry charged with an investigation into the authenticity of the Northern Province's chiefs. By November 1995, the commission had received 406 claims to chiefly status, but also numerous submissions in which the legitimacy of chiefs was being challenged. According to Boshielo, many people welcomed the installation of the commission in the hope that their chiefs would be deposed. The scale of the investigation by the Commission was ambitious: the cut off date for its historical research was 1927, the date of the introduction of the Native Administration Act. Other important vetting points were 1951 (introduction of the Black Authorities Act) and 1971 (Black Homelands Constitution Act). Boshielo expected that this inquiry would result in a reduction of the number of chiefs by about 40 percent.

The installation of this commission had the full support of the acting Paramount Chief of Sekhukhuneland, K.K. Sekhukhune. But his motives were rather different from those of Benny Boshielo or the "commoners" who welcomed the weeding out of illegitimate chiefs. K.K Sekhukhune believed that this purge would serve to restore "tradition", i.e. the power of the paramountcy. If the creatures of bantustan rule were swept aside, the remaining "legitimate" chiefs would be accountable to the paramountcy, as it was before the introduction of Bantustan Authorities. A historical injustice would be undone: the pre-colonial BaPedi Kingdom would be recreated.[22] This was definitely not the intention of the Commissioner for Traditional Authorities in Pietersburg.

---

[22] K.K. Sekhukhune referred to himself both as 'King' and as Paramount Chief; much of the literature on the subject uses the colonial terminology of "Paramount Chief".

The status of the heir to the BaPedi kingdom was also being challenged from other sides. If the Zulu and perhaps the BaPedi can have a king, why should other tribes not have a king? Venda and Shangaan chiefs also submitted claims to paramountcy status. After all, king Goodwill Zwelithini's annual salary was in the range of R.350.000 - R. 400.000, plus benefits. That was almost tenfold the salary of an ordinary Northern Province chief.

Royal blood versus ANC patronage

However, the overriding concern in the life of K.K. Sekhukhune (commonly known as KK) over the years was not the House of Traditional Leaders or the claims from upstart Shangaan or Venda chiefs. His one enduring torment was his half brother Rhyne Thulare who also claimed the right to the BaPedi throne. When the throne vacated in the 1980s, Rhyne made it known that he was not a candidate. KK was duly installed as acting Paramount Chief. The — undisputed — incumbent is KK's eldest son, who at the time was still an infant. Later Rhyne changed his mind and staked a claim to the paramountcy. His claim was supported by the then prime minister of Lebowa, Nelson Ramodike. On the other side, KK's alliances were geared towards the ANC. He was on good terms with the UDF leadership and he was one of the early members of CONTRALESA. During the 1994 elections he campaigned openly for the ANC. He won the court case in which Rhyne challenged his right to the throne. The Lebowa government appealed to the Appellate Division of the South African Supreme Court, but KK won again, at great financial expense to his tribe and himself. But his half brother did not give up. The Lebowa government created a new tribe, the Bapedi Thulare, and installed Rhyne as the chief of this new tribe. KK went to court to challenge this decision and again won his case. The provincial government — by now Lebowa had ceased to exist and the ANC formed the provincial government — had to depose Rhyne.

The Commissioner of Traditional Authorities tried to arrange a discussion between the two claimants, but KK refused. Commissioner Boshielo tried again and managed to assemble two delegations from each side in a Pietersburg hotel in an attempt to solve the issue in a consultation of the elders. But the elders from each side refused to recognise the authority of the elders on the side of the rival. In this impasse, the provincial government recognised KK as the acting paramount chief, who would also be entitled to a seat in the House of Traditional Leaders.

Rhyne was still not outmanoeuvred. He now shifted patronage. His previous alliance with the homeland government of Nelson Ramodike was utterly useless under the new masters of the ANC. Rhyne switched to playing the ANC card. He called on his uncle John Nkadimeng, an old guard ANC activist from Sekhukhuneland who rose to prominence during the long years in exile. Nkadimeng arranged an audience for Rhyne with Nelson Mandela. When Rhyne received this prestigious invitation, he replied that he had no transport. Mandela, known to be a great admirer of the institution of chieftaincy, saw to it that Rhyne was given a Mercedes Benz.[23] All of this has of course infuriated KK Sekhukhune. As KK explained in an interview, there are three attributes for recognition as a chief: a car, an office and an account number. Presumably, these requirements come in addition to a genealogical claim. With the donation of the Mercedes by the State President himself, Rhyne had gained a strategic asset. In addition, Rhyne had sidelined the provincial government and taken his case right to the presidential office. This put KK at a disadvantage: while he had access to the provincial government, he had no direct access to the central government. In order to keep up with Rhyne, he also tried to arrange an audience with Mandela. When he did not succeed, he had to satisfy himself with talks with the minister of constitutional affairs Roelf Meyer and with deputy minister Mohammed Valli Moosa. The appointment, in late 1995, of John Nkadimeng as ambassador to Cuba must have come as a great relief to KK Sekhukhune. KK resented the interventions by the politicians after the court had clearly validated his claims. He talked of suing the ANC government for contempt of court, but at the same time he remained keenly aware that he could not afford to alienate the ANC.

The aftermath of the elections

With the national and local elections over and with no substantial rival to contest its hegemony in its African constituency outside of KwaZulu-Natal, the ANC seemed to lose much of its earlier enthusiasm for traditional leaders. One reason was the growing divide between the ANC and CONTRALESA, whose executive had been taken over by a faction headed by Chief Patekile Holomisa and Winnie Mandela. Chairman Holomisa and treasurer Winnie Mandela, both from the Transkei, both known for maverick politics, turned the organisation into their personal powerbase, thus alienating most of their chiefly constituency in the North. Not only did Holomisa liaise with IFP-aligned chiefs in KwaZulu-Natal, he also joined them in calling for a boycott of the local government elections.

But it were probably these local government elections themselves that engendered the more critical stance towards traditional leadership which has obviously inspired the more recent legislation. In 1994, with two elections ahead and the traditional leaders ruling an estimated 40 % of the population, their role in delivering the rural vote could not be underestimated. In his speeches, Mandela was most accommodating towards chiefs. After his release from prison in 1990, Mandela explicitly addressed them: "I greet the traditional leaders of our country — many of you continue to walk in the footsteps of great heroes like Hintsa and Sekhukhune".[24] After a meeting with traditional leaders,

---

[23] See for example the chapters on his childhood in the Transkei in Mandela's autobiography *Long Walk to Freedom*; also Mamphela Ramphele, *A Life*: 202-203.

[24] Nelson Mandela's address to a rally in Cape Town on his release from prison, 11 Feb. 1990, http://www.anc.org.za./ancdocs/speeches/release.html

Mandela stated that the "the role and place of traditional leaders in our society has in the past been systematically undermined by successive racist regimes which sought to reduce their role to enforce repugnant apartheid politics. Today's meeting should be seen in the context of restoring traditional leaders to their rightful place in society." [25]

The question of how to reconcile such a restoration with the introduction of elected local government bodies in rural South Africa was not addressed until after the local elections were held in most of the country. In his first firm statement on the issue since the elections, Mandela asserted in early 1996 that "we want to advise the traditional leaders in our country to abandon the illusion that there can ever emerge a constitutional settlement which grants them powers that would compromise the fundamental objective of a genuine democracy in which the legislature and the executive at all levels are made up essentially of elected representatives."[26]

The outcome of the local elections made the ANC more confident that it could win on its own, without cumbersome alliances with traditional leaders. Even in KwaZulu-Natal, the ANC did better than anticipated. Thus South Africa's definite Constitution is much more non-committal than its predecessor when it comes to defining the position of traditional leaders in post apartheid South Africa. The battle however is far from over. Immediately after the adoption of the Constitution, Inkatha, which had boycotted most of the constitutional process, reasserted its demands that traditional leaders be given greater authority in local government. The party threatened to call for a review of the Constitution in this respect (*Weekly Mail and Guardian*, 11 Oct. 1996).

Although Inkatha is most outspoken in its support of the chieftaincy, the view that there is a place for the institution in the New South Africa is fairly widespread (Pillay and Prinsloo 1995). From the submissions to the Constitutional Assembly, it is evident that there is wide acceptance of a continued role for traditional leaders, although positions differ when it comes to defining their powers and duties. In many submissions, it was emphasised that chieftaincy ought to be a non-partisan institution (Oomen 1996: 139-151).

Conclusion

In conclusion, it can be stated that the position of traditional leaders in post apartheid South Africa remains thoroughly ambivalent. The come back of the chief has been effected with the support of the ANC, but the battle between traditionalists, modernists, African nationalists and communists within the ANC is far from over. In the transition phase, the ANC and the chiefs perceived a mutual benefit in co-operation. By now, the

---

[25] ANC statement on the meeting between president Mandela and traditional leaders, 1995. http://www.anc.org.za./cgi-bin/mfs/01/tradlead.

[26] Speech, January 1996. http://www.anc.org.za./ancdocs/history

honeymoon between ANC and CONTRALESA has ended. CONTRALESA itself seems to be disintegrating due to leadership squabbles, thereby losing its value as interlocutor. Within the ANC, irritation is mounting about excessive demands emanating from traditional authorities and about attempts by a number of chiefs to obstruct the local elections. But although ANC enthusiasm seems to be waning, it is much too early to predict the definitive demise of the chieftaincy. Moreover, traditionalists continue to have a vocal advocate in the IFP, although Inkatha thus far has not been able to transcend its Zulu ethnic power base.

The institution of chieftaincy has been transformed by the experience of British colonial rule and subsequently by the apartheid scheme of bantustans. Now it faces a new challenge of transformation under the new masters of the ANC government. Even during the decades of bantustan rule, the institution, although operating within strict boundaries, allowed at least for some mode of expression of popular concerns. It remains to be seen whether the elected local councillors succeed in obtaining a wider popular legitimacy. Chiefs have proven that the institution is adaptable to changing times. The case of K.K. Sekhukhune illustrates this flexibility. KK's trials and tribulations reveal how the Paramount Chief attempted to safeguard his position by combining the resources of tradition, modernity and liberation politics. The dispute with Rhyne was fought with arguments invoking tradition: "my royal blood is thicker than his." But his good standing with the ANC was — at least in a certain period — also helpful in propping up his position. In the dispute about the composition of the House of Traditional Leaders, KK's arguments were borrowed from the discourse of liberation politics: "One Chief, One Vote: that is our democratic right."

If traditional leaders are perceived as non-partisan, they can play a valuable role in local communities, e.g. in the sphere of conflict resolution and justice. But if chiefs remain dependent on government patronage, they can easily be manipulated by the government of the day. The central issue remains unresolved: do chiefs derive their legitimacy from state recognition or from popular support?

References

BANK, Leslie and Roger SOUTHALL
1996   Traditional Leaders in South Africa's New Democracy. Pp. 407-430. In: *Journal of Legal Pluralism*, nos. 37 & 38 (Special issue on the New Relevance of Traditional Authorities in Africa, ed. by E.A.B. van Rouveroy van Nieuwaal and D.I. Ray)

BEKKER, Jan C.
1994   The role of chiefs in a future South African constitutional dispensation. Pp. 76-83. In: *The Future of the Institution of Hereditary Rule and Customary Law in South Africa*. R.S. Ndou and Essy M. Letsoalo (eds.). Marshalltown

BOTHMA, C.V.
1976   The political structure of the Pedi of Sekhkhuneland. Pp. 177-205. In: *African Studies*, 35, 3-4

CONTRALESA *Newsletter*, 1, 1 [n.d. 1990]

DELIUS, Peter
1989   Sebatakgomo: Migrant organization, the ANC and the Sekhukhune revolt. Pp. 581-615. In: *Journal of Southern African Studies*, 15, 4

1990   Migrants, Comrades and Rural revolt: Sekhukhuneland 1950-1987. Pp. 2-26. In: *Transformation* 13

EWING, Deborah
1995   The cause of the King. Pp. 31-42. In: *Leadership*, 14, 2

JUNG, Courtney
1996   Understanding Zulu identity. Pp. 47-54. In: *Indicator SA*, 13, 2

KESSEL, Ineke van
1993   From Confusion to Lusaka': the youth revolt in Sekhukhuneland. Pp. 593-614. In: *Journal of Southern African Studies*, 19, 4

1996   'Beyond our Wildest Dreams': The United Democratic Front and the Transformation of South Africa. Leiden: PhD. Thesis

KONRAD ADENAUER STIFTUNG
1994   Seminar report: The Role of Traditional Leaders in Local Government in South Africa, 27-28 Oct. 1994

LODGE, Tom
1983   *Black Politics in South Africa since 1945*. Johannesburg: Ravan Press

MANDELA, Nelson
1994   *Long Walk to Freedom: the Autobiography of Nelson Mandela*. Boston: Little, Brown and co.

MATLALA, Padi
1993   Can Chiefs change? Pp. 2-4. In: *New Ground*, Spring issue

MBEKI, Govan
1984   *The Peasants' Revolt*. London: International Defence and Aid Fund (first published in 1964)

MCINTOSH, Alistair and Anne VAUGHAN
1994   Towards a system of rural local government for the Northern Transvaal. Development Bank of South Africa. Policy Working Paper 34

MZALA
1988   *Gatsha Buthelezi: Chief with a Double Agenda*. London: Zedbooks

NEW WEBSTER Dictionary and Thesaurus
1992   Danbury CT: Lexicon Publications

OOMEN, Barbara
1996   Talking Tradition: the position and portrayal of traditional leaders in present-day South Africa. Amsterdam: unpublished M.A. thesis

PAYZE, Catherine
1992   The elimination of political opponents: the Maphumulo assassination. Pp. 247-258. In: *Patterns of Violence: case studies of conflict in Natal*. Anthony Minnaar et al (eds.). Pretoria: Human Sciences Research Council

PILLAY, Nirmala and Cas PRINSLOO
1995   Tradition in Transition? Exploring the role of traditional authorities. In: *Social Update*, Pretoria: Human Sciences Research Council

RAMPHELE, Mamphela
1995   *A Life*. Cape Town: David Philip

RITCHKEN, Edwin
1989   The KwaNdebele Struggle against Independence. Pp. 426-445. In: *South African Review*, 5

ROUVEROY VAN NIEUWAAL, E. Adriaan B. van
1987   Chiefs and African States: some introductory notes and an extensive bibliography on African Chieftaincy. Pp. 1-46. In: *Journal of Legal Pluralism, nos.* 25 & 26

SACHS, Albie
1992   *Advancing Human Rights in South Africa*. Cape Town: Oxford University Press

SEEKINGS, Jeremy F.
1990   Quiescence and the Transition to Confrontation: South African Townships 1978-1984. Oxford: PhD. thesis

1986   *Saspu National*, 7, 4 (Nov.-Dec. 1986): South African Students Press Union

RACE RELATIONS SURVEY
1987-88   Johannesburg: South African Institute of Race Relations

TRANSVAAL RURAL ACTION COMMITTEE
1988   KwaNdebele—The Struggle against 'Independence'. Pp. 114-135. In: *Popular Struggles in South Africa*. W. Cobbett and R. Cohen (eds.). London: James Currey

ZUMA, Thando
1989   The role of the Chiefs in the struggle for liberation. Pp. 65-76. In: *African Communist*, 121

THE 'ANGLOPHONE PROBLEM' AND CHIEFTAINCY IN ANGLOPHONE CAMEROON

Piet Konings

The political agenda in Cameroon has become increasingly dominated of late by the 'Anglophone problem'. This issue poses a major challenge to the postcolonial state's efforts to forge 'national unity' and 'national integration'. It has led to the reintroduction of 'federalism' and 'secession' into the national political discourse.

The root of the 'Anglophone problem' may be traced back to 1961, when the political elites of two territories with different colonial legacies - one French and the other British - agreed on the formation of a federal state. Contrary to Anglophone expectations, federalism did not result in an equal partnership of both parties, nor in the preservation of the cultural heritage and identity of the Anglophone minority. It proved merely a transitory phase in a movement towards total integration of the Anglophone region into a strongly centralized, unitary state. Gradually this has created an Anglophone consciousness: the feeling of being 'marginalized', 'exploited', and 'assimilated' by the Francophone-dominated state, and even by the Francophone population as a whole. It was not until the political liberalization process in the early 1990s that part of the Anglophone elite began openly organizing in a variety of associations and pressure groups to protest against the alleged subordinate position of the Anglophones and to press claims for self-determination and autonomy. Whereas the major Anglophone movements initially called for a return to the federal state, the Biya government's persistent refusal to discuss constitutional reforms along such lines has since led them to adopt a secessionist stand.

In this article I examine the role that chieftaincy in Anglophone Cameroon has played in these struggles for self-determination and autonomy. I will show that Anglophone chiefs greatly contributed to the achievement of reunification and federalism. In return, the political elite allowed them a large measure of autonomy during the era of federalism and an - admittedly limited - political role in a House of Chiefs in Anglophone Cameroon. But after the promulgation of the unitary state in 1972, the political elite abolished the House of Chiefs and tried to integrate chieftaincy into the state apparatus in a subordinate position. The role of Anglophone chiefs in the current struggles demonstrates that these integrative efforts have never been fully successful. The majority of such chiefs have strongly resisted the persistent efforts by the Francophone-dominated state to use them to protect the unitary state. They have instead supported the Anglophone calls for a return to the federal state or for outright secession.

The emergence and development of the 'Anglophone problem'

The Federal Republic of Cameroon was born on 1 October 1961 (cf. Johnson 1970; Le Vine 1971; and Benjamin 1972). Its birth marked the reunification of two territories which had undergone different colonial experiences since the First World War, when the erstwhile German Kamerun Protectorate was partitioned into French and British Mandate/Trust Territories. Of great significance for this reunification was the fact that the southern part of the British Mandate/Trust Territory, which came to be called the Southern Cameroons, had been integrated into the administrative system of Nigeria. It had been administered as an integral part of the Eastern Region of Nigeria until 1954, when it achieved a quasi-regional status and a limited degree of self-government within the Federation of Nigeria. In 1958, it attained full regional status, placing it on a parity with the other regions in the federation. It is beyond any doubt that the administration of the Southern Cameroons as an appendage of Nigeria - which led to a blatant neglect of the region's development as well as a dominant position of Nigerian migrants, mainly Ibo and Efik-Ibibio, in the Southern Cameroonian economy - was a key factor in the development of a Cameroonian identity among the regional elite and the decision of the majority of the regional population to vote for reunification with Francophone Cameroon, rather than for integration into Nigeria, in the 1961 United Nations plebiscite. Nonetheless, it is also certain that the British-Nigerian colonial experience had a lasting effect on the construction of an Anglophone identity among the regional elite.

The birth of the Federal Republic of Cameroon simultaneously marked the start of a unique experiment in federalism in Africa. However, federalism in Cameroon was to be 'more shadow than reality' (Stark 1976). During negotiations on the federal constitution, particularly at the Foumban Conference from 17 to 22 July 1961, it was already evident that the bargaining strength of the Francophone delegation was much greater than that of the Anglophones. Compared to the Francophone region, the size and population of the

Anglophone region was small, comprising only nine per cent of the total area and about a quarter of the total population of the federation. More important, by the time of these negotiations the former French Trust Territory of Cameroon was already an independent state, having been renamed the Republic of Cameroon, while the British Trust Territory of Southern Cameroons was, under the terms of the United Nations plebiscite, still to realize its independence by *joining* the sovereign Republic of Cameroon. Capitalizing on his territory's 'senior' status, Ahmadou Ahidjo, the then Prime Minister of the Republic of Cameroon and leader of the Francophone delegation, was able to dictate the terms for the federation. John Ngu Foncha, Prime Minister of the Southern Cameroons and leader of the Anglophone delegation, had proposed a loose form of federalism, which he regarded as a guarantee for equal partnership of both parties and for preservation of the cultural heritage and identity of the Anglophone minority. But Ahidjo eventually forced him to accept a highly centralized form of federalism. Ahidjo, who was to become President of the Federal Republic of Cameroon, looked upon federalism merely as an unavoidable transitory phase in the total integration of the Anglophone minority into a strongly centralized, unitary state. To achieve this objective he employed a number of tactics. One of them was to play off Anglophone political factions against each other and eventually integrate them into a single party, the Cameroon National Union (CNU). Another was to eliminate from positions of power any Anglophone leaders who remained committed to federalism, replacing them by others who favoured a unitary state. Still another tactic was to create 'clients' among the Anglophone elite. By granting top posts in the federal institutions and in the single party to representatives of significant ethnic and regional groups in the Anglophone region, Ahidjo tried to control these groups. He also did not shrink from repressing any opposition. Through these and other tactics he succeeded in abolishing the federation. On 6 May 1972, he announced in the National Assembly that he intended to transform the Federal Republic into a unitary state, provided that the electorate supported the idea in a referendum to be held on 20 May 1972. Given the autocratic nature of his regime, it was not surprising that the Cameroonian population voted massively for the draft constitution, which would immediately establish the United Republic of Cameroon. Ahidjo's justification for this 'glorious revolution' was that federalism fostered regionalism and impeded economic development.

A growing proportion of the Anglophone elite, however, was inclined to attribute the emergence of 'regionalism' and the lack of economic development not to federalism *per se,* but to the hegemonic tendencies of the Francophone-dominated state. They began to complain about the loss of regional autonomy and the subordinate position of the Anglophone minority in the unitary state. Their numerous grievances were mainly political, economic and cultural. They concerned in particular the underrepresentation and inferior role of the Anglophones in the national decision-making councils, the neglect of the region's infrastructure, the exploitation of its rich economic resources, especially oil, and the attempts at 'Frenchification'.[1]

To reduce the danger of any united Anglophone action against the Francophone-dominated state, Ahidjo had decided after the 'glorious revolution' to divide the erstwhile Federated State of West Cameroon into two provinces, the South West and North West Provinces. In making his decision he was well aware of the internal contradictions within the Anglophone community between the coastal/forest people (the South West Province) and the Grassfield people (the North West Province).

One major reason for these internal conflicts was the loss of hegemony by the South West elite in the Anglophone region. The coastal population had been exposed to early contact with Western trade, religion and education, giving it a head start over the Grassfield population. An intelligentsia emerged in the coastal area, notably among the Bakweri, and it quickly came to the forefront in the nationalist struggle and dominated the Anglophone political scene up to the end of the 1950s. The transfer of power from the South Westerner, Dr Emmanuel Endeley, to the North Westerner, Mr John Ngu Foncha, was a political event with significant repercussions for the South West-North West relations. From that point onwards the North West elite has played a predominant political and economic role at the regional and national level. In pre-empting for itself the choicest jobs and the best lands in the South West, it has provoked strong resentment among South Westerners (Kofele-Kale 1981). South Western sentiments have been intensified by the gradual success of the 'entrepreneurial' North Westerners in dominating most sectors of the South West economy, in particular trade, transport and housing (Rowlands, 1993). Another source of the South West-North West divide was the UN plebiscite of 1961. On that occasion, the South West had shown considerable sympathy for alignment with Nigeria, and the choice for Cameroon prevailed mainly on the strength of the North West votes. A final source of tensions was the massive labour migration from the North West to the South West, where a plantation economy had been established during the German colonial era (1884-1914) (Konings 1993).

Lack of unity and severe repression precluded the Anglophone elite from openly expressing its grievances about Francophone domination until 1982, when President Biya took power. Following a limited degree of liberalization introduced by the new president, Anglophones began voicing their long-standing grievances. In 1983 the Biya government issued an Order modifying the Anglophone General Certificate of Education (GCE) examination by introducing French as a compulsory subject, without the corresponding requirement of English for the Francophone baccalaureate. The publication of this Order sparked off an Anglophone student boycott of classes, and demonstrations at Yaoundé University and in the urban centres of Anglophone Cameroon, which were brutally suppressed. In 1984 the Biya government changed the

---

[1] For a specification of the numerous Anglophone complaints, see, for instance, All Anglophone Conference (1993)

official name of the country from 'United Republic of Cameroon' to simply 'Republic of Cameroon'. The Anglophone elite strongly protested, recalling that the new name was identical to the one Ahidjo had given to independent Francophone Cameroon before reunification. In 1985 a prominent Anglophone lawyer, who was also a chief in the North West, Fon Gorji Dinka, was arrested for distributing a leaflet declaring the Biya government unconstitutional and calling for the independence of the Southern Cameroons, to be rebaptized the Republic of Ambazonia. In the same year, at the Bamenda Congress of the single party, two memoranda were submitted by members of the North West and South West elite who resided in Douala. The documents drew attention to the Anglophone plight and argued that the Anglophone elite felt sidelined from political power.[2]

Two factors fuelled Anglophone frustration with the Francophone-dominated state in the late 1980s. First, there was the increasing monopolization of economic and political power by the Beti elite, members of the president's ethnic group. Takougang (1993) reports that as of August 1991, 37 of the 47 senior prefects, three quarters of the directors and general managers of parastatal companies, and 22 of the 38 high-ranking bureaucrats appointed at the newly created office of the Prime Minister were Beti. These new *barons* were seemingly much bolder in staking out claims to the state's resources than Ahidjo's *barons* had been. Secondly, there was the deepening economic crisis and the subsequent Structural Adjustment Program (SAP). Anglophones were inclined to attribute the crisis first and foremost to the corruption and mismanagement of the Biya regime. They claimed that during the economic crisis their region failed to benefit of the revenues derived from its rich oil resources, in the form of increased investments in its ailing economy and neglected infrastructure. Oil revenues tended instead to be used by the Francophone-dominated state to feed the bellies of its allies or to stimulate the economy in the Francophone region. SONARA, the oil refinery near Limbe (or Victoria, as Anglophones prefer to resume calling it), continued to be headed by a Francophone and staffed predominantly by Francophones. There was also great anxiety in Anglophone Cameroon that its major agro-industrial enterprises, especially the Cameroon Development Corporation (CDC) and Pamol, would be either liquidated or sold to Francophone and French interests during the economic crisis and SAP (Konings 1995a).

Political liberalization and Anglophone-organized opposition

Given the Anglophone frustration with the Francophone-dominated state, it was not surprising that the first opposition party in the country was formed in Anglophone Cameroon. In 1990 the Social Democratic Front (SDF) was founded at Bamenda, the capital of the North West Province. Its chairman was John Fru Ndi, a librarian by profession, who was to achieve wide popularity among the urban masses because of his great courage and populist style of leadership. Its massive launching rally on 26 May

---

[2] These documents can be found in Mukong (1990)

1990 ended in the killing of six young Anglophones by government troops. The state-controlled media tried to deny government responsibility for this bloody event or to distort the facts. Leading members of the government and the ruling party, the Cameroon People's Democratic Movement (CPDM), strongly condemned the Anglophones for their 'treacherous' action. The government's reaction to this peaceful demonstration shocked the Anglophone community. On 9 June 1990, the Anglophone architect of the federal state, John Ngu Foncha, resigned from his function as the First Vice-President of the CPDM. In his resignation letter, he declared:

> The Anglophone Cameroonians whom I brought into union have been ridiculed and referred to as 'les Biafrais', 'les enemies dans la maison', 'les traitres' etc., and the constitutional provisions which protected this Anglophone minority have been suppressed, their voice drowned while the rule of the gun replaced the dialogue which the Anglophones cherish very much.[3]

Under considerable internal and external pressures, the Biya government eventually introduced a larger measure of political liberalization. In December 1990 it announced multi-partyism and a certain degree of freedom of mass communication, association, and holding of public meetings and demonstrations. As a result, one could subsequently observe the establishment of several political parties, associations and pressure groups, and private newspapers in Anglophone Cameroon, which began to express and represent Anglophone interests. The SDF then extended its influence from the North West to the South West Province, making it the major opposition party in Anglophone Cameroon. However, it remained far more popular in the North West than in the South West, for the South West elite continued to be suspicious of the aspirations of the party's predominantly North Western leadership, fearing renewed North West domination. Personal animosities, on the other hand, prevented the South West elite from forming a strong party there.

For some time the SDF was instrumental in turning the Anglophone region into one of the hotbeds of rebellion, organizing several serious confrontations with the regime in power, especially the 'ghost town' campaign of 1991.[4] The impact of its oppositional stand on the Anglophone community was particularly visible during the 1992 presidential elections. On that occasion, John Fru Ndi received respectively 86.3 and 51.6 per cent of the votes cast in the North West and South West Provinces. John Fru Ndi's loss in these fraudulent elections was a traumatic experience in Anglophone Cameroon. After the elections, violent protests broke out in Bamenda and throughout the North West Province against 'Biya's theft of John Fru Ndi's victory'. Biya imposed a

---

[3] Dr J.N. Foncha's Letter of Resignation from the C.P.D.M., reproduced in Mukong (1990).
[4] This was a campaign of civil disobedience organized by the opposition parties to force the Biya regime to call a national conference. It involved the stoppage of all work, all trade, and all traffic in towns, except for Friday evenings and Saturdays, resulting in huge personal financial losses and an aggravation of the economic crisis.

state of emergency on this province for three months and John Fru Ndi was kept under military surveillance in his house at Bamenda. Paradoxically, despite its great contribution to Anglophone consciousness and action, the party began presenting itself as a 'national' rather than an Anglophone party, and this was also evidenced by a growing Francophone membership. The party adopted a rather ambivalent attitude towards the call of the newly emerging Anglophone pressure groups for a return to the federal state. Its 1992 national convention at Bamenda emphasized 'devolution of powers', and 'decentralization' was the rhetorical focus the following year at Bafoussam, where not once in his keynote speech did John Fru Ndi use the word 'federalism' (Krieger 1994). The party, however, has given the green light to SDF members to freely belong to any Anglophone association and pressure group. It would nevertheless appear that the party is losing its initial appeal in Anglophone Cameroon, due to its half-hearted stand on the 'Anglophone problem'.

Following political liberalization in 1990, several associations and pressure groups were indeed created or expanded by the Anglophone elite to represent and defend Anglophone interests. Some of them, like the Free West Cameroon Movement (FWCM) and the Ambazonia Movement of Fon Gorji Dinka, advocated outright secession. Most, however, initially championed a return to the federal state, the major ones being the Cameroon Anglophone Movement (CAM) and the All Anglophone Congress (AAC). There are also Anglophone associations which are pro-federalist but with a more restricted agenda, relating in particular to the education question, such as the Teachers' Association of Cameroon (TAC), the Confederation of Anglophone Parents-Teachers' Association of Cameroon (CAPTAC), and the Cameroon Anglophone Students' Association (CANSA) (Nyamnjoh 1996).

These Anglophone associations and pressure groups have regularly organized demonstrations, strikes and boycots in their struggles against the Francophone-dominated unitary state. Participation by different strata of the Anglophone population in these actions demonstrates that the 'Anglophone problem' can no longer be perceived as simply and solely an elitist problem. Interestingly, the actions are directed in part against the discourses, myths, and symbols produced by the unitary state. Anglophone movements have boycotted the celebration of the national holiday on 20 May, the 'day of the 1972 glorious revolution', declaring it a 'day of mourning'. They have called upon Anglophones to celebrate their own holidays, namely the 'day of independence' on 1 October and the 'day of the plebiscite' on 11 February.

In addition, the Anglophone associations have begun referring to Anglophone Cameroon as the 'Southern Cameroons'. The reintroduction of this name serves at least two purposes. First, the associations allege that the union between Anglophone and Francophone Cameroon has proceeded without any constitutional base, because the proper procedures for the enactment and amendment of the federal constitution were not followed by Ahidjo.[5] In this perspective, Anglophone Cameroon still finds itself in the pre-reunification phase as the Trust Territory of the Southern Cameroons. Consequently, the United Nations should shoulder its political responsibility for this territory and condemn the 'annexation of the Southern Cameroons' by the Republic of Cameroon. The hoisting of the United Nations flag in Anglophone Cameroon in recent years is a symbol of the Anglophone belief in the continuing responsibility of the United Nations for the Southern Cameroons. A second purpose of the reintroduction of the name Southern Cameroons is to lay a historical and geographical foundation for Anglophone identity (Sindjoun 1996).

A major challenge to the Francophone-dominated unitary state occurred in 1993 when the Anglophone elite and their various organizations placed themselves under the canopy of one pressure group, the All Anglophone Conference (AAC). One week after the regime's announcement of a national debate on constitutional reform, on 2-3 April 1993, over 5,000 members of the Anglophone elite met at Buea, the ex-capital of the Southern Cameroons, at an 'All Anglophone Congress', 'for the purpose of adopting a common Anglophone stand on constitutional reform and of examining several other matters related to the welfare of Ourselves, our Posterity, our Territory and the entire Cameroon Nation'.[6] Three convenors of this conference, Messrs Sam Ekontang Elad, Simon Munzu, and Benjamin Itoe, were members of the South West elite; only one, Mr Carlson Anyangwe, was from the North West elite. Apparently, the North West elite had largely left the AAC leadership to the South West elite in order to foster unity among the Anglophone elite.

At the close of this historic meeting, the AAC issued the 'Buea Declaration' which laid down multiple Anglophone grievances about Francophone domination and called for a return to the federal state. It also called into being an Anglophone Standing Committee of 65 members. On 26 May 1993, this committee submitted a Federal Draft Constitution to the Technical Committee for Constitutional Reform. This Draft Constitution proposed a framework for far-reaching political, financial, and fiscal autonomy of the two federated states. It recommended a separation of powers between the executive, legislative, and judiciary. It proposed a Senate and a National Assembly at the federal level and a House of Chiefs and a House of Representatives for each of the federated states. One significant additional proposal was a rotating presidency of the Federal Republic: after at most two consecutive mandates of five years each, an Anglophone was to succeed a Francophone (or vice versa).

Confronted with the Biya government's persistent refusal to discuss the AAC constitutional proposals, the CAM, one of the most important organizations affiliated to the AAC, declared the 'zero option' on 3 December 1993 - total independence for the Southern Cameroons. The CAM's shift from federalism to secession was more or less

---

[5] See All Anglophone Conference (1993: 11-13). For a critique, see Olinga (1994)
[6] All Anglophone Congress (1993: 8)

confirmed during the Second All Anglophone Conference (AAC II), organized at Bamenda from 29 April to 2 May 1994. In its final document (referred to as the Bamenda Proclamation), the conference stated that if the government 'either persisted in its refusal to engage in meaningful constitutional tasks or failed to engage in such tasks within a reasonable time', the Anglophone Council should inform the Anglophone people and 'thereupon, proclaim the revival of the independence and sovereignty of the Anglophone territory of the Southern Cameroons, and take all measures necessary to secure, defend and preserve the independence, sovereignty and integrity of the said territory'. The Proclamation added that following such a declaration of independence, the Anglophone Council should 'without having to convene another session of the All Anglophone Conference, transform itself into the Southern Cameroon Constituent Assembly for the purpose of drafting, debating and adopting a constitution for the independent and sovereign state of the Southern Cameroons'. Delegates voted to replace the name AAC with the Southern Cameroons Peoples Conference (SCPC), and the newly created Anglophone Council was rechristened the Southern Cameroons National Council (SCNC).

Both the Anglophone Standing Committee and the SCNC have made strenuous efforts to sensitize the Anglophone community on their strategies to create a federal state or an independent Southern Cameroonian state, and to mobilize it for any planned action. They have also engaged in a diplomatic offensive to gain international support for the Anglophone cause. They have particularly focused on the United Nations and the Commonwealth (Konings 1996c).

The SCNC intends to declare the independence of the Southern Cameroons in the near future. The SCNC is hopeful that its diplomatic offensive will at least raise international awareness to the point where military intervention by the Biya regime upon declaration of independence will be difficult. Nevertheless, the SCNC does not rule out the possibility of a 'long-drawn war', and is therefore considering the creation of a 'defensive force' in the Southern Cameroons.

Chieftaincy and Anglophone Struggles for Autonomy

In any discussion of the role of chieftaincy in the current Anglophone struggles for self-determination and autonomy, one has to keep in mind the large contribution of Anglophone chiefs towards the achievement of reunification and federalism in 1961 (Johnson 1970; Nkwi & Warnier 1982; Fogui 1990). Of particular importance was the contribution of North Western chiefs.

Towards the end of the 1950s, 57 per cent of the population of the then Southern Cameroons was made up of North Westerners. The North Western population was largely controlled by powerful, or even sacred, chiefs (or *Fons* as they are called throughout the North West), whose authority was highly respected by their subjects, including the newly created elite. The position of chiefs in the highly centralized states of the North West contrasted sharply in this respect with that of their colleagues in the segmentary societies of the South West. In the latter region chieftaincy was a weak institution in most cases, often a colonial creation (Geschiere 1993; Fisiy 1992 and 1995). The high population density and firm support for chieftaincy in the North West could be crucial in the event of elections.

The general elections of 1959 were generally regarded beforehand as decisive for the political future of the Southern Cameroons. Two major parties were contesting these elections, and they were engaged in a relentless struggle for hegemony. One of them was the ruling party, the South West-based Kamerun National Convention (KNC), led by the serving Prime Minister, Dr Emmanuel Endeley. The other was the largest opposition party, the North West-based Kamerun National Democratic Party (KNDP) under Mr John Ngu Foncha. Broadly speaking, Endeley's party championed the cause of integration with Nigeria, with the tacit approval of the British authorities, while Foncha's party crusaded for secession from Nigeria and (eventual) reunification with Francophone Cameroon (Chem-Langhëë 1995). It was generally understood that the victor in the 1959 elections would proceed to negotiate the terms of union with either Nigeria or Francophone Cameroon.

A brief description of the personalities of the two leaders and their respective attitudes towards chieftaincy may throw some light on the outcome of the elections. The articulate physician, Emmanuel Endeley, boasted constantly of being the most highly educated citizen in the Southern Cameroons. He regarded his political contemporaries as mere intellectual minions, and the villagers as outright natives. He spoke a sophisticated English and even in the heat of the election campaign he refused to speak to the North Western chiefs in the language they understood (pidgin) with the excuse 'I am sorry about speaking my "big" English...but I cannot speak any other way'. Though a Bakweri prince (some even said the heir-apparent) of the Buea Endeley dynasty, he made many mistakes in dealing with the symbols and spokesmen of 'tradition' in the territory. He would offend the fons by shaking their hands, sitting at their side on stools reserved for their fellow fons, or by addressing them by the wrong title or at the wrong times. He is reported to have treated one of the most important North Western chiefs, Fon Galega I of Bali, with levity. One version holds that on a trip to London, after alighting from the plane, he peremptorily asked the fon to carry his bag! The fon never forgot or forgave him thereafter. Endeley's attitude towards chieftaincy was nevertheless complicated. He was by no means unaware of the chiefs' prestige, since he was himself the son of the most important Bakweri chief. But he was also a modernist, a highly educated person living in an era when power was obviously shifting from the traditional to the modern elite. He acknowledged he could not do without the chiefs' support completely. He was therefore not opposed to their repeated demands for a House of Chiefs.

His opponent, the North Westerner John Ngu Foncha, was an uncomplicated, devout Catholic headmaster who perhaps felt more secure speaking pidgin English or indigenous languages than standard English. Foncha was basically a grassroots politician who would walk all day to reach a remote village of voters. He presented himself as an African who was proud of wearing a sumptuous traditional boubou rather than a suit and tie, and preferred eating African food to European food. A story has it that on one visit to London, Foncha carted along *achu* (a Grassfields delicacy), which he publicly munched to show his attachment to things African. Above all, Foncha displayed great respect for 'tradition' and for those who were the symbols of tradition. His attitude to them was scrupulously deferential if not reverent. This attitude, needless to say, endeared him to the fons.

During the election campaign Foncha and other KNDP leaders such as Augustine Ngom Jua and Solomon Tandeng Muna spent considerable time lobbying influential chiefs and chiefs' conferences. Their main strategy was to portray the KNDP as a party that upheld traditional norms and symbols and the KNC as inimical to tradition and traditional rulers. They also alleged that the KNC's championing of unification with Nigeria would leave the position of the Ibo in the Southern Cameroons intact - the Ibo would not only continue to dominate the regional economy but would go on exhibiting disrespect for traditional norms and authority in the Southern Cameroons. They stressed that the KNDP was a predominantly North Western party which was more likely than the South West-based KNC to defend the interests of the North Western population in general and the North Western chiefs in particular. Thus while Endeley and the KNC relied to a large extent on newspapers for the 1959 elections, the KNDP attempted to court chieftaincy, placing more confidence in the voice of the traditional rulers.

The KNDP leaders succeeded in winning over the powerful chief of Bali, the most educated among the North Western chiefs who used to be a strong KNC supporter. This chief had been excluded by Endeley from the Southern Cameroonian delegation to the constitutional conference at London in 1957 because of personal animosities (see above). He was to become the principal mobilizer of North Western and even South Western chiefs against Endeley. On 27 August 1957, he reported to the Southern Cameroons Chiefs' Conference at Kumba that he had been replaced by a non-traditional leader - clear proof of Endeley's lack of respect for traditional authorities. During the conference of North Western chiefs at Bamenda in January 1958, it was evident that the mobilizing efforts of the chief of Bali and the persistent lobby of KNDP leaders had been effective: most KNC chiefs dissociated themselves from the KNC, expressing disappointment with Endeley's continual disrespect for traditional authority and rejecting his call for political integration with Nigeria. The KNDP leadership then incited North Western chiefs to militant action. These chiefs then ordered their subjects to impede Dr Endeley from campaigning in the North West. During a conference of North Western chiefs at Bamenda on 3 May 1958 it was even decided that any chief who failed to prevent a victory of Endeley's party in his area of jurisdiction would not be eligible for a seat in a future House of Chiefs (Nkwi 1979; Nkwi & Warnier 1982).

The alliance between the KNDP and North Western chiefs was soon supported by a growing number of South Western chiefs, including some in the Bakweri area, the home region of Dr Endeley. There were several reasons for this support. Bakweri and other South Western chiefs were afraid Endeley would limit the role of chieftaincy in the administration of the future independent state. Moreover, as early as 1948 Bakweri chiefs had been calling for the eviction of the Ibo, and they therefore strongly resented Dr Endeley's pleas for integration of the Southern Cameroons into Nigeria.[7] In addition, Dr Endeley and his younger brother Sam Endeley had been constantly meddling in Bakweri chieftaincy affairs. Both were insisting that the serving Bakweri Paramount Chief of Buea, their uncle, had been installed only as a regent after the death of their father in 1925, and that the chieftaincy should thus be theirs (Geschiere, 1993). Many Bakweri chiefs, including Chief G.M. Endeley, joined the KNDP. In reply, Dr Endeley attempted to depose them and replace them by his own men, but he failed.

He then sought to recapture the chiefs' support by entreating the administration to establish the proposed House of Chiefs ahead of schedule and before the elections, so he could take credit for the innovation. This ultimately made matters worse, because Foncha, distrusting the motives for this move, claimed that Endeley intended to interfere with the chiefs' affairs by putting his own stooges into the House, or that he would use the promise of a position in it to bring pressure to bear on the chiefs. At the instigation of Foncha, the Fon of Bali assembled most of the Southern Cameroonian chiefs at Kumba, where they firmly rejected the idea of inaugurating the House of Chiefs before the elections. As the Fon of Bali stepped up his campaign to mobilize chiefs against the KNC, Endeley shifted his position on the role of chieftaincy in politics. In May 1958 he stated that

> We shall also expect that in their own interest chiefs and traditional rulers must keep clear of party politics... Any chief who persists, despite this timely advice, to participate in party politics does so at his own risk (quoted in Johnson 1970: 164).

Endeley's loss of support from the chiefs, particularly in the North West, was evidenced by the KNDP's victory in the 1959 general elections. It won 14 of the 26 seats. In the 1957 elections, the then newly created KNDP had won only 5 of the 13 seats. The alliance between the KNDP and chieftaincy also proved decisive in the 1961 United Nations plebiscite, when the majority of the Southern Cameroonian population voted for reunification with Francophone Cameroon. The influence of (North Western) chieftaincy on domestic politics was clearly recognized by Endeley's principal coalition partner, Mr N.N. Mbile, leader of the South West-based Kamerun People's Party (KPP). Mbile's

---

[7] See BNA, file Pc/h/1948/1, which deals with the anti-Ibo sentiments of the 1940s and 1950s

testimony to the United Nations Fourth Committee in 1959 on the mechanisms for deciding the political future of the Southern Cameroons is instructive on the shift in locus of political power away from the coastal areas and the role of chiefly authority:

> Much of the present struggle was really between the grassland tribes in Bamenda and the people of the southern coastal forest belt. His own opinion was that even a plebiscite would not serve to make clear what the real wishes of the people were, for they were still loyal to their tribal leadership, especially in the Bamenda Grassfields, and might well vote against that own interest if such was the wish of their chiefs.[8]

The KNDP was grateful for the massive support of the chiefs. One of the KNDP government's first measures was to set up the long proposed Southern Cameroons House of Chiefs (Chem-Langhëë, 1983). It met for the first time on 5 September 1960. Its members were divided into two categories: 4 ex-officio members and 18 elected members. Ex-officio members were the four most important North Western fons: the paramount rulers of Kom, Bafut, Bali, and Nso. The powers of the House of Chiefs were very limited, however. It was to give advice and to assist the government in exercising its legislative authority. As a legislative body it could not initiate bills, but it could postpone or prevent the adoption of a bill. It was presided over first by the British High Commissioner and, after independence and reunification, by one of the 'modern' political rulers.

Interestingly, while few elements of Anglophone cultural heritage were eventually incorporated into the federal constitution, the Anglophone delegation at the 1961 Foumban Conference, under the leadership of John Ngu Foncha, did succeed in safeguarding the continued existence of the House of Chiefs in the Federated State of West Cameroon. Initially, the leader of the Francophone delegation, Ahmadou Ahidjo, was not in favour of creating an 'autonomous' power base for chieftaincy in Anglophone Cameroon, especially because no House of Chiefs existed in Francophone Cameroon. He finally agreed, in recognition of the key role that chieftaincy in Anglophone Cameroon had played in reunification. A potentially dangerous disequilibrium was thus created between the two federated states, which could in the long run frustrate the chiefs in the Federated State of East Cameroon.

Little wonder that Ahidjo's 'hegemonic project' (Bayart 1979) entailed the abolition of this inequality and the subordination of chieftaincy throughout the national territory to the same statute. Ahidjo, however, was well aware that he had to manoeuvre carefully in view of his own fragile power base during the early years of federalism and the continuing powerful position of certain Anglophone chiefs, notably North Western ones. It was only with the gradual co-optation of the Francophone and Anglophone elite into the Francophone-dominated state and the subsequent promulgation of the unitary state in

---

[8]   UNGA A/C.4. SR 885 of 24 September 1959

1972 that Ahidjo dared to abolish the West Cameroon House of Chiefs. It took still another five years before he subjected chieftaincy in the United Republic of Cameroon to uniform statutory provisions. Decree number 77/245 of 15 July 1977 reinforced the process of integrating chieftaincy into the state apparatus. This decree was justified by the political elite in terms of the necessary modernization of traditional structures, but a close reading of the decree reveals its true objective: the bureaucratization of chieftaincy, the turning of chiefs into mere auxiliaries of the administration so as to take advantage of their control over the local population and local resources. This is clearly illustrated by Article 19:

> Under the authority of the Minister of Territorial Administration the traditional chiefs are responsible for assisting the administrative authorities in their mission of capturing ('encadrement') of the local population.

As auxiliaries of the administration, chiefs were to receive a monthly salary. Suspension of payment is one of the sanctions stipulated in the decree to make chiefs comply with the directives of the administration. In addition, sinecures or appointments to prebends were sometimes provided in exchange for anticipated co-operation. Such cases include the appointments of the Fons of Bafut and Bali as members of the Management Board of the North West Development Authority (MIDENO).

The bureaucratization of chieftaincy is one factor that tends to draw chieftaincy closer to the state. Another such factor, as Geschiere (1993) rightly observes, is that the distinction between chiefs and the modern state elite has become increasingly blurred. It is no longer unusual for chiefs in Anglophone Cameroon to have an academic degree or be involved in modern business enterprises. Moreover, some chiefs had been given access to high positions in the state apparatus either before or after their enthronement. Nevertheless, the relationship between chieftaincy and state has remained complex. When chiefs perceive that a net gain can be derived, they readily enter into an alliance with the state elite. On the other hand, when they stand to lose, they are inclined either to adopt confrontational tactics or to devise new strategies to maintain political control. Fisiy (1992; 1995) has demonstrated how North Western chiefs have been able to manipulate the 1974 Land Ordinances to their advantage.

This already complex relationship has been further complicated by the political liberalization process and the concomitant polarization of the local population starting in 1990 (Konings 1996a). With emerging political pluralism, chiefs were suddenly confronted with the competing demands of different political parties. Previously, in the one-party state, they had usually identified with the ruling CPDM. When the Anglophone region, and in particular the North West Province, emerged as the hotbed of opposition, chiefs were often pressured to sever their links with the ruling party. As a result, chieftaincy has become divided into pro- and anti-government, as well as 'neutral', factions.

Not surprisingly, the pro-government faction has been privileged by the regime. In the days of the one-party state, Biya had passed a law that prohibited chiefs from participating in national politics. However, following the introduction of political pluralism, he changed his position. Some influential chiefs have been elevated to high positions in the CPDM party. For example, Fon Angwafor III of Mankon in the North West Province was appointed First Vice-President of the CPDM in 1990, replacing John Ngu Foncha. The latter had resigned from the party because of the marginalization of the Anglophone region by the Francophone-dominated state and the brutal repression of North Western opposition by the Biya regime. Underlying Biya's strategy was the belief that the successfully wooing of chiefs would produce a trickle-down effect. In other words, the local population would readily vote for his CPDM, if so instructed by the chief. Unfortunately for the powers that be, circumstances have changed with the emergence of 'modern' values, institutions and authority patterns. There is a new generation of subjects who no longer profess blind allegiance to traditional authority. The 1992 parliamentary and presidential elections provide evidence for this change. Although Biya still relied on the pledge of some North Western chiefs that their subjects would vote en masse for him and his party, they voted overwhelmingly for the opposition and its candidate, John Fru Ndi of the SDF. Where pro-government chiefs resorted to fraud to ensure victory for the CPDM and Biya in their area of jurisdiction, violent confrontations ensued between them and their subjects, sometimes resulting in the destruction of royal property. Fon Galabe Doh Gah Gwanyin of Bali-Kumbat in the North West Province was (temporarily) divested of authority and his palace stormed for his purported rigging of the 1992 parliamentary elections in favour of Biya's CPDM. Fon Angwafor III of Mankon, who was believed to have engaged in a similar practice at the 1992 presidential elections, had his official resthouse burnt by an unidentified group of furious subjects.

One can also observe this division of chieftaincy into pro- and anti-government factions in the current Anglophone struggles for self-determination and autonomy. While both groups acknowledge the 'marginalization, exploitation, and assimilation' of the Anglophone region by the Francophone-dominated state, pro-government chiefs agree with the Biya regime that a solution to this problem is not to be sought in the two-state option (the return to the federal state) but rather in the ten-state option - the granting of a large measure of autonomy to the ten existing provinces within the unitary state. Opposition of chieftaincy to the increasingly militant Anglophone associations and pressure groups appears stronger and more widespread in the South West Province than in the North West Province. South Western CPDM chiefs are inclined to look upon these Anglophone movements as 'organs' of the North West-based SDF, and are afraid that a return to the federal state or outright secession will lead to a renewed domination of the North West over the South West.

One of the leading CPDM chiefs in the South West Province is Chief Sam Endeley, Bakweri Paramount Chief of Buea. He is the younger brother of Dr Emmanuel Endeley, the former nationalist leader who died in June 1988. He is a retired Chief Justice and ex-president of the Fako Section of the CPDM. His wife has been the president of the Fako Section of the CPDM Women. He has been the only Anglophone in a nine-member commission, the so-called Endeley Commission, appointed by the Biya regime in 1991 to investigate the brutalities of the security forces against Bamilike and Anglophone student activists at the University of Yaoundé in that year. The findings of the commission, which have been summarized as 'no rape, no death, and no disappearances', were at complete variance with the available evidence, but suited the Biya regime splendidly (Mbu 1993). In return for his loyal services, the regime approved, shortly after the report's publication, Endeley's installation as Bakweri Paramount Chief of Buea, a seat vacant since 1982 (Geschiere 1993).

Chief Endeley and other important South Western CPDM chiefs, such as Nfon Victor Mukete of Kumba, hold leading positions not only in the South West Chiefs' Conference but also in the South West Elites' Association (SWELA). SWELA was founded in 1991, uniting all the existing elite organizations in the South West into one single body. Its leadership continually claimed it was a non-political pressure group whose main objective was to promote the socioeconomic development and cultural revival of the South West Province. The South West was to be restored to its 'former glory', after having been marginalized by the Francophone-dominated state and subjected to 'Grassfield imperialism'. Clearly, fear of renewed North West domination over the South West was one of the underlying motives for the association's foundation. SWELA, in fact, came into existence after the launching of the SDF and the latter's subsequent expansion into the South West. On several occasions, SWELA leaders, especially those closely allied with the ruling regime, issued public statements blaming the SDF for acts of violence and anti-government activities in the South West.

A major split occurred in SWELA in 1993, dividing it into two camps:

- One group which continued to maintain close links with the Biya regime and the ruling CPDM party, and which often displays strong anti-North West sentiments. This is why many people continue to see SWELA as a CPDM appendage and a resurrection of VIKUMA - the Victoria, Kumba, Mamfe alliance propagated in the mid-1960s by Walter Wilson Mbong to destroy 'Graffi' domination over the South West (Johnson 1970). The group is composed of older and younger CPDM barons, like Emmanuel Tabi Egbe, Peter Agbor Tabi, Joseph Takem, as well as the most important South Western chiefs. It opposes the return to the federal state advocated by Anglophone pressure groups. Like the CPDM government, it champions the ten-state option, which would retain the present separation between the South West and North West Provinces and thus safeguard South West autonomy.

- Another group which is more critical of government policies and is often allied to opposition parties, including the SDF. This group vehemently condemned the military 'occupation' of the South West during the 1993 anti-smuggling campaign. It advocates closer cooperation between the South West and North West as a necessary precondition for effective representation of Anglophone and South West interests. It strongly supports the Anglophone demand for a return to the federal state. Some South Western chiefs, like the militant Chief Joseph Agbor Tabi of Mamfe, are members of this group.

A large delegation of the Anglophone chiefs participated in the All Anglophone Conference (AAC) held at Buea from 2-3 April 1993, and eleven of them were nominated to represent chieftaincy in the 65-member Anglophone Standing Committee created by the AAC. The Federal Draft Constitution which was eventually drawn up by this committee included a section on chieftaincy. Its provisions aimed at restoring the relatively autonomous position that chieftaincy had enjoyed in the era of federalism, and it proposed the re-introduction of a House of Chiefs. Significantly, one provision prohibited chiefs from actively participating in party politics.[9]

One week later the South West Chiefs' Conference met at Mamfe. During this meeting some CPDM chiefs tried to dissociate the South West Province from the AAC and the Buea Declaration. They failed, because most participants were opposed to this move. Fon Angwafor III of Mankon, the First Vice-President of the CPDM, tried to convene a meeting of the North West Fons' Conference on 17 May 1993 to dissociate the North West from the AAC and the Buea Declaration. He proposed that Mr Achidi Achu, the then Prime Minister hailing from the North West, should be invited to address the conference. His proposal was opposed by most North Western chiefs who tended to be firm supporters of the SDF and the Anglophone struggles. At first they insisted that Mr Achidi Achu could not be invited since he was not a traditional ruler. Later they declared that they would only accede to Mr Achidi Achu's presence if the chairman of the SDF, Mr John Fru Ndi, were also invited. This was a bitter pill to swallow for Fon Angwafor and the meeting was called off at the last minute.[10]

On 23 September 1993, nine CPDM chiefs from the South West led by Chief Endeley undertook a mission to the Unity Palace at Yaoundé to pledge their unalloyed allegiance to President Biya. They told him that 'they were alarmed at the numerous demonstrations, blackmail, civil disobedience, rebellious attitudes and recurrent activities designed to destabilize the state and the government'. In what the chiefs referred to as massive incitement to rebellion and secession, they drew the president's attention to the consequences of compromising the peace and unity of Cameroon. They vehemently condemned any attempts at partitioning Cameroon on the basis of Anglophone and Francophone cultures, and they assured the president that they 'were prepared to use all orthodox and unorthodox methods to ensure calm and quiet in their

---

[9] Le Comité Permanent de la 'All Anglophone Conference', 'Avant-Projet de Constitution de la République Féderale du Cameroun', July 1993, pp. 114-115
[10] *The Herald,* 20-27 October 1993, p. 5; *Cameroon Post,* 27 October-3 November 1993, p. 10

province'. They asked the President to transform the present ten provinces into ten or more autonomous provinces, stressing that

> the Governor, Legislative Assembly and Local Governments must be elected by the indigenes of the Province, so as to get rid of those who want to consolidate their grip on, and dominate, the South West people in perpetuity. Such a profound constitutional change is capable of defusing all the present threats and thereby secure and consolidate you in your office as president and also save us from any form of domination.

At the end of the meeting, they pointed out that the South West Province had been discriminated against after reunification in the distribution of 'strategic posts'. All the top positions reserved for Anglophones in the Federal as well as Unitary State reserved had continued to be occupied by North Westerners. On their return, these 'self-seeking' chiefs were strongly attacked by the Anglophone movements for 'selling their people into slavery in exchange for the contents of khaki envelopes'.[11]

One week later, on 29 September 1993, a North West delegation likewise travelled to Yaoundé to pay homage to President Biya. Its mission took place after the President of the Mezam Section of the CPDM had campaigned throughout the North West Province for a motion of support for President Biya that would outstrip that of the South West chiefs. His campaign met with little response. The four major fons (the paramount chiefs of Kom, Bafut, Bali, and Nso) and most other traditional rulers simply refused to join the North West delegation.[12]

On 1 October 1993, the Anglophone movements commemorated the independence of the Southern Cameroons which was achieved on 1 October 1961. On that day there were attempts by CAM activists to hoist the federation flag. The governors and certain CPDM leaders and chiefs in Anglophone Cameroon perceived this as a 'plot' by the Anglophone movements to declare secession and independence, and they called on government troops to suppress the subversive activities.[13]

Strikingly, when the government announced the privatization of the Cameroon Development Corporation (CDC) on 15 July 1994, a temporary alliance developed between the Anglophone movements and the Bakweri CPDM chiefs. The CDC is one of the oldest and by far the largest agro-industrial parastatal in the country. Its estates are located mainly on the fertile, volcanic soils around Mount Cameroon in the coastal area of Anglophone Cameroon. Most of its estate lands are Bakweri lands. These lands were expropriated during the German colonial period for plantation production and were leased by the British Trusteeship Authority to the CDC at its foundation in 1946/47 for a

---

[11] *The Herald*, 3-10 November 1993, p. 6
[12] *The Herald*, 13-20 October 1993, p. 1
[13] *Cameroon Post*, 27 October-3 November 1993, p. 10

period of sixty years (Konings 1993; 1995b). Anglophones perceived the privatization of the CDC as a further step in the emasculation of the Anglophone cultural and economic heritage by the Francophone-dominated state, claiming that it was 'an ill-disguised plot to hand over the corporation to the French and Francophones' or 'a plan of Biya to compensate his "tribesmen" and allies with a slice of the parastatal cake'. There were protest marches in the Anglophone towns, organized by the SDF and Anglophone pressure groups. On 30-31 July 1994, the CAM National Executive met, condemning the privatization of the CDC as a declaration of war against the people of Southern Cameroons and calling upon Anglophones to observe the 16th of August 1994 as a day of protest and solidarity with the CDC. In that month, the Biya government sent a delegation composed of high-ranking Anglophone allies to the capitals of the two Anglophone provinces to try to appease the population. They were jeered and asked whether they would 'benefit of the spoils'.

Being the owners of the CDC lands, the Bakweri felt particularly aggrieved by the announced privatization of the CDC. On 23 July 1994, the Bakweri chiefs and elite met at Buea, under the chairmanship of Paramount Chief Sam Endeley of Buea and Paramount Chief F. Bille Manga Williams of Victoria to discuss the implications of the government decision. The meeting strongly opposed the announced privatization, on the grounds that the CDC lands were Bakweri lands and thus could not be sold to non-natives without Bakweri consent. After some lengthy and passionate discussions, an Ad Hoc Committee was elected by acclamation to prepare a detailed memorandum on the Bakweri position, which was to be presented to the government and all other interested parties.

On 4 August 1994, over 500 Bakweri chiefs and elite, assembled at the Buea Youth Cultural and Animation Centre, approved the memorandum drawn up by the Ad Hoc Committee and later presented it to the Provincial Governor for onward transmission to President Biya. On the same day, Professor Ndiva Kofele-Kale, the eminent Bakweri scholar who had acted as the secretary of the Ad Hoc Committee, was designated Counsel for the Bakweri people with instructions to present their case to the United Nations and other international fora.

The Bakweri case was firmly supported by the Anglophone movements. In a strongly worded petition to the Head of State, co-signed by the Anglophone pressure groups and the Bakweri chiefs, it was reiterated that the Bakweri had never relinquished ownership of the CDC lands and that the corporation could not be sold without Bakweri consent. It was also pointed out that the Bakweri had never been paid for the use of their lands since the CDC's foundation in 1946/47.

Concerned about the mounting anger within the Bakweri community, the Biya government sent the above-mentioned delegation of Anglophone allies to Buea to discuss the issue with the traditional and modern Bakweri elite. It was led by Chief

Ephraim Inoni, the then Deputy Secretary General at the Presidency and chief of Bakingili, a village located in the territory of a Bakweri sub-group. Though speaking on behalf of the government, Chief Inoni appealed to the Bakweri representatives not to forget he was one of them. He acknowledged that there should have been prior contact between the government and the Bakweri before the corporation's privatization was announced. He denied the widespread rumours in Anglophone Cameroon that the French and some high-ranking Francophones had masterminded the whole operation. The Bakweri Paramount Chief of Buea, Sam Endeley, then took the floor. Under thunderous applause, he declared that the Bakweri were against privatization of the CDC and requested Chief Inoni to report this to President Biya:

> We are in a country where we like to cheat ourselves, where Government hands down decisions through dictatorship... We say no, no [to privatization], go and tell Mr Biya that he cannot afford to go down in history as the man who sold the CDC.

After the delegation had returned to Yaoundé, the government took no further action on the CDC's privatization (Konings 1995a; 1996c).

The alliance was short-lived. Following the 1994 Bamenda Proclamation and the determined efforts of the newly created Southern Cameroons National Council (SCNC) to mobilize the Anglophone community and to gain international support for an independent Southern Cameroonian state, the government continued to use the CPDM leaders and chiefs in Anglophone Cameroon for the defence of the unitary state, giving them adequate reward for their services. These allies began blaming the leaders of the Anglophone movements for their 'demagogic and irresponsible' calls for secession, and disputing their claims to be spokesmen for the Anglophone community. Another government tactic was to create splits within the South West and North West Chiefs' Conferences. Breakaway factions of CPDM chiefs were then presented as the only and 'true' representatives of chieftaincy. This led to a number of severe confrontations between the CPDM breakaway factions on the one side and the authentic North West and South West Chiefs' Conferences and Anglophone movements on the other.

The tactics became particularly visible in July 1995, when a SCNC delegation returned from an apparently successful mission to the United Nations. Frightened by the momentum the SCNC delegation was gathering throughout the region, the Governor of the South West Province hurriedly organized an extraordinary session of the South West Chiefs' Conference on 8 July 1995. The chiefs were supposed to come out with a resolution denouncing the SCNC leaders. This did not happen. The chiefs remained divided on the issue, and only a few CPDM chiefs issued a statement on the eve of the extraordinary session condemning 'this group of irresponsible leaders who preach war, division, secession and disorder', and reaffirming 'the South West commitment to the ten-state option within a sovereign Cameroon state'.[14]

Events took a more dramatic turn in the North West Province. On 11 July 1995, security forces brutally attacked a crowd of unarmed civilians at Bamenda which had assembled at a school compound to welcome the SCNC delegation. On the same day, the Prime Minister, Mr Achidi Achu, and CPDM leaders and fons held a meeting in the Bamenda Congress Hall, in which they appealed to the President of the Republic 'to defend territorial integrity with all the available means'. After this meeting, the angry Bamenda population booed, jeered and stoned the participants.

The Prime Minister, Mr Achidi Achu, had previously sponsored the formation of a small breakaway faction of the North West Chiefs' Conference. Purportedly this action was motivated by the fact that the North West Chiefs' Conference had shown itself too independent on crucial issues such as the Anglophone clamour for separation from the Republic of Cameroon. At its inaugural meeting, the Governor of the North West Province reportedly urged the CPDM faction not to go along with the SCNC's call for an independent Southern Cameroonian state, for 'Cameroon is one and indivisible'.[15] The government-controlled Radio Bamenda refused to broadcast announcements emanating from the Steering Committee of the North West Fons' Conference advising North Western chiefs 'to distance themselves from the pro-CPDM faction led by Fon Galabe Doh Gah Gwanyin of Bali-Kumbat aimed at destabilizing the General Assembly'.[16] Whereas the leader of the CPDM faction, Fon Galabe Doh Gah Gwanyin, used his affiliation to the regime as a licence to launch a war of expansion against the Bafanji people (Jua, 1995), there is ample evidence that he and other members of the CPDM faction were increasingly isolated by their colleagues, who identified with the Anglophone struggles for self-determination. The Fon of Bali, Secretary-General of the Steering Committee of the North West Fons' Conference, has repeatedly repudiated the Prime Minister, Mr Achidi Achu, for what he calls his unstatesmanlike conduct, even to the point of calling him a 'traitor'.[17]

Due to its failure to recruit the majority of the Anglophone chiefs into its camp, the regime has been compelled to resort to intensified repression. Leaders of the Anglophone movements are regularly harassed by security forces, threatened with arrest and subjected to travelling restrictions. Rallies and demonstrations by Anglophone movements are officially banned in the Anglophone provinces. Despite the intimidating presence of a large number of security forces, however, Anglophone actions continue. During the 1995 sensitization tour of SCNC leaders to the urban centres in Anglophone

---

[14] *Cameroon Tribune*, 11 July 1995, p. 1; *The Herald*, 20 July 1995, p. 6
[15] *The Herald*, 14 August 1995, p. 5
[16] *The Herald*, 9 October 1995, p. 2
[17] *The Herald*, 21-24 September 1995, p. 1

Cameroon, the military could not prevent them from entering the towns and addressing the crowds.

Conclusion

This study has attempted to show that chieftaincy in Anglophone Cameroon has played a significant role in the Anglophone struggles for the political future of the Southern Cameroons, both in the late 1950s and in the current campaign for self-determination and autonomy.

In the 1950s struggles, Anglophone chiefs tended to align with Foncha's KNDP and to support its option for reunification, for two main reasons. First, the KNDP appeared to best safeguard the position of chieftaincy after independence and reunification. Second, the option of Endeley's KNC for unification with Nigeria would imply the continuing domination of the Ibo over Southern Cameroonian society and economy. It appears, however, that chiefs in the North West were more likely to serve as vote banks for the KNDP than those in the South West. North Western chieftaincy was at that time still a powerful, even 'sacred' institution and could as such still exercise a large measure of control over the local population's voting behaviour. The controlling power of North Western chiefs was facilitated by the fact that the North West-based KNDP was seen to be more inclined to represent and defend North Western interests than the South West-based KNC. Unlike that in the North West, South Western chieftaincy was generally weak and thus experienced difficulties in controlling the local population, especially because 'traditional' institutions and value systems had been extensively undermined by the introduction of a plantation economy in the coastal areas during German colonial rule (1884-1914) (Konings 1995c). Bakweri chiefs who owed allegiance to the KNDP even came into conflict with a large group of subjects who supported the KNC, the party with strong roots in Bakweri society. These chiefs were often branded as 'KNDP traitors' and fiercely attacked - with arson or murder threats - by their subjects (Geschiere 1993). Such violent resistance was fuelled by the fact that the Bakweri and other South Western elite feared that a KNDP victory would effect a transfer of power from the South West to the North West.

While chieftaincy in Anglophone Cameroon still enjoyed a considerable measure of autonomy in the era of federalism, the unitary state attempted to subordinate chieftaincy to the state and to use it as an instrument of control over civil society. As a result, chieftaincy now experiences great trouble in balancing the demands of the state and civil society. This problem has been enhanced by the increasing politicization of chieftaincy in the wake of government's introduction of limited political liberalization and the emergence of the 'Anglophone problem'.

The role of Anglophone chiefs in the present-day Anglophone struggles for self-determination and autonomy provides additional evidence that the postcolonial state's efforts to co-opt chieftaincy into the state apparatus have never been fully successful (cf. van Rouveroy van Nieuwaal 1987; 1995). The majority of the Anglophone chiefs, in particular North Western chiefs, have identified with the widespread grievances among the Anglophone population about the 'marginalization, exploitation, and assimilation' of its region by the Francophone-dominated state. They have supported the Anglophone movements in their struggles for a return to the federal state or for secession. Only a few Anglophone chiefs, in particular some important South Western chiefs closely allied with the regime in power, have conceded to the persistent requests of the government and the CPDM party to defend the unitary state, either for private gains or for fear of renewed North West domination over the South West after a return to the federal state or secession. However, the events after the government announcement of the CDC privatization show that the Bakweri CPDM chiefs began opposing the government as soon as they perceived that the interests of their ethnic group were being threatened. They have even entered into a (temporary) alliance with the Anglophone movements.

It is noteworthy that Francophone chiefs have never played any significant role in the coming into being of the Federal State, nor in the current Anglophone struggles for a return to federalism or outright secession. Generally speaking, they have enjoyed less autonomy vis-à-vis the state than have Anglophone chiefs (Fogui 1990). Neither have they ever had a House of Chiefs nor have they succeeded to organize in chiefs' conferences. French colonial rule tended to transform them more or less into auxiliaries and administrative subordinates. Decree number 77/245 of 15 July 1977, which coopted chieftaincy throughout the national territory into the lower ranks of the administration, was thus in line with French colonial practice. Some Francophone chiefs have served as vote banks for the ruling CPDM party during the political liberalization process, resulting in severe confrontations with their subordinates in areas dominated by opposition parties, as well as in a further demystification of their sacred position in the strongly hierarchized Bamilike, Bamoun and Fulbe societies (Miaffo 1993; Mouiche 1995a and b). Although there are certain ethnic links between the Anglophone provinces and neighbouring Francophone provinces (Geschiere, 1993; Fisyi, 1995), this has never led to any permanent alliances between Anglophone and Francophone chiefs in defence of their mutual interests against the state, especially with regard to control over land.

References

ALL ANGLOPHONE CONGRESS
1993   *The Buea Declaration, 2-3 April 1993*. Limbe: Nooremac Press

BAYART, Jean-François
1979   *L'Etat au Cameroun*. Paris: Presses de la Fondation Nationale des Sciences Politiques

BENJAMIN, Jacques
1972   *Les Camerounais occidentaux: La minorité dans un état bicommunautaire.* Montréal: Les Presses de l'Université de Montréal

CHEM-LANGHEË, Bonfen
1983   The Origin of the Southern Cameroons House of Chiefs. Pp. 653-673. In: *International Journal of African Historical Studies,* 16, 4

CHEM-LANGHEË, Bonfen
1995   The Road to the Unitary State of Cameroon 1959-1972. Pp. 17-25. In: *Paideuma,* 41

CHIABI, Emmanuel M.L.
1982   Background to Nationalism in Anglophone Cameroon, 1916-54. PhD. Thesis: University of California

FISIY, Cyprian F.
1992   *Power and Privilege in the Administration of Law: Land Law Reforms and Social Differentiation in Cameroon.* Leiden: African Studies Centre. Research Report no. 48

1995   Chieftaincy in the Modern State: An Institution at the Crossroads of Democratic Change. Pp. 49-61. In: *Paideuma,* 41

FOGUI, Jean-Pierre
1990   *L'Intégration Politique au Cameroun.* Paris: Librairie Générale de Droit et de Jurisprudence

GESCHIERE, Peter L.
1993   Chiefs and Colonial Rule in Cameroon: Inventing Chieftaincy, French and British Style. Pp. 151-175. In: *Africa,* 63, 2

JOHNSON, William R.
1970   *The Cameroon Federation: Political Integration in a Fragmentary Society.* Princeton: Princeton University Press

JUA, Nantang B.
1995   Indirect Rule in Colonial and Post-Colonial Cameroon. Pp. 39-47. In: Paideuma, 41

KOFELE-KALE, Ndiva
1981   *Tribesmen and Patriots: Political Culture in a Poly-ethnic African State.* Washington, D.C.: University Press of America

KONINGS, Piet
1993   *Labour Resistance in Cameroon.* London: James Currey

1995a   Agro-Industry and Regionalism in the South West Province of Cameroon during the National Economic and Political Crisis. *Paper* presented at the conference on "Regional Balance and National Integration in Cameroon: Lessons learnt and the future" held at Yaoundé on 16-18 October 1995 (in press)

1995b   Plantation Labour and Economic Crisis in Cameroon. Pp. 525-549. In: *Development and Change*, 26, 3

1995c   Chieftaincy, Labour Control and Capitalist Development in Cameroon. Pp. 261-277. In: *Proceedings of the conference on the contribution of traditional authority to development, human rights and environmental protection: strategies for Africa (Accra and Kumasi, 2-6 September 1994)*. Nana Arhin Brempong, D.I. Ray, & E.A.B. Rouveroy van Nieuwaal (eds.). Leiden: African Studies Centre

1996a   The Post-Colonial State and Economic and Political Reforms in Cameroon. Pp. 244-265. In: *Liberalization in the Developing World: Institutional and economic changes in Latin America, Africa and Asia*. A.E. Fernández Jilberto & A. Mommen (eds.). London/New York: Routledge

1996b   Le 'problème anglophone' au Cameroun dans les années 1990. Pp. 25-35. In: *Politique Africaine*, 62

1996c   Privatization of Agro-Industrial Parastatals and Anglophone Opposition in Cameroon. Pp. 199-217. In: *The Journal of Commonwealth & Comparative Politics*, 34, 3

KRIEGER, Milton
1994   Cameroon's Democratic Crossroads, 1990-4. Pp. 605-628. In: *The Journal of Modern African Studies*, 32, 4

LE VINE, Victor T.
1971   *The Cameroon Federal Republic*. Ithaca, N.Y.: Cornell University Press

MBU, Aloysius N.T.
1993   *Civil Disobedience in Cameroon*. Douala: Imprimerie Georges Frères

MIAFFO, Dieudonné (éd.)
1993   *Chefferie Traditionnelle et Démocratie: Réflexion sur le destin du chef en régime pluraliste*. Yaoundé: Editions LAAKAM

MOUICHE, Ibrahim
1995a   Le Royaume Bamoun, Les Chefferies Bamileke et l'Etat au Cameroun. Unpublished paper, University of Yaoundé II

1995b   Ethnicité et pouvoir au Nord-Cameroun. *Paper* presented at the 8th General Assembly of CODESRIA, Dakar (26 June-2 July 1995)

MUKONG, Albert W. (ed.)
1990   *The Case for the Southern Cameroons*. CAMFECO (USA)

NKWI, Paul N.
1979   Cameroon Grassfield Chiefs and Modern Politics. Pp. 99-115. In: *Paideuma*, 25

NKWI, Paul N. & Jean-Pierre WARNIER,
1982   *Elements for a History of the Western Grassfields*. Yaoundé: SOPECAM

NYAMNJOH, Francis B.
1996   *The Cameroon G.C.E. Crisis: A Test of Anglophone Solidarity.* Limbe: Nooremac Press

OLINGA, Alain D.
1994   La 'Question Anglophone' dans le Cameroun d'aujourd'hui. Pp. 292-308. In: *Revue Juridique et Politique,* 3

ROUVEROY VAN NIEUWAAL, E. Adriaan B. van
1987   Chiefs and African States: Some Introductory Notes and an Extensive Bibliography on African Chieftaincy. Pp. 1-46. In: *Journal of Legal Pluralism,* nos. 25 & 26

1995   State and Chiefs in Africa: Are Chiefs Mere Puppets? Pp. 49-88. In: *Proceedings of the conference on the contribution of traditional authority to development, human rights and environmental protection: strategies for Africa (Accra and Kumasi, 2-6 September 1994).* Nana Arhin Brempong, D.I. Ray, & E.A.B. van Rouveroy van Nieuwaal (eds.). Leiden: African Studies Centre

ROWLANDS, Michael
1993   Accumulation and the Cultural Politics of Identity in the Grassfields. Pp. 71-97. In: *Itinéraires d'accumulation au Cameroun.* P. Geschiere & P. Konings (eds.). Paris: Karthala

SINDJOUN, Luc
1996   Rente identitaire, politique d'affection et crise de l'équilibre des tensions au Cameroun. *Paper* to be published in: *Afrique Politique.* Paris: Karthala

STARK, Frank
1976   Federalism in Cameroon: The Shadow and the Reality. Pp. 423-442. In: *Canadian Journal of African Studies,* 10, 3

TAKOUGANG, Joseph
1993   The Demise of Biya's New Deal in Cameroon, 1982-1992. Pp. 91-101. In: *Africa Insight,* 23, 2

WACHE, Francis K.
1991   The Plebiscite: Thirty Years After: The Choice between Fire and Deep Water. Pp. 6-10. In: *Cameroon Life,* 1, 8

OBSCURED BY COLONIAL STORIES. AN ALTERNATIVE HISTORICAL OUTLINE OF AKAN-RELATED CHIEFTAINCY IN JAMAICAN MAROON SOCIETIES

Werner Zips

Introduction

In late 1993 a new Colonel was elected as the head of the Accompong state (as the Maroons refer to their leaders). He had lost in the heartland of Accompong Town against his contender, a former Colonel. But the votes from Montego Bay and Kingston decided the election for him.[1] At the time (and to my knowledge until today) he was serving as a member of the Jamaican Constabulary Police Force. Being a grandson of the highly reputed historian and (lifelong) secretary of state (Mann O. Rowe) from a family which had several times supplied the Colonel in the history of Accompong, the kinship relations he could materialize as his social capital during the election campaign were excellent. His reported vigour and expected mediatory capabilities (as an employee of the Jamaican state) were seen as favourable assets, which could be interpreted as symbolic forms of capital, counterweighing his relative young age. Though he was not exactly welcomed by the whole community as their new chief, most Maroons decided to go along with the tide and to watch how things would develop.

As early as at the beginning of 1994, there were numerous public discussions, "noisy" council meetings and active lobbying going on. One of the main issues of what slowly developed into a chieftaincy dispute was the continual residence of the Colonel outside

---

[1] Interview with Wayne Rowe on 27.2.1994

of the Accompong community and his absence from the seat of government for most of the time. Outsiders (like myself) would have noticed the great amount of "altercations and quarrels" in Accompong and might have applied a similar description for Maroon "self-government" like the one of the "dispute-ridden town" given to the Maroon settlement by the colonial observers some 250 years ago. For two years the fractions and frictions over the chief went on with accusations and counteraccusations of the two "camps". The dispute climaxed in February 1996 when a meeting of (what the press referred to as) "the rebels" voted to oust the Colonel and set up a 15 member interim committee to run the affairs of the Accompong Maroon Council until a new Colonel would have been elected. Jamaica's daily newspapers headlined "New development in the Maroons' saga" and a few days later "Maroons locked in leadership crisis" (Earle 1996: 10C).

At the same time in Brooklyn, New York, a group was formed by "expatriate" Maroons which called itself "Maroons United for Democracy in Accompong" with the purpose of supporting the acting Colonel and to restore "democracy" in Accompong. When I met some of their leading representatives a few months later in New York, I was reassured that it was not a "family thing" (regardless of their actual kinship ties) but a political statement for democratic rule. Every Maroon, no matter from which part of the world, would comment on the situation in Accompong and participate in a way affordable to her or him. The media continued to have a "field day" with all the divergent statements issued by Maroons. Jamaican government officials appeared quite satisfied at the "process of dissolution", a dissolution which their British colonial predecessors had thought to observe all over their reign in Jamaica. Regrettably this interest-loaden view got support from part of the historiography of the Maroons, too uncritical of the colonial "writing of history" (cf. Campbell 1990: 254; or Kopytoff 1973: 360).[2] With this contribution I am therefore attempting an alternative historical outline of "chieftaincy" in Jamaican Maroon societies. I will apply a comparative perspective (informed by theoretical concepts taken mainly from Bourdieu and Habermas) to look at Jamaican Marronage within the context of African cultures (especially the Akan).

The emergence of African expressions of authority and leadership in the Caribbean date back to the first people of African descent who formed social groups in the forced surroundings of total dehumanization.[3] Certainly, such processes were already taking place on the slave ships and on the plantations among the enslaved. Most uprisings and revolts depended on the existence of effective leadership. This included religious and

---

[2] This criticism applies to some interpretations of the authors cited which appear theoretically unsound and lacking of the African cultural context (cf. Brathwaite 1994 who argued along a similar critical line). But in their ethnohistorical depths and the amount of archival material used, the work of these authors (especially Kopytoff who has also done extensive fieldwork in Accompong) is very impressive and useful for further analysis.

[3] The first African-American Maroon is said of having arrived on the first slave ship to reach the Americas within a decade of Columbus' landfall (Price 1992: 62).

ritual authority as well as political manoeuvre and strategic military planning. But slavery was a system too brutal and totally controlling the lives and socio-cultural practices of the enslaved to allow for an elaborate social reorganization. Only those who fled and escaped the plantations had a chance to build on their political experiences of the Motherland. These groups were called Maroons (or Cimarrones in Spanish, or Marrons in French)[4] throughout the so-called New World, now called the African Diaspora, in following a paradigmatic shift.[5]

Maroon communities in the Caribbean and both Americas showed a good deal of similarities, especially in tactics of guerilla warfare, but also in their general reliance on the African religious, cultural and political experiences. Yet, the differences between particular societies were also considerable. Social groups formed by Africans who escaped plantation life varied from tiny bands that survived less than a year to powerful states encompassing thousands of members that survived for generations and even centuries.[6] Where their descendants managed to endure until today they still form autonomous political entities such as those in Jamaica, Suriname, French Guiana, Colombia and Belize. They are, in some cases at least, governed by their own authorities, continually claim sovereign rights, and stay faithful to their cultural traditions forged during the earliest days of African-American history (Price 1992: 62).

This achievement of socio-political distinctiveness can only be grasped adequately if conceived in relation to structural changes in the external political system. For heuristic reasons, three historical periods will be differentiated in this context. Firstly, the time starting with the formation of free Black social goups following the invasion of Jamaica by the British in 1655. These early Maroon groups fought alongside the Spaniards (though not exactly with the same cause) before the former occupants of Jamaica were driven away to neighbouring Cuba. Once free of bondage, surrender was no option. Except for short intervals of relative tranquility, Maroons fought vigorously against the British colonial armed forces until the danger of a general uprising of the enslaved brought enough pressure to "persuade" their foes to sue for peace in the year of

---

[4] The Dutch chose to call these groups of freedom fighters "Bush Negroes", a notion which came out of use fairly recently because of its apparent pejorative connotations (see Price 1972 for a more detailed discussion).

[5] For an overview of Maroon communities past and present see Bilby and Baird N'Diaye 1992; Price 1983; Agorsah 1994.

[6] Maroons of several parts of the hemisphere have caught the interest of ethnohistorians, archaeologists and cultural anthropologists. For comparative data to the Jamaican Maroon case presented in this article see e.g. Rosa Corzo (1988 and 1991), Roll (1977), and Oppel (1994) on Cimarrones in Cuba; Price (1990), Price and Price (1991), Price (1984) on Saramaka Maroons of Suriname; Beet and Sterman (1981) on Matawai Maroons of Suriname; Bilby (1996) on Maroon Ethnogenesis of the Aluku of Suriname and the Windward Maroons of Jamaica; Marshall (1976) on Marronage in Dominica; Kent (1983), and Hofbauer (1995) on Quilombos and Palenques in Brazil; Pereira (1994) on Maroon heritage in Mexico.

1738/39.[7] Secondly, the time after the peace treaties (from 1738/39 until Jamaican independence in 1962) with its fundamentally different legal/political position of Maroon enclaves within the plantation colony. During this period of territorial control and political autonomy in continual contest with the sovereignty claims of their colonial treaty partners, the Maroons successfully protected their cultural integrity by political action directed at their internal social control and the external seclusion of the colonial authority. All this in defiance of the recurrent attempts by the colonial administration to gain more control through the internationally tried practices and means of indirect rule. And thirdly, the ongoing developments since national independence in 1962[8].

Until today the Maroons still withstand the much more subtle challenges to their independent status in the post-colonial situation. The ideological constraint to contribute to a national identity by severing historical bonds to the Maroon lands and thereby renounce all claims to sovereignty is supported by hegemonial legal and economic structures of the national state. "Out of many people, one nation", the Jamaican national motto, is but one example speaking to the rising pressure for gradual assimilation into the general population.

Yet, contrary to expectations by state agencies, Maroon societies in Suriname (cf. Pakosie 1996) and Jamaica are not prepared to dissolve the basis of their corporate existence as sociocultural entities. They are today self-governing groups with systems of leadership comparable to forms of traditional authority within the context of African chieftaincy. In these two countries Maroons enjoy a factual legal position close to "states within states" (Price 1983: 293; Zips 1993b). As with traditional systems on the African continent, their actual social, economic and political situation depends largely on the diplomatic skills of their chiefs to negotiate favourable conditions for their autonomous existence.[9] Yet, the diplomatic frame is determined by the general attitude of the statical political system towards the "competing (traditional) power". Autonomy without financial means, legal "justice", civil rights and so on has little to offer even for people fiercely proud of their unique historical heritage. State institutions and traditional authority compete over legitimacy in the field of power .

I will first attempt a historical reconstruction of the (re-)emergence of chieftaincy in the Jamaican Maroon context, in order to define a frame for a preliminary discussion of the

---

[7] The example of Haiti demonstrated the possible "explosion" of Maroon resistance into a general revolution against the slaveholding plantocracies in the Caribbean. See Fouchard (1981), Parkinson (1980: 21) and James (1984) for an analysis of the Haitian revolution at the turn of the 18th to the 19th century.

[8] Certainly these three periods could be much more differentiated according to important structural changes. Foremost the gradual abolition of slavery from 1834-1838 changed the political conditions of Maroon existence considerably. The simplification to three periods is only undertaken in this context in consideration of the necessary condensation of my argument.

[9] See van Rouveroy van Nieuwaal (1998) for the analogous observations in the West African context.

different bases of state and Maroon authorities. This appears essential not alone for a better understanding of the ongoing competition between the "modern" state and "traditional" Maroon authorities with its ambivalent tendency to conflicts over sovereign rights, but also for possible solutions to the dilemma of the "legal pluralism colonial heritage". The (social) recognition of (legitimate) authority functions as the currency of exchange between subordination to state dominance and submission to traditional Maroon authority. Actual power of these traditional authorities depends largely on the political abilities of contemporary chiefs. History and tradition become rhetorical devices in the highly charged arena of competition between state and Maroon leaders over their legitimacy. Only if a chief succeeds in convincing his people of his "better" leadership in the interests of the community through action and rational argumentation, his authority is regarded as supreme to the state, in the sense of more legitimate. Therefore history as such, be it related to the ancestors, old customs, or traditions does not sufficiently legitimate the authority of a particular chief. Rather, chiefs have to make good use of history (or more precise, historical rhetoric) to mediate the link between the past, the present and the future. Their power base is integrally linked to this successful mediation. Maroon citizens are subjects of the Jamaican state and the Maroon (quasi-) state. They have a certain choice to bestow (supreme) legitimate authority on either or. A chief conceived as a guarantor for (dynamic) continuity is thus equalled with his predecessors (in office). Change and continuity in traditional authority are more than just compatible: they seem to condition each other in a process that could be described as the "continual tranformation" of chieftaincy. Certainly, the most radical transformation occurred at the very beginning of the process of (re-)creating chieftaincy structures based on African origins in the mountainous Jamaican interior. I will first outline some central aspects of this formative process.

The recreation of leadership in Jamaican Maroon societies

For an accurate reconstruction of even the most basic aspects of Maroon leadership in the formative days of their social history there is little material. Oral history of the Maroons barely mentions even the existence of organized groups who resisted the British on the side of their former Spanish enslavers in 1655 (cf. Harris 1992: 73).[10] Their oral testimonies begin with Nanny, Kojo, Kwako, Accompong and other leaders, "...who placed our community on the road of freedom".[11] These were the leaders who were actually in power before and during the conclusion of peace. Written sources

---

[10] In a series of conversations with Colonel C.L.G. Harris of the Moore Town Maroons the heritage of the first "Spanish Maroons" was mentioned. Harris also insisted that some spanish words survived in this Maroon society by oral tradition until today (interview on 26.2.1994). But I was not able to gather more detailed oral information on the first Maroons. The Maroons of Accompong (on whom my research is based) hardly make any reference to the time before their cultural heroes Kojo and Nanny. The notion of First Time always refers to these Maroon leaders at the turn of the 17th/18th century.

[11] Interview with Melvin Currie on 6.1.1989 (documented on film; see Zips 1991: 65-66).

generated by their colonial counterparts possess very little information on internal structures of authority among the first people who became known as Maroons in Jamaica. Their general content is occupied with the possible strategies to eradicate this "eminent danger for the plantation system" (Black 1979: 56). The picture painted by the first authors on the Maroon wars carries the full weight of their hostility towards the Maroons. Such planter historians like Bryan Edwards (1796)[12] and Edward Long (1774) invented accounts of Maroon organizational principles and personal characters of their leaders that should be read as expressions of what Lewis (1983:7) has called "the mindless labyrinth of the white racist psyche". Their economic existence depended on slave labour. Marronage meant the biggest threat to their livelihood on the sugar plantations (Campbell 1990: 22). On the symbolic level, this economic and physical military threat played havoc with an ideology that had Caribbean Africans as lazy, irresponsible, mendacious, sexually aggressive, mentally inferior, and biologically retarded un-persons, close enough to animals to be kept as property.[13]

Therefore, every achievement and victory of Maroons became reinterpreted as weakness, stubbornness or defeat in the colonial reports. Thus, the writing of history (and culture) served a legitimizing function for the doctrine of racial superiority and colonial control. The same happened to the first known chief of the Maroons whose name is given in the historical sources: Juan de Bolas, a possible spanish pronounciation of the African name (Gyani?) Lubolo. His group was one of (at least) three main Black communities with recognized leaders in the year following the British conquest of Jamaica. Lubolo showed political flexibility in accepting the British offer of partial independence in exchange for loyalty and cooperation with the British. The "charter to the said Negroes", issued in a Council meeting of February 1, 1662/63 honored Lubolo with the new title Colonel of the Black Regiment and made him and others of his men magistrates with jurisdiction over his people in all ordinary matters except cases of great consequence and "cases of Life and Death".[14]

This recognition as equals appears as one of the most valuable symbolic capitals in the context of the institutionalized total unequality set up by slavery.[15] The context of the declaration by the Jamaican governor and the Council reveals striking similarities with the later peace treaties of the Leeward and Windward Maroons in Jamaica, various Maroon societies in Suriname (and other countries of the African Diaspora where such treaties have been concluded) and also the much later politics of indirect rule in Africa

---

[12] The publication of 1796 has been reprinted in Richard Price's book on Maroon Societies (1983) to which I will refer in this contribution.

[13] See Lewis (1983: 8-12) for his critical analysis of this sort of "eighteenth-century literary primitivism" which constitutes the main part of "primary" source material on Maroon social history.

[14] Colonial Office (CO), 140/1, Council meeting, February 1, 1662/63.

[15] I use the notion of symbolic capital as a recognized form of cultural and social capital in this case in the sense of Bourdieu' analysis of the forms of capital (cf. 1986: 246).

which (at least partially) substituted the legitimacy of traditional authority held by African chiefs with the "naked power" of colonial domination.[16] Thus, bringing the chiefs into the ambivalent position of standing on thin ice between the colonial state and their (former) subjects. Shortly after receiving colonial recognition through the charter mentioned above, Lubolo was killed and his men defeated by another Maroon group known as the Los Vermahalles[17] under the leadership of one Juan de Serras.

Individual runaways strengthened the Maroons in numbers. Occasional attacks on outlying plantations provided their tiny social entities with goods for their subsistance and with new recruits of both sexes. But it was not until the uprisings of whole plantations that the situation came close to a war of independence. The so-called Sutton's rebellion became especially famous because of the great number of escaped rebels.[18] Carrying along their seized arms they reinforced already existing groups in the Cockpit Country who may or may not have been earlier followers of Juan de Serras. Reportedly, the revolt was led by the father of Captain (or General) Kojo, who was to become the most famous Maroon chief through his command at the signing of the peace treaty in 1738/39 (Kopytoff 1973: 71; Schafer 1973: 64). It was the period following this revolt that consolidated chieftaincy structures in the Maroon communities and set the pace for later developments.

The consolidation of West African-type chieftaincy among the Maroons

There is general consent among scholars that Kojo and his father were of Akan origin. It is assumed that Kojo was born in Jamaica whilst his father came from the former Gold Coast. At the end of the 17th century, as the time in question, there existed powerful chiefdoms in the area covered by the Ghanaian state today. Around that time (after 1700) when Kojo must have taken over leadership from his father in Jamaica, the kingdom of Denkyira was supplanted by Asante as the principal Akan power in the former Gold Coast.[19] Maroons today refer to Ashanti (Asante) in giving their ethnic origins (Harris 1994: 36). This should be read on a symbolic level in coherence with the interests in a "powerful genealogical narration". However, structures of chieftaincy or

---

[16] See Giddens (1971: 156-163) for a discussion of Weber's differentiation of three ideal types of legitimacy. According to Weber (1976: 124), traditional authority is based on the everyday belief of the subordinate (something close to the structures of perception in Bourdieu's habitus concept) in the sanctity of age old traditions which also legitimize the authority of certain rulers who are in turn bound by tradition.

[17] The Los Vermahalles were named after the location where they had built their Palenque (fortified camp): the Vermahollis Savanna in the Cave Valley between the parishes of Clarendon and St. Ann (Hart 1985: 6).

[18] It was reported that about 500 enslaved had participated in the rebellion of the estate of one Mr. Sutton. Some 150 may have escaped into the mountains (Hart 1985: 18).

[19] See McCaskie (1995: 58-63) for historiographic examples of authority in the early Asante state. For the struggle with Denkyira see Tufuo and Donkor (1989: 25-40).

African kingship form the experiental background of Maroon leadership. These were the (African) cultures the Maroons came from and should therefore be considered in a structural comparative frame, as Brathwaite (1994: 120) has argued recently. Linguistic research has thoroughly established the great portion of Twi terms in the remaining fragments of African languages still known today (Dalby 1971: 31-51).[20] What the former Colonel of the Moore Town Maroons has to say in relation to the old Kromanti (Kramanti) language could aptly be expanded by inference to the creative consolidation of a new dynamic social system that drew on the cognition of West African traditions:

> One of the most important sociological issues among the Maroons of Moore Town and Charles Town in Portland was the ancestral language, known as 'Kramanti'. It was spoken freely up to some six decades ago - in the early 1930s...'Kramanti', as my ancestors knew it to be called, is regarded as a hybrid having Twi, the Ashanti language of the Gold Coast (now Ghana in West Africa), as the more vigorous of its parents (Harris 1994: 39).[21]

It is generally understood that no Maroon culture has ever come into existence as a directly transplanted African system, no matter how homogenous the original founders of a particular society were in terms of their ethnic and cultural origins. Between them and the Motherland lay not only the dreadful experience of the so-called middle passage, but also entirely new conditions of survival that could never allow for a simple revival of any specific social, political, religious, or aesthetic system of African origin. The search for African "survivals" or retentions, in order to trace specific ethnic origins has therefore been widely replaced by an analytical approach, conscious of the "African character" of Maroon organizational principles but also aware of their continuous inventions in all social fields (Price 1992: 64).

Such an analytical perspective does not have to prevent making the connection between Caribbean cultures and their African sources; especially if we consider the analogous

---

[20] Note that the usage of "First Time" language is ritually sanctioned and therefore not spoken in public (except in ceremonial contexts or when the "dead" participate) nor for research purposes. During my research in Accompong, Nana Rowe, who is the widely acknowledged expert on Kromanti songs and language, refused repeatedly to transmit her knowledge to other Maroons as well as to outsiders like myself (interview with Nana Rowe, 16.2.1994).

[21] Kromanti or Kramanti is a notion used by Maroons to refer to their deep "original" culture. All captured Africans shipped away from the British Forts of the former Gold Coast were categorized with a quasi-ethnic signifier as Coromantees, regardless of their "real" ethnic affiliation as Fanti, Akim, Ashanti, Ga or Guang. It referred to the first important British Fort of the area in a village still called Kormantse in Ghana today (van Dantzig 1980: 21-32). Originally meaning "those being shipped from Fort Kromantyne", the notion was soon extended to all Africans who have been taken away from this coastal region by the British. For the Maroons the application of the notion Kromanti should not be read as an acceptance of a colonial categorization but rather as an attempt to create a basis for ethnic cohesion out of diversity (see Zips 1996b for a more detailed discussion of Maroon ethnicity; cf. Hart 1985: 9).

flexibility of African systems of leadership and chieftaincy that are traditional in the most dynamic sense of traditio as a process of communicating custom, knowledge and social norms (Calhoun 1993: 77). This traditio structures the socially constituted, cognitive capacity that Bourdieu (1979: 165; and 1986: 255) has called habitus. Its conception offers a (praxeological) theoretical grasp for a processual understanding of the empirically observed "African character" of Maroon cultures. Their cultural uniqueness rests firmly - as Price (1992: 64) has remarked - on their fidelity to "African" cultural principles at the deeper levels of an internal dynamism of West (and Central) African cultural systems than on the frequency of their isolated "retentions" in form. The concept of habitus seeks to account for the ability to grow and change, attributed to the dynamic setting of these African systems, without leaving its inventiveness to explications based on the exclusive subjective consciousness and individual deliberation of outstanding leaders and other social actors.

According to Bourdieu's theory (of practice), the habitus is a system of relatively durable, transposable dispositions which generate and organize practices and representations (cf. Bourdieu 1979: 165). As "accumulated history" (Bourdieu 1986: 241) the "Maroon habitus" was strucutured by the inculcation of various African principles of perception, interpretation and action, complemented by their early contact with Amerindian cultures. At the same time the objective social conditions of slavery, warfare and other interactions with the Europeans were also incorporated. This necessarily produced a similarity in the habitus of agents sharing a common group experience. Speaking of a "Maroon habitus" thus refers to their ability to generate practices adjusted to the specific conditions of continual military threat and the constraints of economic survival as well as the difficulties of socio-political recreation. Seen in such a light, the remarkable number of direct and sometimes spectacular continuities from particular African peoples found in Maroon cultures does not contradict the transformation of African experiences from a variety of societies nor the strategic calculation of social organization and action in relation to the concrete circumstances.[22] I want to suggest that this process of habitus formation lies at the root of grasping a situation seemingly paradoxical at first sight: that Maroons in Jamaica (and elsewhere) "...have built systems that are at once meaningfully African and among the most truly 'alive' and culturally dynamic of African-American cultures" (Price 1992: 64).[23]

---

22   Also see Johnson (1993: 4-6) for an outline of the theoretical concept applied in this context.

23   Such an analyis contradicts some of Bourdieu's critics (e.g. Garnham and Williams 1980) who overstated the extent to which Bourdieu's concept of habitus focuses on reproduction. In contrast to such a reading of habitus Bourdieu clarified his position repeatedly (e.g. Bourdieu and Wacquant 1992: 133): "Habitus is not a fate that some people read into it. Being the product of history, it is an open system of dispositions that is constantly subjected to experiences, and therefore contantly affected by them in a way that either reinforces or modifies its structures. It is durable but not eternal!" From this theoretical point of view, revolution or armed freedom struggle (as in the case of the Maroons) does not break with the habitus, but is rather based on it (cf. Calhoun 1993: 75). Habitus is the conceptual frame for the social and individual capacity for structured improvisation (Postone, LiPuma and Calhoun 1993: 4).

Various Maroon groups existed on the island in the decades predating the peace treaties. There were apparent differences in their political organizational efforts. It is hence not possible to define one system of "chieftaincy" in Maroon societies; not even with validity for a very limited period. But this is yet another reflection of the precolonial situation in Africa. A great spectrum of particular expressions of precolonial authority came under the diminutive European discourse of "the" African chief. The contra factum generalization served well the colonial purposes of reducing the status of rulers such as the Oba of Benin; in precolonial times he considered himself, and was considered by his subects, a king (Crowder and Ikime 1970: ix). For the European colonialists there was no chief except the one recognized as an intermediary agent for the enactment of colonial rule. Their dismantling as genuine traditionally legitimate African authorities in the precolonial context was accompanied by a narrative of primitivism and ridicule. Such was the case with both leading figures in Jamaican Maroon societies of the time. Maroon oral traditions insist that Nanny and Kojo were kin. As sister and brother they led the different groups in the east (called Windward Maroons) and the west (Leeward Maroons). Living Maroon historians such as Mann O. Rowe in Accompong emphasize the continual interaction of both Maroon groups.[24]

But the picture changes radically if the written historical sources on the pre-treaty authorities are consulted. In my view, the historical account of chieftaincy structures in Maroon societies suffers in credibility from two ideological problems and one practical deficiency. For the colonial observers it was quite impossible to imagine (and much less to accept) an elaborate political/social/religious system of authority among the "wild negroes" (the etymological meaning of the term Maroon). But it was still even more unthinkable to these literary foes of the Maroons to conceive a Black woman in the complex position of a female chief or queen mother comparable to her African counterparts. Thus, Kojo's status was reduced to military leadership while Nanny was branded with the typical mark for nonsubmissive women of the time: that of a witch (cf. Thicknesse 1790: 69-74; and Dallas 1803: 34 and 74). In short, the two main ideological deficiencies of the contemporary authors result from the habitualized historic figurations of absolute white and male supremacy. On the practical "methodological" level, the most important obstacle for any, at least fairly, accurate ethnohistorical account of the Maroon political system (at "First Time") appears in the "method" of gathering the relevant data. All primary colonial sources before the peace treaties were based exclusively on access to Maroon societies by warfare and related interactions; the latter being such means as interrogation of captured guerillas or information by Black spies who had been sent to the mountain villages in exchange for their later manumission from slavery. The military reports as the most important written sources for the reconstruction of Maroon chieftaincy reveal the ideological and "methodological" reduction of "history". Thinking of the representational politics involved in the most recent "Gulf War"-mise en scène in a time with alleged media

---

[24] This account was repeated by Mann O. Rowe in many interviews and conversations (e.g. on 21.1.1994).

transparency seems sufficient to imagine the distortions inherent in this "colonial reportage".

However, the political picture, created rather accidentally by reporting soldiers on which the later narrations of Dallas (1803), Edwards (1796), or Long (1774) are based, differentiates sharply between the Leeward and the Windward Maroon system. Following these contemporary sources, the Windward Maroons are generally described as a loose-knit federation with shifting alliances and an "ad hoc leadership". Consequentially, authority is perceived as weakly developed and divided in different spheres, such as the military, political and religious fields (Kopytoff 1973: 75-89; cf. Bilby 1996: 121). In contrast to the undifferentiated "ad hoc rising" of Windward Maroon headmen, Kojo's autocratic rule over the Leeward Maroons is juxtaposed (Kopytoff 1973: 89). I have argued recently that the picture changes drastically if the situation is recontextualized comparatively with West African systems of complementary male and female leadership (Zips 1998). Emanating from the theoretical concept of habitus one can hypothesize that African structures of authority were incorporated in the relations of power in Maroon societies. Where the habitualized African structures were the predominant source for socio-political reorganization, the reemergence of female leadership needs less explanatory efforts than its absence would require. Female participation (of the queen mother) in the process of determining (or "making") a king was a prerequisite for the reproduction of political structures in most West African societies that informed the habitus (as the "structuring structures") of Maroon political practices.

The available written (colonial) sources allow at least for a reading of Nanny as representing a possible female leadership role analogous to the West African context. Many authors based their conclusions of a loose federacy among the Windward Maroons on the reported existence of various Maroon villages in the east, each of which appeared to be governed by their own headmen (e.g. Kopytoff 1973: 77). Furthermore, Nanny's invisibility during the negotiations of peace and the sole signature of Captain Quao (Kwao) on the document were interpreted as sufficient support for her "non-political" role among the Windward Maroons. The sole position granted to her became the one of a witchcraft specialist (cf. Robinson 1969: 53). This seems to me a very reductionist view of female political roles on the one hand and of African organizational principles on the other.[25]

For the contemporary West African context complementarity and differentiation of political functions was a defining feature of such early states as Asante. The Asante government knew of various institutions constituting a deliberative (conciliar) system,

---

[25] As I have argued elsewhere (Zips 1998), Nanny's role was rather coherent with the position of female leaders or queen mothers in the Akan dual system of leadership. Then her role should be interpreted as extending in the military, political, legal, and religious sphere. With great certainty Nanny's participation or guidance was tantamount for all processes of deliberation in reaching political decisions.

such as a privy council, a cabinet, council of state, Council of Kumase, House of Commons, high council, senate, Grand Assembly, Kotoko Council, Supreme Council of the Empire,[26] and the like. Their highest conciliar body was the Asantemanhyiamu (literally the Assembly of the Asante Nation; McCskie 1995: 146; Wilks 1975: 146). Membership in this Assembly was on a territorial basis. Its origins may be assumed to date from the very beginning of the Asante kingdom at the turn of the 17th century (Wilks 1975: 387-388).[27] This coincides exactly with the time we are looking at as the pre-treaty period of Maroon history in Jamaica. Following from the structural comparison with the West African political system of the Asante - as the one, Maroon oral tradition strongly identifies with - the existence of territorial units under their own headmen or chiefs does not necessarily suggest a loose federation of independent units. Just as Kumase in Asante, the Windward Maroons had one principal town. And this was the settlement named after Nanny. There is of course hardly any chance to validate further speculations on a territorial hierarchical division of the Windward Maroons political entity. Also, the sources supporting an evaluation of Nanny as a queen mother or acting chief are certainly limited and almost exclusively of the oral tradition. All we can say with certainty is that the African cultures later Maroons came from, knew of such traditions. Akan history saw queen mothers at the very top of affairs, foremost in times of crises, when male leaders were not available, or competing over legitimate authority, or occupied with military affairs (Arhin 1983: 95-96; Aidoo 1990: 68-69).[28]

Nanny's "invisibility" at the conclusion of peace is rather supportive of her apical political role, if judged from an West African context. Queen mothers or chiefs would hardly negotiate with emissaries considered as being below them in rank. Above all, traditionally, the role of queen mothers was played out "behind the scene", as the one being consulted for the final decision making. However elusive Nanny's actual role before the peace treaty may appear from the written sources, living Maroons more than 250 years after this time refer to her as Mother of all Maroons, Queen of the mountains and the "original owner of the Maroon treaty lands" (cf. Bilby 1996: 125). On the most general level we can conclude from our discussion that the Windward Maroons had a system of leadership with a divisional territorial organization and an acting chief, whether or not on behalf of yet another superior in the person of Nanny.

In the case of the Leeward Maroons the position of Kojo is much less disputed. But even there the picture of an autocratic ruler given by the written (colonial) sources, on which modern accounts are generally based (cf. Kopytoff 1973: 89), seems doubtful. There were at least two large settlements in the west, namely Kojo's Town and

---

[26] The capitalization follows Wilks (1975: 146) who refers to the literature on these institutions.

[27] In fact many of the core structures pre-date this period.

[28] See also Zips (1998) for an extended discussion of "forefront" queen mothers in Akan history.

Accompong Town.[29] The latter was named after yet another Maroon leader, known as the brother of Kojo. Oral traditions in Accompong today speak of the existence of a deliberative body, called the Council of Elders before the peace treaty. Kojo is also said of having had (at least) two brothers in leading positions as well as several sub-chiefs.[30] This is also supported by the last article (no. 15) of the peace treaty 1738/39 which sought to alter the rules of succession among the Maroons. It declared the legitimacy of Captain Cudjoe (English spelling for Kojo) as lifelong leader and intended to determine a line of succession. Equivalent designations were made by clause 14 in the treaty with the Windward Maroons (barely four months after "Kojo's treaty", on 23rd of June 1739). Nanny has been completely neglected by this document; which should be interpreted restrictively as an omission on the side of the British. This must not necessarily indicate the subordinate political role of Nanny. In fact - one might speculate - it could have been to the contrary, given the Maroon tendency to disguise or "camouflage" their cultural and political institutions, leaders and practices to protect these from outside intervention.

However, the text of the treaties certainly reveals the degree of consolidation Maroon leadership had achieved during the 85 years of a continual state of war.[31] Yet, the two sides had sharply conflicting interpretations of the treaties. These documents present very complex problems for interpretation that reflect the adverse legal and political perspectives of Maroons and colonialists. I will only sketch certain aspects of these issues to shed some light on the dynamics of change in Maroon leadership following the transition from military conflict to peaceful (but ambivalent) diplomacy.

The Peace Treaties of 1738/39 and its effects on Maroon chieftaincy

Generations of Jamaican Maroons lived on the cutting edge of extinction. They were always subject of being overrun by the then superpower Great Britain. In the event of complete detection of their villages and hiding places, such a fate would have been unescapable and in fact happened to many Maroon groups in most parts of the African Diaspora. On the other hand, the colonialists lived in constant fear of a general Black uprising. Greatly outnumbered by the enslaved, they were terrified by the myth of invincibility spun around the supernatural practices and actual military devices of such commanders as Kojo or Nanny. Considering their master/slave mentality it must have shaken this racial order to sue for peace with the dreaded "animalized" rebels whom they had depicted as barbarians for well over 80 years (see e.g. Edwards 1796). It is in

---

[29] Kojo's Town was renamed Trelawney Town after the peace treaty, which is most likely where Maroon Town is located today.

[30] Interview with Captain Melvin Currie on 6.1.1989.

[31] There were of course periods of relative military tranquility, but even then regular military skirmishes occurred (see Hart 1985: 1-60).

this symbolic sense that most "modern" authors have agreed to conceive the peace treaties as an unparalleled historic achievement for the Maroons. But their actual political meaning has rather been seen by some of these authors as a successful introduction of "indirect (colonial) rule" and "diplomatic submission" of the Maroons (e.g. Patterson 1983: 272; Campbell 1990: 129; Kopytoff 1973: 363)[32]:

> ...one can find no ancient precedents of rebel slaves and their ex-masters signing treaties conjointly. And it is in this sense that the Treaty is historically important, that it is a triumph for the Maroons. In practical terms, though, it is another matter, for the Treaty, in effect, represents more a victory for the colonial power than for the Maroons, who were never defeated in battle by the British. It represents the triumph of diplomacy over warfare, demonstrating that what the British could not gain on the battlefield, they now gained in full measure over the negotiating table (Campbell 1990: 129).

In my view, this statement seems to reflect the basic ingredients of the old colonial stereotype, which the historical sources wanted their contemporaries and following generations to believe as fact: that, in reality, the "bloodthirsty" Maroons finally gave in to British superiority allegedly grounded on "intelligent diplomacy". But is it really so intricate to overcome source-positivist readings by decoding the symbolic interests of such vivid descriptions as Dallas' (1803: 56) "account" of the signing of peace (between Kojo and the British emissary John Guthrie) published more than 60 (!) years after the historic event? It reads like this:

> (Kojo) threw himself to the ground, embracing Guthrie's legs, kissing his feet, and asking his pardon. He seemed to have lost all his ferocity and to have become humbly penitent and abject. The rest of the Maroons, following the example of their chief, prostrated themselves, and expressed the most unbounded joy at the sincerity shown on the side of the white people.

The portrayal of the Maroon chief as a clown vis-a-vis the noble white Colonel hints at the distortions written into "history". It further gives an idea of the opposite interpretations occuring between both parties involved of the "legal history" and meanings of the treaty contents. Kojo and Kwao, who signed the treaties on behalf of the Leeward and Windward Maroons were most likely not able to read English (Harris

---

[32] It is doubtful whether the notion of "indirect rule" should be applied comparatively to the 18th century post-treaty era in Jamaica (as done by Kopytoff 1973: 346-365, in her conclusions). The policy was formally introduced by Lord Lugard in 1919 for Northern Nigeria. I agree with van Rouveroy van Nieuwaal (in a personal communication) who felt reluctant to compare the British "Maroon policy" to the later indirect rule system in the African colonies. However, the indirect rule interpretation for Jamaica can only cover the intentionalist perspective of the British search for colonial control and not the strategies of the Maroon struggle for power to self-control.

1994: 47). Certainly they were not trained in the "international law" of treaties. When they put their mark X under the treaties, they must have agreed to what had been negotiated verbally in the course of arriving at a peace conclusion. Even the very act of concluding the treaty was perceived in radically different terms between the two sides. For the Maroons - as all oral traditions related to the treaties vigorously insist - it was the exchange of blood between the Whites and the Maroons that "made peace". Hence these treaties are still called "blood treaties".[33] From a legal doctrinal point of view, the exchange of blood was apparently seen as constitutive by the Maroons, whereas the signature on the written document had a mere declarative (or affirmative) character.[34]

But the differences in interpretation go far beyond the divergent evaluation of symbolic action. With the exchange of blood the Maroons associated a statement of equality. Only equal nations and sovereigns would conclude peace in such a way, seen from the perspective of the African societies they came from. For them, the blood pacts were sacred agreements (Kopytoff 1979: 45). Any attempt to tamper with the treaties or to realize their revocation would have meant to call for a new exchange of blood; in other words: war (Zips 1993a: 117; Martin 1973: 176).

For the English, the treaties were political instruments to "pacify" a dangerous enemy. It was not intended to turn the "rebels", as the Maroons were still called, into a sovereign nation. Rather, they should have become a special class of free subjects to the Crown, serving the colony for the maintenance of slavery and as a military force in case of a foreign invasion. In relation to chieftaincy that meant to undermine the traditional authority of the chief and to substitute it for the legal authority of the colonial administration. Kopytoff (1973: 352-364) and other authors might be quite right to assume that the formulations of the written treaties were intended by the British to let them gradually win control over internal Maroon affairs with the passing of time. Yet, it is difficult to accept a historical analysis that arrives at the success of such a colonial policy, if one experiences the chieftaincy politics (and chieftaincy disputes, to be sure) that are still very much alive now in Maroon societies, 35 years after the British administration ended and Jamaica gained its independence in 1962. Let us examine the three clauses of Kojo's treaty (see Zips 1993b: 343) which had the most effect on traditional authority, in order to assess whether the hypothesized "patron-client relationship with flexible parameters" (Kopytoff 1979: 50) and exclusive colonial sovereignty is not merely reflecting the interpretation of only one of the involved parties. The colonial state had the means to "write" history rather than to merely transmit or tell history. It also attempted to give "official" interpretations of the treaty.

---

[33] According to the Maroon historian Mann O. Rowe (filmed interview on 12.1.1989, cf. Zips 1991: 72), the Maroons and the Whites cut their veins, caught the blood in a calabash basin, mixed it with rum and weed and then drank it.

[34] According to a doctrinal differentiation, declarative legal acts ascertain rules or rights whereas constitutive legal acts actually shape these (cf. Adamovich and Funk 1980: 219).

The three clauses in question concern the chief's right of jurisdiction (except for capital offence and/or sanction), the nomination of white intermediaries, and the question of leadership and succession:

12th
That captain Cudjoe, during his life, and the captains succeeding him, shall have full power to inflict any punishment they think proper for crimes committed by their men among themselves, death only excepted: in which case, if the captain thinks they deserve death, he shall be obliged to bring them before any justice of peace, who shall order proceedings on their trial equal to those of other free negroes.

14th
That two white men, to be nominated by his excellency or the commander of chief for the time being, shall constantly live and reside with captain Cudjoe and his successors, in order to maintain a friendly correspondance with the inhabitants of this island.

15th
That captain Cudjoe shall, during his life, be chief commander in Trelawney-Town; after his decease, the command to devolve on his brother captain Accompong; and, in case of his decease, on his next brother captain Johnny; and failing him, captain Cuffee shall succeed; who is to be succeeded by captain Quaco and, after all their demises, the governor, or commander in chief for the time being shall appoint, from time to time, whom he thinks fit for that command.

It has been argued that these provisions turned the Maroon settlements into "incomplete polities" (Kopytoff 1973). This consequence was attributed to the regulations of chieftaincy which were interpreted as undercutting the power of the chiefs. I am quite convinced that the British had in mind to undermine the authority of the chiefs by interfering with its base of legitimacy. The three strategies for structural changes were apparently intended to alter the legitimacy base on the part of the chiefs. Their legitimation was sought to become dependent on colonial approval. A strategy generally used by any colonial power to gain control of "traditional" authority. Given these intentions, the question remains if these hegemonial aims became realized in the case of the Jamaican Maroons. To answer this I will draw on the paradigmatic shift as outlined by the theory of practice (Bourdieu 1979).

Intended structural changes depend for their effect on the desired political practices of the actors. These political practices are already structured by a habitus which is in itself the product of a long process of inculcation of earlier political structures, or, as mentioned above, "accumulated history" (cf Bourdieu 1986: 241; Calhoun 1993: 83). In this competition between "old and new", or between incorporated structures and newly imposed ones, the new colonial political structures of chieftaincy would have had to be enforced by (the colonial) power. Maroon history reveals, as I am suggesting with this discussion, that colonial politics were not always successful. At least not in full.[35] To interpret the (treaty) intentions as actual (structuring) structures or social facts means to read colonial aims into the historical analysis.[36] Kopytoff (1973: 112 and 125-126) has given the following summary of the major treaty points in regard to chieftaincy:

> The treaties recognized the authority of the leaders to mete out any punishment but death for crimes committed within the settlements (crimes whose definition was itself left to the Maroons) and established life tenure for the head men; they also recognized the superior power of the British government by reserving to it the death penalty and by keeping for the Governor the power to appoint the Maroon chiefs after the lines of succession set up in the treaties had run out. The British further involved themselves in Maroon affairs by stationing White men to live in their towns as their representatives...The insuring of life tenure for the chief, the reservation of the death penalty for the Crown, the presence of White superintendents in the towns, all had profound effects on Maroon political organization, and most particularly on the headman. The result was a state that the British called 'disorder', and in the ensuing years they passed numerous laws trying to bolster the authority of the Maroon chiefs and the White superintendents, to insure order and government in the dispute-ridden towns, but they had little success.

For the British colonial government in the first half of the 18th century, the structures and according practices of African-type chieftaincy must have been as obscure as the Maroon military practices before the peace treaty. Completely misunderstanding the guerilla tactics of hit and run, the colonial militia had usually thought of having defeated their enemies when the Maroons escaped back into the forest - until their forces were "milked" again in yet another ambush.[37] In relation to political processes of decision making, the British had equally no experience to grasp these "disputes" and "quarrels" among the Maroons as the discoursive means of argumentation and convincing by means of "better" reasons to reach a decision backed (or legitimized) by a procedure of communicative rationality. Council or public meetings presided over by the chief were and still are the institutionalized settings for the communicative integration of divergent views. Both, in Jamaica and Ghana, traditional councils share common features in

---

[35] See van Rouveroy van Nieuwaal (1998) and Mann and Roberts (1991) for a comparison with African colonial situations.

[36] This approach misses the point of a structural history "...which finds in each successive state of the structure under examination both the product of previous struggles to maintain or to transform this structure, and the principle, via the contradictions, the tensions, and the relations of force which constitute it, of subsequent transformations" (Bourdieu and Wacquant 1992: 91; also cf. Calhoun 1993: 82).

[37] See Zips (1993a: 83-99; and 1987) for a detailled discussion of military practices.

practice.[38] Reasoning and discourse are given all the necessary time needed for reaching a consensus based on rational argumentation. For outside observers today, used to the formalisms of representative European democracies, where party interests rule over rational arguments, such interactive (and many times vivid) procedures might appear as chaotic disputes. The colonial reporters had of course additional interests to represent their old adversaries as totally incapable of and inefficient in governance. In applying an alternative reading to the reported failure of the Maroon leaders to govern their people after the treaties, one might turn this observation from standing on its head to its feet. Then, the continual existence of communicative practices in reaching (rational) decisions rather demonstrates the prevalence of Maroon political structures rooted in negotiations, despite the colonial attempts to throw them under central autocratic control. By these "Maroon political structures", I am referring to "deeper" habitualized forms of communicative deliberation from the African experiences. In his analysis of the society and state of precolonial Asante, McCaskie (1995: 86) elaborated the clear and obvious limitations of the coercive capacity on the part of the Asante state's authority:

> It (the coercive capacity) was in and of itself a necessary but not a sufficient condition of the state's authority. The state's ability to coerce society ultimately depended upon society being structurally complicit in, or consenting to, its subjection to the state's interventions. But the bases of consent were not an agenda of neutral agreements. They had to be identified by the state, and then ideologically structured and articulated to serve the discrete objects of power.

This ideological structuration of jural corporateness by discussions, reasonings and rational argumentations might have well been the visible features of Maroon politics, misunderstood by the colonial observers as disputes and taken as a sign for an apparent lack of coercive capacities of post-treaty Maroon leaders. But the concern on the side of the colonial administration to "bolster the authority of the Maroon chiefs or the White superintendents" rather indicates the failure of this prelude to "indirect rule", due to the very refractoriness of the various actors within the Maroon political system to loosen the ties between coercive actions and their concurrence with social consensus. In other words, Maroon society did not give away the power to define authority to the colonial administration. Neither did the Maroons allow the British to dismantle their way of

---

[38] In the Maroon council of Accompong, all important matters are discussed. During my research I was allowed to observe such meetings quite frequently. The process to come to a decision was never a univocal, "silent" affair. Rather, controversial argumentations had the walls shaking at many occasions. Similarly, traditional councils in Ghana are fora for open discourse. Chiefs, supported by their linguists and elders try to make full use of their symbolic power, based on the social knowledge and recognition of their social and cultural capital. At such an occasion, in the traditional council meeting in Adukrom, on 10.9.1994, two chiefs alternated with each other in their divergent views of the adequate procedure for a meeting with the Regional Minister. It took several hours until a decision was reached with the participation of almost all chiefs present.

political decision making and to alter the situational legitimation through consensus-oriented communicative procedures.[39]

It was the peace treaties, their rooting in the successful war, and their procedural conclusion through the exchange of blood which the Maroons interpreted as a reciprocal recognition of sovereignty that marks the difference to the African situation some 150 years later. Maroon chiefs appear of having enjoyed far more latitude in shaping the relations to the colonial administration than their African counterparts in the 19th century. An overall picture of the cautious colonial dealings with the Maroons reveals the unwillingness of the British to risk a renewal of the "atrocities" linked to the guerilla tactics of Maroon warfare. Even though the strategies employed by the colonial power to gain control over the Maroon communities are quite comparable to the later methods preparing for indirect rule on the African continent, its efficient introduction was repeatedly frustrated by the "(African) Kromanti" conceptions of authority and the practices to secure its legitimacy.

Clearly, the peace treaty and the historic colonial narrations surrounding it reveal the hope of the British to make the Maroon chiefs dependent on the colonial authorities. With the colonial Native Authority System in Africa (first introduced in Northern Nigeria in 1919) the British administration intervened in the legitimacy base of traditional authorities. A wide variety of "indigenous African sources" for the right to rule became suspended by the recognition through the colonial government (Crowder and Ikime 1970: x-xi). Just as in these later times on the African continent, the British must have envisioned the role of a Maroon leader as that of a go-between as well as an administrator mediating between the colonial administration and "his" society. After a period of nominated successors to Kojo (authorized by their position in Maroon society) they have also hoped to appoint new chiefs (see clause 15 of the peace treaty). Yet, apparently that has never happened, as Kopytoff (1973: 126) writes, in what seems to me as a clear contradiction to her own parallelizations between the post-treaty Maroon chieftaincy and later indirect rule policies on the African continent:

> The British claimed for themselves the right to appoint new chiefs after the lines of succession established in the treaties had run out. One never hears of this power having been exercised; the Governor may have relied on the Maroons to select their own leader and then put his seal of approval on him, or he may have selected a man who was an obvious natural leader in the community. But even the best Maroon chiefs often had trouble in commanding obedience in their towns.

In yet another contradictory passage in her study, Kopytoff (1973: 357-358) seems to arrive at a different interpretation. I will quote from this author at some length because

---

[39] See Habermas (1992: 45-58) for theoretically conceptualizing the legitimacy of rules as being indissolubly linked to a compliance with procedures of communicative rationality.

she offers (unknowingly as it may be) a key to the understanding of internal and external Maroon chieftaincy politics which were still based on a strategy of "camouflage" as a means to struggle for the conservation of self-government:

> The British viewed the incomplete polities they had thus helped to shape, and maintain, as being in a state of chronic disorder. But the treaty arrangements insured that no satisfactory resolution could be given to the disorders and the factionalism which simmered and periodically erupted in the post-treaty Maroon towns. The era of dramatic factional disruptions of post-treaty Maroon towns seemed to taper off after the first 30 years or so of the post-treaty period. While the quarrels still occurred, and the absence of a visible chain of command in the exercise of authority continued to disturb the British, and interferred with their efficient administration of the Maroons, overt challenges to the chieftaincy and attempts to establish splinter settlements virtually disappeared; violence was rare. We suggest as an explanation that, as time went on, the Maroons were becoming ever more homogenous and developing a network of social accommodation and control not visible even to the Whites living among them...'Disorder' and quarreling went on, but were resolved without creating major factional disputes threatening the corporate existence of the towns.

In shifting the paradigm from the intentionalist perspective of the colonial administration to the practical level of confirmed Maroon actions, I want to read the written sources against their grain. Then, the failure of an "efficient colonial administration of the Maroons" must be attributed precisely to the failing superimposition of autocratic rule based on a legal, "counter-traditional" authority of colonial gratification (or legitimation). The advantage of a praxeological approach, as outlined by Bourdieu (1979), lies in its concentration on the actual implementation of practices intended of being structurally generated by the formulation of rules. It is true that the requirement of two white superintendents residing in the Maroon communities (as contained in clause 14 of the peace treaty with Kojo) "...was the most blatant attempt of the authorities to control Maroon destiny" (Campbell 1990: 134). But to further interpret this provision as representing "...an inchoate form of the indirect rule the British were to practice so successfully in Africa", reveals the theoretical blindspots of source-positivist thinking.

It is therefore misleading to view chieftaincy among the Maroons as an expression of indirect rule (in its inchoate or fully fledged form). In practice, following generations of Maroons and their leaders used the peace treaties for support of stability in their external affairs with the colonial government and "exploited" its general provisions for internal selforganization and political flexibility. The presence of superintendents in their settlements, intended to secure the "functioning" of the chiefs under the disguise of the colonial officers, seems to have worked in the opposite direction or rather to have been diverted by the Maroons for their own needs. Instead of subordinating Maroons, these government officials were rather treated as a sort of ambassadors. They were again used by the Maroons to handle outside affairs for them, to advise them, represent their interests, and intercede with the government on their behalf (Kopytoff 1973: 341). And finally, clause 12 of the peace treaty regulating the chief's legal powers brought recognition to the chief's jurisdiction and legislation. It is cited even today as a "(quasi-)contitutional" guarantee for the juridico-political powers of Maroon chiefs. The removal of the death penalty from the catalogue of possible punishments administered by the chief can hardly be seen as having had the effect of creating hegemonial control or a subordination of the chief to the colonial courts. It is doubtful if the death penalty has had much importance before the treaties. Furthermore, the Maroon chiefs were given the right to expel a delinquent to the outside courts if they felt the death penalty to be appropriate. This in turn could have relieved them from a situation potentially causing much public unrest.

To sum up the consequences of the peace treaties for the "traditional" Maroon authorities, the intended limitations of their powers did not materialize as planned by the colonial designers of the treaty texts. After all, their attempts to turn the Maroon chiefs into some sort of henchmen (or a proto type of "indirect rulers") were frustrated by the Maroons' unwillingness to relinquish the "unchangeable statement of equality" seen in the "blood ritual" of the peace conclusion. This "failure" of colonial strategies becomes even more salient if we look on the change in colonial politics towards the Maroons following the post-emancipation period.

The search for colonial control in the post-emancipation period

As soon as the emancipation of enslaved people finally came through, following a period of "apprenticeship" (from 1834-1838), the British made a significant change in their "Maroon policy". Again, they hoped to find an ultimate solution to the "Maroon problem" which consisted (for them) in its provocative display of a model of Black self-determination. Physical force was still shunned by the British, after the Trelawney Town Maroons had proven their continual military abilities in the so-called Second Maroon War of 1795/96.[40] Instead, a law was passed in 1842 which formally abrogated all previous laws respecting the Maroons, including the peace treaties.[41] This so-called Maroons Land Allotment Act stated that all Maroon lands as guaranteed by the treaties were revested in the Crown, to be resurveyed and patented to individual Maroons. Additionally, it declared the Maroons' status to be that of ordinary citizens. But the only

---

[40] See Hart (1985: 157-190) for an ethnohistorical treatment of these highly interesting historical events which finally led to the repatriation of these Maroons to Africa (Sierra Leone) some years after their exile in Nova Scotia.

[41] Maroons Land Allotment Act, Act No. 3465, PRO: CO 137/39; see Kopytoff (1973: 384-391) for a reprint of the law.

provision that became effective in practice was the removal of the white superintendents from the Maroon settlements. Nothing was done on the side of the colonial administration to actually implement the new law. And it is doubtful whether the Act has ever been properly publicized among its "addressees". Present day Maroons have no knowledge of such legal provisions and amusedly argue that the British authorities might have felt insecure to address their forefathers directly. However, the complete absence of coercive actions taken to implement the Act and the lack of publicizing the provisions amongst the Maroons raises questions as to its effectiveness and therefore its legal validity (cf. Fischer and Köck 1980: 117). The historical context suggests the law be interpreted as yet another expression of colonial "wishful thinking" or possibly as a (symbolic) political action ventilated to appear as a firm stand on the colonial monopoly of sovereignty. Kopytoff (1979: 55) came to a similar conclusion:

> The Governor thought the Maroons were best left undisturbed. When the Colonial Secretary insisted on the new law against his protests, the only way left to avoid possible "Maroon trouble" was to obfuscate, to present only the advantages of the new law and not to mention the revocation of the treaty acts or the underlying intent to merge the Maroons in the general population.

Onesided legal provisions (enacted by colonial laws) could not change the Maroons' jural corporateness. The removal of the white intermediaries did not alter the legitimacy of Maroon authorities substantially. It may have raised the stress on the chiefs to mediate between the interests of "their" people and the colonial administration. But this seems to be a regular feature of chieftaincy also in the African context. Whenever imposed outside hegemonial claims get into conflict with "customary" rule and its feedback in communicative procedures which are ideologically (pre-) structured as self-determination, the chief's diplomatic skills are at stake. The practical employment of these personal abilities in negotiation determines his recognition as a leader and therefore his political survival. The Primus inter Pares, as chiefs are generally circumscribed in the West African context - expressing a positioning of the chief which results from such an ideological structuration - is expected to occupy this "uncomfortable position" as a go-between (cf. van Rouveroy van Nieuwaal 1997). It is up to the individual office-holder to keep a balance between the responsibilities and loyalties to his people and the demands of strict loyalty issued by the external (state) government. And it is in this sphere of political manoeuvre that internal public criticism should not be misunderstood as a "chronic structural problem" of Maroon (or African) leadership (see Kopytoff 1973: 363-364), or worse, as an expression of a "colonial-dependency syndrome" (see Campbell 1990: 254), but rather as a "democratic" quality of "traditional rule".

After the Maroons Land Allotment Act has been passed and barely anybody - certainly not the Maroons - (except for the removal of the white superintendents) had taken notice of it, the subsequent colonial governments adhered to the policy of leaving the

Maroons fairly undisturbed. Occasional conflicts did arise over the question of communal landownership. Up to the present the succeeding Maroon chiefs felt bound by the original disposition of the territory with which the cultural hero Kojo is credited: according to oral tradition, Kojo had ordered the so-called treaty lands to be prescribed eternally "for the born and the unborn". This circumscription of communal landownership is seen as an essential principle of Maroon jural corporateness. It is not just a custom that might be changed or adjusted by legislation. In that respect, communal landownership as the core of social cohesion in Jamaican Maroon societies reminds one of jural corporateness as a supreme immemorial custom that ordered the community (called aman mmu) in the precolonial Asante state (cf. McCaskie 1995: 87). Any infringement on the inviolable principle of communal landownership would have indeed threatened the corporate Maroon identity as a nation in its own right. The treaty land was and still is understood as the backbone of Maroon national sovereignty and therefore beyond the discretionary authority of disposition on the part of chiefs (cf. Kopytoff 1979: 57-58).

If the colonial government was quite unsuccessful to "creep in" on treaty lands (as Maroons call the gradual shifting of boarder lines), this is even more true so for their attempts to alienate the chiefs from their people. There is an uninterrupted succession line of Colonels (chiefs) following Kojo at least as far as Accompong is concerned. From the names given by former Colonel Wright (1994: 70), it appears that "...there was a strong tendency towards a kinship-based network or that leadership rested with dominant family groups." Throughout the colonial and post-colonial period Maroons managed to preserve their treaty right of being self-governed. Until the 1930s the post of a Colonel in Accompong was generally for lifetime. In Moore Town this customary view of lifelong tenure of the office still prevails (though not unanimously) in practice. Oral traditions in Accompong describe customary succession as being vested in the nominational right of the preceding Colonel. But the actual appointment of a candidate had to be approved by public consent.[42]

Interestingly enough change did not come about as a consequence of external pressure, but from within Maroon society in Accompong. Following the dismissal of Colonel H.R. Rowe (who had reportedly attempted to "sell out" lands to the government) in the 1930s and a chieftaincy dispute in its aftermath, the election of a new chief was changed to public voting by all adult Maroons.[43] Nowadays a Colonel in Accompong is elected every five years, but can remain in office for (legally) indefinite subsequent terms. A clear concludent recognition of the representational power of the Colonel can be read

---

[42] This description has been given among others by Mrs. Cora Rowe (interview on 17.2.1994). There is some uncertainty in relation to when the practice has been changed and to what degree the nomination by a preceding Colonel was seen as binding a public meeting. I will try to investigate these and some other questions of personal qualification and succession in chieftaincy during a research trip in 1997.

[43] Interview with Cora Rowe on 24.1.1994

from the participation of Jamaican state institutions in the electoral process assisting the Maroons in the organization of polling outside their communities.[44]

There is yet another organizational "change from within" that sheds some light on the readiness of Maroons to respond to political developments in the state. On the early eve of Jamaican national independence, the then Maroon authorities apparently saw the danger of being left out in the foreseen agreement between the colonial state and its successor. In 1942 the Accompong Maroons Council under the leadership of T.J. Cawley drafted a constitution certainly aimed at anticipating The Jamaican Constitution (of independence).[45] In its inscription this (Maroon) constitution declared:

> This town shall be governed by a constituted body of officers namely Colonels, administrators, majors, captains, lieutenants, secretaries, town clerks, treasurers, auditors, generals, registrars of trustees and clerk of courts also an organized police force.

Merely symbolic or not, the constitution was generated generations after their foreparents had been "written off" - by authors (e.g. Campbell 1990: 254; or Patterson 1973: 281) who arguably misinterpreted the interest-loaden obscurations of the colonial reportage. This led to a conclusion that interpreted the Maroons as a cadre of colonial-dependent "mimic men" who had lost their self-confidence, inculcated a feeling of helplessness, and negated their own cultural values (esp. Campbell op. cit).

The praxeological approach (as outlined by Bourdieu 1979) enables to contrast the (colonial) state-centered perspective written into the archival material with the "other" (Maroon) perspective. Then, the colonial state does not appear as an apparatus programmed to accomplish domination but rather as a field where constant struggles between agents and institutions take place. And this is the essential difference in the analysis: struggles, and thus historicity (Bourdieu and Wacquant 1992: 102):

> When the dominant manage to crush and annul the resistance and the reactions of the dominated, when all movements go exclusively from the top down, the effects of domination are such that the struggle and the dialectic that are constitutive of the field cease.
>
> There is history only as long as people revolt, resist, act. Total institutions - asylums, prisons, concentration camps - or dictatorial states are attempts to institute an end to history.

---

[44] Since quite a number of Maroons live in Kingston or Montego Bay this assistance is necessary to allow for their voting: A Journey to Accompong - to use Dunham's (1971) book title metaphorically - is still a "journey" even today.

[45] I am referring to a typed copy of the handwritten original by Colonel Harris N. Cawley, a son of the author T.J. Cawley who was reigning Colonel at the time of the constitution.

Eurpean plantocracies in the Caribbean were certainly such "totalitarian" attempts. The "colonial reportage" shares the dominant perspectives of the planters, military personnel and administrators simply because it was written predominantly by these very people. If the colonial state perspective is brought into a dialectical tension with Maroon practices, as delivered through oral traditions and oral history, or through direct observation today, we will arrive at a picture which is possibly less dependent on written (colonial) source material, than on contextual and comparative thought. It is in this context that the recently begun practice of Maroon officials boldly stamping tourists' passports with the Accompong Military State imprint should be located.

Conclusion and outlook

I have argued against a historiography (re-)presenting Maroon self-government as becoming increasingly dysfunctional. The history of Maroon chieftaincy has been obscured by the "colonial reportage" (and the source-positivist interpretations based on it) as a "process of dissolution". Is there not another lesson to be learned from the Maroon history? Let us first summarize the political history of the Maroons to reach a conclusatory answer. As outlined throughout this contribution, succeeding colonial governments were not able to solve the "Maroon problem" which at the time simply meant to extinguish the autonomous communities. In changing the strategy, the colonialists sought to subdue the Maroon authorities by altering their base of legitimacy through their submission under colonial superintendents - a strategy resembling the later policy of indirect rule in Africa. Yet, this was a far cry from being a success as their next change of policy showed. But even the succeeding period of marginalization by "leaving them undisturbed" did not succeed. The Maroon communities did not simply give up their identity and gradually melt into the larger Jamaican populace after the abolition of slavery as the colonial policy of isolation had intended. Until the end of colonial rule the British tried their best to annihilate the basis of Maroon corporate existence by confiscating their lands in clear disregard of treaty rights. But the Maroons did not refrain from defending the treaty as the basis of their sovereignty and political distinctness. Since the Jamaican national state inherited "the Maroon problem" with the proclamation of independence in 1962, the Maroons were faced with an entirely new situation. There is no official recognition on the Jamaican side of what has been derogatively called a "colonial treaty"; though one can argue that concludent recognitions are manifold (Zips 1993b: 341). It is quite manifest from the 35 years of relative stable relations between the Jamaican state and the various Maroon communities that the Jamaican government has little intention to extinguish Maroon autonomy forcefully. Rather, a peaceful process of assimilation can be read from economic, social, educational, health care and so on policies. The "dissolution" of Maroon authority is certainly believed to accelerate the coming end of the ongoing competition over sovereignty (and its implicit spheres of jurisdiction, taxation, territorial control, economic self-determination and so forth). "Disputes and quarrels" are read as clear signs of dissoluble processes for the centuries-long Maroon jural corporateness.

I want to end with an alternative view which relies on a theoretical conception of rationality that differentiates between "communicative rationality" and "functionalist rationality" (Habermas 1992: 24-32; and 1985: 180).[46] Habermas' criticism of European representative democracies in short focusses on the juridico-political processes based solely on preliminary decisions of dominant interest groups who determine politics in accordance with democratically irrevocable purposes. But without a procedure of rational discourse based on argumentation, the parenthesis combining legality and legitimacy, law and justice, legislation and democratic validity is lost - according to this criticism. Let me give an example from my own country to illustrate what is meant by this. During legislation on the national budgets for 1996 and 1997, the Austrian parliament enacted 96 new laws in 4 days (29 of which were enacted within one and a half hours). Some representatives to parliament openly admitted after this "tour de force" that they had little idea of what they had actually enacted (see Zips 1996b: 12-13). Even though this event may be a rather extreme example, it reflects a general tendency in "Western" political systems to forget about the legitimation of political decision making through rational discourse, argumentation and reasonable persuasion. Purposive action based on an instrumental (often technological) rationality looses its necessary embodiment in rational communicative negotiation; necessary at least if democratic legitimation is an acknowledged aim. Its result is social disintegration, a weakening of social solidarity and alienation of the subjects from their political "representatives" which has been noted by critical sociologists such as Habermas (1992: 12-13).

In contrast to such a development which characterizes many (imported) "modern" state legal systems in Africa and the Caribbean, traditional authorities depend (and have to depend by public demand) on discursive means to render legitimacy to their policy, legislation, jurisdiction and, finally, their authority. Traditional authority or chieftaincy in African countries and among the African-Caribbean Maroons have been disqualified

---

[46] In my view (certainly not generally shared) the outlines of Bourdieu's praxeological action theory and Habermas' discourse ethic or communication theory are quite complementary, or can be operationalized complementarily for empirical research. Both authors are heirs to the tradition of critical theory - as Calhoun (1993: 63) suggested - and both propose projects that substantially reformulate the foundations of critical theory. Furthermore they share an analytic focus on agents or agency, while avoiding the philosophy of the subject. Their theoretical approaches also appear compatible due to the shared attempts to overcome the opposition between theory and practice, their critical reading of Weber's account of rationalization and their materialist perspective to power and the abuse of power (see the more detailed discussion of Calhoun 1993: 61-67, and 82-84; see also the affirmative remark of Habermas 1985: 218 in relation to Bourdieu's work). It is revealing in this context to compare their criticism of neoliberalism or neoconservativism (e.g. Bourdieu 1996: 2; and Habermas 1985: 30-35; and 141-163) which reach to similar inferences. Habermas appears more useful to me for the critical analysis of processes of political decision making, whereas Bourdieu seems preferable for the empirical analysis of the distribution of social power and the processes of its reproduction in a given society.

as undergoing a long process of dissolution. Seen from a praxeological and discourse-theoretical perspective the actual communicative practice of "traditional rule" might in fact (in some cases at least) give evidence to the very contrary: a practice of successful social integration amidst a hegemonial and often hostile environment of another political entity competing over sovereignty. And, what we look at then with all the chieftaincy disputes is not a continual state of dissolution but rather situational series of solutions or attempts to find such solutions. Occasionally these also fail, to be certain. In the case of the Jamaican Maroons, analysed with this contribution in a comparative framework, such a failure has not occurred yet. Arguments, as the visible practices of a discursive integrational social and political process, have occurred throughout their history and do so (in present time) on a daily basis. Instead of marking a deficiency, these rational (though vivid) communications could as well be read as a decisive quality in a situation of legal pluralism that determined their social existence ever since their foreparents were forcefully taken off the African shores. Their politics of deliberation have been continually obscured by a malevolent discourse built on notions of "uncivilized disputatiousness" and "primitive inability for self-determination". Despite such an unfavourable portrayal (continued by some modern scholars) the Maroons have managed to keep their political integrity (dynamically) intact from the time of their social (re-) formation in the 17th century.

This observation is more of a starting point or a working thesis for further empirical research. I am not suggesting a sharp distinction between "African-type" and "European-type" juridico-political systems by way of categorizing the first as embedded in communicative rationality and the second in instrumental (or functionalist) rationality. The Maroon case I have presented here and legal case studies of "traditional African fields of law" indicate their orientation to reach instrumental decisions and guidelines for purposive political action. Therefore, instrumental rationality is certainly not monopolized by "European-type" representative democracies. "African (traditional) politics" are not just stuck in endless discussions. But the difference to representative democracies might show in their far stronger reliance on the communicative rational process. Further research, analytically organized by a discourse theory of law (such as Habermas 1992), would have to concentrate on the link between purposive (political) action and its grounding in "communicative rationality". This link appears integral in the society studied here, in the sense of securing the legitimation of political authority. An authority that depends on its backing through procedures of argumentation and reasonable persuasion. Empirically, such procedures of communicative rationality can be seen in all discoursive means to communicate and empower concrete (proposals for) decisions. These processes have been obscured by colonial stories as mere disputes. It is about time to counter this hegemonial discourse in favour of European concepts by bringing the communicative rational contents of "traditional authority" to the light.

References

ADAMOVICH, Ludwig K. und Bernd-Christian FUNK
1980   *Allgemeines Verwaltungsrecht.* Wien, New York: Springer-Verlag

AGORSAH, Kofi E. (ed.)
1994   *Maroon Heritage. Archaeological Ethnographic and Historical Perspectives.* Kingston, Jamaica: Canoe Press

AIDOO, Agnes Akosua
1990   Asante Queen Mothers in Government and Politics in the Nineteenth Century. Pp. 65-78. In: *The Black Woman Cross-Culturally.* Filomina Chioma Steady (ed.). Rochester (Vermont): Schenkmann

ARHIN, B. Kwame
1983   The Political and Military Roles Of Akan Women. Pp. 91-98. In: *Female and Male in West Africa.* C. Oppong (ed.). London: George Allen & Unwin

BEET, Chris, de and Miriam STERMAN
1981   *People in Between. The Matawai Maroons of Suriname.* Utrecht: Rijksuniversiteit te Utrecht

BILBY, Kenneth
1996   Ethnogenesis in the Guianas and Jamaica. Two Maroon Cases. Pp. 119-141. In: *Power and Identity: Ethnogenesis in the Americas.* 1492-1992. J.D. Hill (ed.). Iowa City: Univ. of Iowa Press

BILBY, Kenneth and Diana Baird N'DIAYE
1992   Creativity and Resistance: Maroon Culture in the Americas. Pp. 54-61. In: *Festival of American Folklife*, Smithsonian Institution (ed.). Washington DC: Smithsonian

BLACK, Clinton V.
1979   *History of Jamaica.* Kingston, Jamaica: Collins Educational

BOURDIEU, Pierre
1979   *Entwurf einer Theorie der Praxis auf der Grundlage der kabylischen Gesellschaft.* Frankfurt am Main: Suhrkamp (translation of Esquisse d'une théorie de la pratique, précédée de trois études d'ethnologie kabyle 1972).

1986   The Forms of Capital. Pp. 241-258. In: *Handbook of Theory and Research for the Sociology of Education.* John G. Richardson (ed.). New York: Greenwood Press

1996   Krise des Wohlfahrtsstaates: Eine Polemik des französischen Soziologen Pierre Bourdieu. In: *Die Zeit,* nr. 45, 1. Nov. 1996: 2

BOURDIEU, Pierre and Loic J. D. WACQUANT
1992   *An Invitation to Reflexive Sociology.* Oxford: Polity Press

BRATHWAITE, Kamau E.
1994 Nanny, Palmares & the Caribbean Maroon Connexion. Pp. 119-138. In: *Maroon Heritage. Archaeological Ethnographic and Historical Perspectives.* E. Kofi Agorsah (ed.). Kingston (Jamaica): Canoe Press

CALHOUN, Craig
1993 Habitus, Field, and Capital: The Question of Historical Specificity. Pp. 61-88. In: *Bourdieu: Critical Perspectives.* Craig Calhoun et. al. (eds.). Oxford: Polity Press

CALHOUN, Craig, Edward LiPUMA and Moishe POSTONE (eds.). *Bourdieu: Critical*
1993 *Perspectives.* Oxford: Polity Press

CAMPBELL, Mavis C.
1990 *The Maroons of Jamaica 1655-1796. A History of Resistance, Collaboration & Betrayal.* Trenton (New Jersey): Africa World Press

CROWDER, Michael and Obaro IKIME
1970 Introduction. Pp. vii-xxix. In: *West African Chiefs. Their Changing Status under Colonial Rule and Independence.* Michael Crowder and Obaro Ikime (eds.). Ile-Ife, Nigeria: Univ. of Ife Press

DALBY, David
1971 "Ashanti Survivals in the Language of the Windward Maroons in Jamaica". Pp. 31-51. In: *African Language Studies*, 12

DALLAS, Robert C.
1803 *The History of the Maroons.* London: Strahan, Longman and Reese

DANTZIG van Albert
1980 *Forts and Castles of Ghana.* Accra: Sedco

DUNHAM. Katherine
1971 *Journey to Accompong.* Westport, Connecticut: Negro Univ. Press

EARLE, Sharon
1996 Maroons locked in leadership crisis. *The Sunday Gleaner,* March 31: 10C

EDWARDS, Bryan
1796 Observations on the Disposition, Character, Manners and Habits of Life, of the Maroon Negroes of the Island of Jamaica; and a Detail of the Origin, Progress and Termination of the Late War between those People and the White Inhabitants. Reprinted in *Maroon Societies. Rebel Slave Communities in the Americas.* R. Price (ed.). 1983, Baltimore: The John Hopkins Univ. Press

FISCHER, Peter und Heribert Franz KÖCK
1980 *Allgemeines Völkerrecht. Ein Grundriß.* Eisenstadt: Prugg

FOUCHARD, Jean
1981 *The Haitian Maroons. Liberty or Death.* New York: Edward W. Blyden Press

GIDDENS, Anthony
1971   *Capitalism and Modern Social Theory. An analysis of the writings of Marx, Durkheim and Max Weber.* Cambridge: Cambridge Univ. Press

HABERMAS, Jürgen
1985   *Die Neue Unübersichtlichkeit.* Frankfurt am Main: Suhrkamp

1992   *Faktizität und Geltung. Beiträge zur Diskurstheorie des Rechts und des demokratischen Rechtsstaates.* Frankfurt am Main: Suhrkamp

HARRIS, C.L.G. Col.
1992   The Maroons and Moore Town. Pp. 73. In: 1992 *Festival of American Folklife.* Smithsonian Institution. Washington DC: Smithsonian

1994   The True Traditions of my Ancestors. Pp. 36-63. In: *Maroon Heritage. Archaeological Ethnographic and Historical Perspectives.* E. Kofi Agorsah (ed.). Kingston, Jamaica: Canoe Press

HART, Richard
1985   *Blacks in Rebellion. Slaves who abolished Slavery.* Kingston, Jamaica: The Herald Publ

HOFBAUER, Andreas
1995   *Afro-Brasilien. Vom weißen Konzept zur schwarzen Realität: historische, politische, anthropologische Gesichtspunkte.* Wien: Promedia

JAMES, C.L.R.
1963   *The Black Jacobins.* London: Allison & Busby

JOHNSON, Randal
1993   Editor's Introduction: Pierre Bourdieu on Art, Literature and Culture. Pp. 1-27. In: *The Field of Cultural Production. Essays on Art and Literature.* P. Bourdieu (ed.). Cambridge: Polity Press

KENT, R. K.
1983   Palmares: An African State in Brazil. Pp. 170-190. In: *Maroon Societies. Rebel Slave Communities in the Americas.* R. Price (ed.). Baltimore and London: The Johns Hopkins Univ. Press

KOPYTOFF, Barbara Klamon
1973   *The Maroons of Jamaica: An Ethnohistorical Study of Incomplete Polities, 1655-1905.* Pennsylvania: Univ. of Pennsylvania (unpubl. PhD. Thesis).

1979   Colonial treaty as sacred charter of the Jamaican Maroons. Pp. 45-64. In: *Ethnohistory,* 26

LEWIS, Gordon K.
1983   *Main Currents in Caribbean Thought. The Historical Evolution of Caribbean Society in its Ideological Aspects.* Kingston, Port of Spain: The John Hopkins Univ. Press

LONG, Edwards
1774   *History of Jamaica.* London: T. Lowndes

MANN, Kristin and Richard L. ROBERTS (eds.)
1991   *Law in Colonial Africa.* London: James Currey

MARSHALL, Bernard A.
1976   Maronage in Slave Plantation Societies: A Case Study of Dominica, 1785-1815. Pp. 26-32. In: *Caribbean Quarterly* Vol. 22, nos. 2&3: 26-32

MARTIN, Thomas
1973   *Maroon Identity: Processes of Persistance in Moore Town.* Riverside: Univ. of California (unpubl. PhD. thesis)

McCASKIE, Tom C.
1995   *State and society in pre-colonial Asante.* New York: Cambridge Univ. Press

OPPEL, Sonja
1994   *Sklaverei und Widerstand in Kuba 1762-1886.* Wien (Univ. Dipl. Arb.)

PAKOSIE, André
1996   Maroon Leadership and the Surinamese State (1760-1990). Pp. 263-278. In: *Journal of Legal Pluralism,* nos. 37 & 38

PARKINSON, Wenda
1980   *"This Gilded African" Toussaint L'Ouverture.* London: Quartet Books

PATTERSON, Orlando
1973   *The Sociology of Slavery. An Analysis of the origins, development and structure of Negro slave society in Jamaica.* Kingston/Jamaica: Sangster's

1983   Slavery and Slave Revolts: A Sociohistorical Analysis of the First Maroon War, 1655-1740. Pp. 246-292. In: *Maroon Societies. Rebel Slave Communities in the Americas.* R.Price (ed.). Baltimore: The John Hopkins Univ. Press

PEREIRA, Joe
1994   Maroon Heritage in Mexico. Pp. 94-108. In: *Maroon Heritage. Archaeological Ethnographic and Historical Perspectives.* E. Kofi Agorsah (ed.). Kingston, Jamaica: Canoe Press

POSTONE, Moishe, Edward LIPUMA, and Craig CALHOUN
1993   Introduction: Bourdieu and Social Theory. Pp. 1-13. In: *Bourdieu: Critical Perspectives.* Craig Calhoun et. al. (eds.). Oxford: Polity Press

PRICE, Richard
1972   "The Guiana Maroons: Changing Perspectives in 'Bush Negro' studies." Pp. 82-105. In: *Caribbean Studies,* 11 (4)

1983   *Maroon Societies. Rebel Slave Communities in the Americas.* Baltimore and London: The Johns Hopkins Univ. Press

1990   *Alabi's World*. Baltimore and London: The Johns Hopkins Univ. Press

1992   Maroons: Rebel Slaves in the Americas. Pp. 62-64. In: *1992 Festival of American Folklife*. Smithsonian Institution (ed.). Washington DC: Smithsonian

PRICE, Richard and Sally PRICE

1991   *Two Evenings in Saramaka*. Chicago and London: The Univ. of Chicago Press

PRICE, Sally

1984   *Co-wives and Calabashes*. Ann Arbor: The Univ. of Michigan Press

ROBINSON, Carey

1969   *The Fighting Maroons of Jamaica*. Kingston: William Collins and Sangster

ROLL, Zoila Danger

1977   *Los Cimarrones de El Frijol*. Santiago de Cuba: Editorial Oriente

ROSA CORZO, Gabino la

1988   *Los Cimarrones de Cuba*. La Habana: Editorial de Ciencias Sociales.

1991   *Los Palenques del Oriente de Cuba. Resistencia y Acoso*. La Habana: Editorial Academia

ROUVEROY van NIEUWAAL, E. Adriaan B. van

1998   Law and Protest in Africa: Resistance to Legal Innovation. Pp. 70-118. In: *Sovereignty, Legitimacy and Power in West African Societies. Perspectives of Legal Anthropology*. E. Adriaan B. van Rouveroy van Nieuwaal and Werner Zips (eds.). Münster & Hamburg: LIT Verlag

SCHAFER, Daniel Lee

1973   *The Maroons of Jamaica*. Minnesota: Univ. of Minnesota

THICKNESSE, Philip

1790   *Memoirs and Anecdotes of Philip Thicknesse*. Dublin: William Jones

TUFUO, J. W. and C. E. DONKOR

1989   *Ashantis of Ghana. People with a Soul*. Accra: Anowuo

WEBER, Max

1976   *Wirtschaft und Gesellschaft. Grundriß der Verstehenden Soziologie*. Tübingen: J.C.B. Mohr

WILKS, Ivor

1975   *Asante in the Nineteenth Century. The structure and evolution of a political order*. London: Cambridge Univ. Press

WRIGHT, Martin-Luther Colonel

1994   "Accompong Maroons of Jamaica." Pp 64-71. In: *Maroon Heritage. Archaelogical, Ethnographic and Historical Perspectives*. E. Kofi Agorsah (ed.), Kingston, Jamaica: Canoe Press

ZIPS, Werner

1987 "The were Children in the Forest but we were Children of the Forest." Kulturökologische Aspekte des Befreiungskampfes der Maroons von Jamaica. Pp. 113-124. In: *Mitteilungen der Anthropologischen Gesellschaft*, 117

1991 Widerstand in Jamaica. Staatsoberhäupter - Statement von Colonels und des Staatssekretärs. Film C2281/6 des ÖWF. Wien: Österreichisches Bundesinstitut für den Wissenschaftlichen Film 1990. Wiss. Film (Scientific Film) 43: 71-72

1993a *Schwarze Rebellen. Afrikanisch-karibischer Freiheitskampf in Jamaica.* Wien: Promedia

1993b "Staat im Staat". Die vertraglich garantierte Autonomie der Maroons von Jamaica. Pp. 338-345. In: *Verband Österreichischer Historiker und Geschichtsvereine (Hg.).* 19. Österreichischer Historikertag. Tagungsbericht. Graz: VÖHG

1996a Laws in Competition. Traditional Maroon Authorities within Legal Pluralism in Jamaica. Pp. 279-306. In: *Journal of Legal Pluralism*, nos. 37 & 38

1996b Verkommt unsere Demokratie zur Marionettokratie? Ein Plädoyer für ein Mindestmaß an Vernunft in der Parlamentarischen Gesetzgebung. Pp. 12-13. In: *Falter No. 29*

1998 Nanny: Nana of the Maroons? Some Comparative Thoughts on Queen Mothers in Akan and Jamaican Maroon Societies. Pp. 191-227. In: *Sovereignty, Legitimacy and Power in West African Societies. Perspectives of Legal Anthropology.* E. Adriaan B. van Rouveroy van Nieuwaal and Werner Zips (eds.). Münster & Hamburg: LIT Verlag

Interviews

CURRIE, Melvin, 6.1.1989, in Accompong Town
HARRIS, C.L.G., 26.2.1994, in Moore Town
ROWE, Cora, 17.2.1994, in Accompong Town.
ROWE, Cora, 24.1.1994, in Accompong Town
ROWE, Mann O., 12.1.1989, in Accompong Town
ROWE, Mann O., 21.1.1994, in Accompong Town
ROWE, Nana, 16.2.1994, in Accompong Town
ROWE, Wayne, 27.2.1994, in Accompong Town
VALERA, Hermes, Babalao, 7.12.1992 in Havanna, Cuba

Other Sources

Maroon Constitution, dated 3rd of August 1942, typewritten transcription from handwritten original by Colonel Harris N. Cawley, dated 6th of August 1981
Maroons Land Allotment Act, Act No. 3465, PRO: CO 137/39
Peace Treaty 1738/39, original copy kept by Mann O. Rowe in Accompong Town

About the authors

Jan Abbink studied anthropology and history in Nijmegen and Leiden (the Netherlands). His dissertation research was on the Ethiopian immigrants in Israel. From 1989 to 1992, he was a postdoctoral research fellow at the Royal Netherlands Academy of Arts and Sciences, engaged in field research on the political culture and ethnic relations in Southern Ethiopian groups in the Käfa (Southern) Region. Other interests are the history and theory of anthropology, and epistemological and applied aspects of anthropology. He has taught at the Universities of Amsterdam and Nijmegen, and since 1994 he has been a research fellow at the African Studies Centre, Leiden University, where he belongs to the research theme groups Globalisation and Sociocultural Transformation in Africa and Conflict, Conciliation and Control in Africa.

Dirk Beke is a professor at the Faculty of Law of the University of Ghent and at the Institute of Development Policy and Management of the University of Antwerp (Belgium). He teaches non-western law, comparative constitutional law and public administration in developing countries. Between 1973 and 1977, he taught administrative law in Algiers (Algeria). Since 1977 he has continued his academic career at the University of Ghent, obtaining his PhD in 1983 with a study on politics, administration and administrative law in Algeria. Since 1988 he has also been teaching at the University of Antwerp. He has done research and served as a visiting professor in several developing countries, most of them in Africa. His present research focuses on decentralisation in multiethnic developing countries. He is editor of the Belgian multidisciplinary journal *Africa Focus*.

Wim van Binsbergen is head of the theme group Globalisation and Sociocultural Transformations at the African Studies Centre (Leiden), Professor of Foundations of Intercultural Philosophy, Faculty of Philosophy, Erasmus University, Rotterdam, the Netherlands.

Rijk van Dijk is affiliated to the African Studies Centre, Leiden, as a member of the theme group Globalisation and Sociocultural Transformations. He did extensive fieldwork in Malawi during his research on the rise of charismatic Pentecostalism in the country's main urban areas. He was part of a UNDP observation team at Malawi's first free elections in 1994. He recently published a contribution entitled 'Christian Fundamentalism, Gerontocratic Rule and Democratisation in Malawi: the Changing Position of the Young in Political Culture', in *Religion, Globalization and Political Culture in the Third World*, edited by Jeff Haynes (Macmillan, 1998). His current research focus is the charismatic Pentecostal churches in Accra and Kumasi and their relations with diasporic communities in The Hague.

Gerti Hesseling, a legal scholar, wrote her PhD thesis on constitutional law in Senegal, *Histoire Politique du Sénégal - Institutions, droit et société* (Karthala 1985). She has considerable research experience in West Africa, specialising in land tenure, decentralisation processes and constitutionalism. She was a member of the *Club du Sahel* and has carried out many consultancies for international organisations such as the World Bank. She has been affiliated to the African Studies Centre (Leiden) since 1978 and was appointed its Director in 1996.

Ineke van Kessel is a researcher with the African Studies Centre (Leiden), specialised in the contemporary history and politics of South Africa. She has completed a PhD thesis on internal anti-apartheid resistance in South Africa in the 1980s, entitled *'Beyond Our Wildest Dreams': the United Democratic Front and the Transformation of South Africa* (1995), to be published by the University of Virginia Press (USA).

Piet Konings is a Senior Research fellow at the African Studies Centre (Leiden). He has done extensive research on the state, labour and trade unionism in Ghana and Cameroon. His most recent books are *Labour Resistance in Cameroon* (James Currey 1993), *Itinéraires d'Accumulation au Cameroun*, co-edited with Peter Geschiere (Karthala 1993) and *Gender and Class in the Tea Estates of Cameroon* (Avebury 1995).

Christian Lund is a sociologist holding a PhD in International Development Studies from Roskilde University, Denmark. He has done research in Niger, Burkina Faso, Mali and Senegal. He is currently a Research Fellow at IDS, Roskilde University, and is conducting research on land tenure disputes in Burkina Faso.

Barbara Oomen is associated with the Van Vollenhoven Institute, Leiden University, where she is preparing a PhD thesis on the current position of traditional authorities in South Africa. She participated in the Traditional Authority Research Group (TARG), which provided input into the constitutional process on the issue of traditional leadership in South Africa.

E. Adriaan B. van Rouveroy van Nieuwaal is a Senior Research Fellow at the African Studies Centre, Leiden University; and he has been a Professor of Law at the same university since 1983. His most recent publication is *The New Relevance of Traditional Authorities to Africa's Future* (with D.I.Ray), a theme issue of the *Journal of Legal Pluralism*, no. 37/38, 1996. Forthcoming is his *L'Etat en Afrique face à la chefferie – le cas du Togo;* With Werner Zips he edited *Sovereignty, Legitimacy, and Power in West African Societies: Perspectives of Legal Anthropology* (1998, Lit Verlag)

Werner Zips studied law, anthropology and African studies at the University of Vienna. He has been teaching legal and political anthropology, ethnohistory and Caribbean/African studies at the University of Vienna since 1990. He has done research in Jamaica, Tanzania and Ghana. He has published numerous articles and a book, *Schwarze Rebellen, Afrikanisch-karibischer Freiheitskampf in Jamaica* (1993), and he has directed a film project entitled *Accompong - Black Freedom Fighters of Jamaica*. His current research focuses on legal pluralism in Jamaica and Ghana.

Index of cited authors and some organizations

A.C.D.I. (Agence Canadienne de Développement International);   93
Abba, Souleymane;   139, 151
Abbink, Jan G.;   8, 11, 63, 67, 71, 72
Abeles, Marc;   72
Aberra, Jemberre;   53, 72
Adamovich, Ludwig K.;   221, 234
Agorsah, Kofi E.;   209, 234
Aidoo, Agnes Akosua;   218, 234
All Anglophone Congress;   203
Anderson, Benedict;   18
Annor, Kwame P.;   23, 43
Apter, David E.;   97, 130
Apthorpe, Raymond J.;   97, 130
Arhin, B. Kwame;   218, 234
Baerends, Elza A.;   42, 46
Bahru, Zewde;   72
Bailey, Fred G.;   100, 130
Bako-Arifari, Nassirou;   136, 151
Bank, Leslie;   156, 177
Barotseland Agreement, the;   130
Barth, Fredrik;   100, 130, 131
Batabiha, Bushoki;   89, 93
Bayart, Jean-François;   5, 18, 193, 203
Beck, Karl;   11, 18, 34, 35, 39, 43
Beet, Chris de;   209, 234
Beinart, William;   99, 131
Beke, Dirk;   12, 13, 75, 82, 88, 93
Bekker, Jan C.;   6, 18, 165, 177
Benda-Beckmann, Franz von;   21, 43
Benjamin, Jacques;   182, 204
Bentsi-Enchill, Kwamena;   99, 131
Berhane, Ghebray;   55, 72
Bienen, Henry;   25, 43
Bilby, Kenneth;   209, 217, 218, 234
Binsbergen, Wim M. J. van;   7, 10, 13, 29, 99, 103, 101, 111,112, 114, 120, 130, 131, 132
Black, Clinton V.;   212, 234
Blanc-Jouvan, Xavier;   140, 151
Blau, Paul M.;   25, 43
Boissevain, Jeremy F.;   100, 132
Bothma, C.V.;   158, 178

Bourdieu, Pierre;   5, 18, 208, 215, 222, 223, 226, 230, 232, 234
Braeckmann, Colette;   86, 87, 93
Brathwaite, Kamau E.;   214, 235
Brown, Edward D.;   97, 132
Brown, Richard;   103, 132
Buell, Raymond L.;   76, 93
Bukurura, Sufian;   29, 43
Bureau, Jacques;   72
Bustin, Edouard;   105, 132
Calhoun, Craig;   215, 222, 223, 232, 235, 237
Campbell, Mavis C.;   208, 212, 220, 226, 228, 230, 235
Carlens, Ivo;   93
Caverivière, Monique;   137, 151
Chabal, Patrick;   7, 18
Chaïbou, El Hadji Omorou;   30, 42, 43
Chanock, Martin;   101, 132
Charlick, Robert B.;   142, 151
Chem-Langhëë, Bonfen;   190, 193, 204
Chiabi, Emmanuel M.L.;   204
Christopheresen, K.;   153
Claessen, Henry;   24, 43
Clapham, Christopher;   54, 72 x
Contralesa Newsletter;   178
Cour, Jean-Marie;   80, 93
Crowder, Michael;   216, 225, 235
Dalby, David;   214, 235
Dallas, Robert C.;   216, 217, 220, 235
Daneel, Martinus L.;   6, 12, 18
Dantzig, Albert van;   214, 235
De Boeck, Filip;   4, 5, 6, 9, 18
Delavignette, Robert;   37, 44
Delius, Peter;   157, 178
Dhedonga Dheba Chele;   80, 81, 94
Dijk, Rijk van;   7, 18, 19
Djelo, Empenge-Osako;   80, 94
Donham, Donald L.;   51, 56, 72
Donkor, C.E.;   213, 238
Dunham, Katherine;   230, 235
Earle, Sharon;   208, 235
Edwards, Bryan;   212, 217, 219, 235
Ellis, Stephen;   7, 19
Evans-Pritchard, Edward E.;   58, 97, 72, 132
Ewing, Deborah;   163, 178
Fallers, Lloyd A.;   22, 44, 97, 132

Faure, A.; 153
Feierman, Steven; 2, 19
Fischer, Peter; 228, 235
Fisiy, Cyprian F.; 6, 18, 24, 33, 44, 49, 71, 72, 190, 194, 203, 204
Fogui, Jean-Pierre; 189, 203, 204
Fortes, Meijer; 97, 132
Fouchard, Jean; 210, 235
Fournier, François; 41, 44
Frieske, Karl; 32, 44
Fuglestad, Finn; 139, 151
Funk, Bernd-Christian; 221, 234
Gamory-Dubourdeau, Capitaine; 139, 151
Garretson, Peter P.; 57, 61, 72
Gayibor, Nicole L.; 22, 44
Geschiere, Peter; 2, 6, 7, 19, 99, 132, 190, 192, 194, 196, 202, 203, 204
Giddens, Anthony; 213, 236
Gould, David; 79, 94
Griffiths, John; 41, 44, 99, 132
Groff, David H.; 35, 44
Guillemin, Jacques; 139, 152
Haar, Bernhard ter; 23, 44
Haberland, Eike; 52, 60, 61, 72, 73
Habermas, Jürgen; 208, 225, 232, 236
Harris, C.L.G. Col.; 211, 213, 214, 220, 232, 233, 236
Harris, Marvin W.; 58, 73
Hart, Richard; 213, 214, 219, 227, 236
Hawkins, Sean; 2, 19
Hesseling, Gerti; 6, 15, 22, 44, 137, 152
Hobsbawm, Eric; 1, 19, 116, 132
Hofbauer, Andreas; 209, 236
Hollemann, Hans F.; 23, 29, 44
Hutchinson, Sharon E.; 60, 73
Huynh Cao Trí; 93, 94
Ikime, Obaro; 216, 225, 235
James, C.L.R.; 51, 56, 210, 236
Johnson, Douglas W.; 60, 73
Johnson, Randal; 215, 236
Johnson, William R.; 182, 189, 192, 204
Jong, Ferdinand de; 5, 19
Jua, Nantang B.; 201, 204
Jung, Courtney; 163, 178
Kabungulu Kibembi, Pascal; 89, 90, 94
Kanynda Lusanga; 78, 81, 94
Keita, Michel; 137, 152

Kent, R. K.; 209, 236
Kessel, Ineke van; 6, 9, 14, 162, 178
Köck, Heribert Franz; 228, 235
Kofele-Kale, Ndiva; 184, 204
Konings, Piet; 16, 184, 185, 189, 194, 199, 200, 202, 204, 205
Konrad-Adenauer-Stiftung; 165, 178
Kopytoff, Barbara Klamon; 208, 213, 217, 218, 220, 221, 222, 223, 225, 227, 228, 229, 236
Krieger, Milton; 187, 205
Kurczewski, Jacek; 32, 44
Laar, Elly van; 25, 44
Ladley, Andrew; 42, 44
Latour-Dejean, Éliane de; 141, 152
Le Roy, Etienne; 139, 140, 152
Le Vine, Victor T.; 182, 205
Lewis, Gordon K.; 212, 236
Lipuma, Edward; 215, 235, 237
Lodge, Tom; 157, 178
Long, Edwards; 212, 217, 237
Lund, Christian; 6, 15, 135, 136, 140, 147, 148, 152, 153
MacGaffey, William; 88, 89, 94
Mafikiri Tsongo; 88, 94
Mair, Lucy P.; 97, 132
Mandela, Nelson; 175, 178
Mann, Kristin; 223, 237
Marshall, Bernard A.; 209, 237
Martin, Thomas; 221, 237
Mathieu, P.; 153
Matlala, Padi; 167, 178
Mbeki, Govan; 159, 178
Mbembe, Achille; 8, 19
Mbu, Aloysius N.T.; 196, 205
McCaskie, Thomas C.; 2, 19, 213, 218, 223, 229, 237
McClellan, Charles W.; 73
McIntosh, Alistair; 168, 178
Meyer, Birgit; 7, 19
Miaffo, Dieudonné; 203, 205
Miller, Norman N.; 22, 45
Moore, Sally F.; 29, 33, 45
Mouiche, Ibrahim; 203, 205
Mpinga-Kasenda; 78, 94
Mugolongu, Apolinaire; 85, 86, 94
Mukong, Albert W.; 185, 186, 205
Mushi-Mugumorhagerwa; 79, 94

Mzala;   159, 178
N'Diaye, Diana Baird;   209, 234
Ngaido, Tidiane;   136, 142, 143, 148, 152
Nicolas, Guy;   139, 153
Nigerien Législation;   154
Nkwi, Paul N.;   189, 192, 205
Nyamnjoh, Francis B.;   187, 206
Olinga, Alain D.;   188, 206
Olivier de Sardan, Jean-Pierre;   139, 142, 153
Oomen, Barbara;   6, 9, 14, 170, 176, 179
Oppel, Sonja;   209, 237
Ouedraogo, H.;   145, 153
Pabanel, Jean-Pierre;   87, 94
Pakosie, André;   210, 237
Parkinson, Wenda;   210, 237
Patterson, Orlando;   220, 230, 237
Paulus, Jean-Pierre;   77, 95
Payze, Catherine;   164, 179
Pels, Peter;   3, 7, 19, 21, 45
Pereira, Joe;   209, 237
Pillay, Nirmala;   179
Postone, Moishe;   215, 235, 237
Price, Richard;   208, 209, 210, 214, 215, 237, 238
Price, Sally;   209, 238
Prins, Gwynn;   101, 103, 108, 132
Prinsloo, Cas;   179
Proctor, Jack M.;   33, 45
Race Relations Survey;   162, 179
Ramphele, Mamphela;   175, 179
Ranger, Terence;   1, 2, 3, 19, 20, 116, 132
Raulin, Henri;   141, 153
Ray, Donald I.;   4, 9, 20, 21, 23
Raynal, Jean-Jacques;   139, 153
Richards, Audrey I.;   133
Ritchken, Edwin;   161, 179
Roberts, Richard;   35, 45, 223, 237
Robinson, Carey;   139, 217, 238
Robinson, Pearl Theodora;   153
Rochegude, Alain;   137, 143, 153
Roll, Zoila Danger;   209, 238
Rosa Corzo, Gabino la;   209, 238
Rose, Carol;   145, 153
Rothiot, Jean-Paul;   139, 153
Rouveroy van Nieuwaal, E. Adriaan B. van;   4, 6, 7, 9, 10, 20 21, 22, 23, 24, 25, 27, 28,

29, 30, 33, 34, 35, 36, 37, 39, 40, 41, 42, 45, 46, 83, 95, 98, 101, 133, 135, 153, 156, 179, 202, 203, 206, 210, 223 , 238
Rowlands, Michael;   184, 206
Sachs, Albie;   165, 179
Salifou, André;   139, 153
Samba Kaputo;   89, 95
Schafer, Daniel Lee;   213, 238
Schapera, Isaac;   97, 133
Schoffeleers, J. Matthew;   59, 73
Sebald, Peter;   38, 46
Seekings, Jeremy F.;   160, 179
Sekgoma, G. A.;   33, 46
Séminaire-Atelier;   9, 20
Simón, Henryk;   59, 73
Simonse, Simon;   59, 73
Sindjoun, Luc;   188, 206
Skalník, Peter;   9, 20
Skinner, Edward P.;   22, 46
Solomon, Gashaw;   65, 73
Southall, Roger;   156, 177
Spalding, Fred O.;   108, 133
Spittler, Gerd;   22, 34, 35, 46
Stark, Frank;   182, 206
Sterman, Miriam;   209, 234
Suret-Canale, Jean;   139, 154
Taborga, Paul;   80, 93
Takougang, Joseph;   185, 206
Tangri , Roger;   32, 46
Tengan, Edward B.;   59, 74
Teshale, Tibebu;   51, 74
Thicknesse, Philip;   216, 238
Todd, Dave;   52, 74
Tornay, Serge;   57, 74
Transvaal Rural Action Committee;   161, 179
Trotha, Trutz von;   5, 7, 11, 20, 22, 23, 33, 35, 37, 38, 39, 40, 41, 46, 47
Tufuo, J.W.;   213, 238
Turton, David;   58, 59, 74
Vanderlinden, Jacques;   41, 47, 99, 133
Vaughan, Anne;   168, 178
Vaughn, Olufemi;   22, 47
Verboven, Dirk;   75, 93
Wache, Francis K.;   206
Wacquant, Loic J. D.;   215, 223, 230, 234
Wallerstein, Isaak;   89, 95

Wallis, C. A. G.;   77, 95
Warnier, Jean-Paul;   189, 192, 205
Weber, Max;   98, 133, 213, 238
Wendy, James L.;   72
Werbner, Richard P.;   4, 5, 20, 59, 74
Wilks, Ivor;   218, 238
Willame, Jean-Claude;   78, 83, 95
Wright, Martin-Luther Colonel;   229, 238
Young, Crawford;   89, 95
Zips, Werner;   10, 16, 17, 210, 211, 214, 217, 218, 221, 223, 231, 232, 239
Zuma, Thando;   163, 179

**African Studies Centre
(Leiden, The Netherlands)**

Piet Konings
Unilever Estates in Crisis and the Power of Organizations in Cameroon
The current economic crisis and political liberalization process in Africa have led in many cases to a partial withdrawal of the state, creating more space for autonomous forms of organization and action. Most analyses of these developments focus only on the national level, overlooking forms of organization and action at regional and local levels. This monograph tries to fill this gap. It first examines the impact of the current economic crisis on one of the oldest private agro-industrial enterprises in Cameroon, the Plantations Pamol du Cameroun Ltd, or Pamol, as it is still popularly called. It is a subsidiary of the giant Unilever company located in the South West Province of Anglophone Cameroon. The Francophone-dominated Cameroonian state denied any assistance to the ailing company during the crisis, leading to Pamol's liquidation in 1987. Interestingly, the newly appointed liquidator then decided to run the company as an ongoing business until a prospective buyer was found. The book also assesses the roles played by Pamol's trade unions and contract farmers' cooperatives, as well as by newly created regional elite groups and associations, in defence of their members' interests. Their capacity to act appears to be strengthened by the current political liberalization process.
1998, 160 S., 38,80 DM*, br., ISBN 3-8258-3530-8

E. Adriaan B. van Rouveroy van Nieuwaal; Rijk van Dijk (eds.)
African Chieftaincy in a New Socio-Political Landscape
Many contemporary studies of African chieftaincy are devoted to the unravelling of "chiefly tradition". They have tried to unmask chieftaincy as an artefact of modernist projects of colonial rule, missionary activity and postcolonial stateformation. "tradition" and "customs" have been interpreted as products of codification, petrification and coercion, all applied in the furtherance of such projects.
Beyond such processes of imposition, however, African chiefs and their authority have often been focal points in the imagination of social und political power, and in the creation and subjugation of ethnicities. Research on chieftaincy has revealed continuities and discontinuities that are highly pertinent to the understanding of African societies today. This research froms the core of the contribution of this volume. Chiefs are shown to be richly varied in their responses to state authority and to the wishes and contestations of their subjects. They are viewed and analysed here in the light of the many diverse forces that determine their positions, their symbolic functions, and the resources they can mobilise within African societies and polities.
New light is also shed on the precolonial history of chieftaincy and on its diasporic spread to places both insided and outside Africa. The book will give further breath and depth to the study of contemporary African chieftaincy.
The stamp on the front cover was used to authories decisions taken by the office of the late Paramount Chief of the Anufom (or: Tyokossi). Na Tyaba Tyekura, of Sansanné-Mango in northern Togo. Although in colonial times such stamps were imposed on chiefly office, this stamp was accepted by the Paramount Chief in 1969 as a welcome gift, and was included in his chiefly paraphernalia.
1998, 256 S., 38,80 DM*, br., ISBN 3-8258-3549-9

Dick W. J. Foeken; Jan Hoorweg;
R. A. Obudho (eds.)
The Kenya Coast
Problems and Perspectives
This volume is a standard work on the Kenya Coast and its hinterland. By many, the region ist considered relatively undeveloped within Kenya, despite the presence of the country's second town and East Africa's major port, Mombasa, and the large number of foreign tourists visiting the area each year. The book explores the background of this situation by means of presenting the current state of knowledge regarding a broad range of topics related to the development possibilities in the region. In 25 chapters, aspects ranging from physical resources and environment to ethnicity, politics, tourism, education and nutrition are discussed under five main headings: *general background*, *historical background*, *economic resources*, *human resources*, and *development effort*. The book also contains a large bibliography and statistical information. It is a 'must' for anyone with a professional interest in the East-African coastal region in general and the Kenya Coast in particular.
1999, 504 S., 99,80 DM*, gb., ISBN 3-8258-3937-0

LIT Verlag Münster–Hamburg–London
Bestellungen über: Grevener Str. 179 48159 Münster Tel.: 0251–23 50 91 Fax: 0251–23 19 72
* unverbindliche Preisempfehlung